Understanding FRBR

What It Is and How It Will Affect Our Retrieval Tools

Edited by Arlene G. Taylor

LIBRARIES

UNLIMITED

A Member of the Greenwood Publishing Group

Westport, Connecticut • London

Library of Congress Cataloging-in-Publication Data

Understanding FRBR : what it is and how it will affect our retrieval tools /
  edited by Arlene G. Taylor.
    p. cm.
    Includes bibliographical references and index.
    ISBN 978–1–59158–509–1 (alk. paper)
    1. FRBR (Conceptual model) I. Taylor, Arlene G., 1941–
  Z666.6.U53   2007
  025.3—dc22   2007013558

British Library Cataloguing in Publication Data is available.

Library of Congress Catalog Card Number: 2007013558
ISBN: 978–1–59158–509–1

First published in 2007

Libraries Unlimited, 88 Post Road West, Westport, CT 06881
A Member of the Greenwood Publishing Group, Inc.
www.lu.com

Printed in the United States of America

The paper used in this book complies with the
Permanent Paper Standard issued by the National
Information Standards Organization (Z39.48–1984).

10   9   8   7   6   5   4   3   2   1

Contents

Introduction

This book is written for librarians, bibliographic systems designers, library and information science faculty and students, and anyone else who is interested in learning about the Functional Requirements for Bibliographic Records (FRBR) and how following the FRBR model can improve access to information through helpful organization of the metadata records that are surrogates for information resources. It is hoped that the book will be of interest to people who are not cataloging specialists, as well as to those who are. Chapters herein introduce the reader to Functional Requirements for Authority Data (FRAD), as well, and explain the relationship between FRBR and FRAD.

Chapter 1 gives a basic introduction to FRBR, starting with a demonstration of the situation in today's catalogs that begs for the FRBR model for arrangement. It then gives an explanation of the entity-attribute-relationship type of model on which FRBR is based, followed by definitions of terms and examples of entities, attributes, and relationships. FRBR's "user tasks" are shown to be a continuum from Cutter's "Objects" and the Paris Principles, and some practical applications are discussed. In Chapter 2, Glenn E. Patton provides an introduction to FRAD. He explains FRAD's conceptual model for authority data, discusses the entities on which authority records are based, and explains the relationships that are modeled between authority data and bibliographic data and among authority records of various kinds. Chapter 3 is an explanation by Mr. Patton of the relationship between FRBR and FRAD.

In Chapter 4 we learn from William Denton how we got to FRBR from the first major attempts to create cataloging rules. He traces four ideas—the use of axioms, the importance of user needs, the "work," and standardization and internationalization—through the last two centuries of cataloging history and shows how they are coming together in FRBR. Edward T. O'Neill gives us, in Chapter 5, a look at the research and development that has been done in the FRBR realm. He observes the wide acceptance of the general FRBR model, but at the same time acknowledges the challenges involved in codifying it. In Chapter 6 Richard P. Smiraglia discusses the fact that "constellations of works exist with abundance in the bibliographic universe," variously called "superworks" or "bibliographic families." He points out what a challenge it is to organize these constellations so that individuals within them are easily related to each other as well as findable, and shows how FRBR promises a more sophisticated approach. Finally, in this group of chapters discussing general applications and interpretations of FRBR, Barbara B. Tillett relates the process that is going into using FRBR as a basis for *RDA: Resource Description and Access,* a new set of cataloging rules to follow after the *Anglo-American Cataloguing Rules.*

The final six chapters look at issues involved in applying FRBR in environments other than traditional general library settings: archives, art, cartographic materials, moving image materials, music, and serials. Alexander C. Thurman argues in Chapter 8, that the FRBR model has limited relevance to archives because of the incompatibility of the FRBR definition of work with the central unit of archival control, the collection. He points out that archival collections are typically unique aggregations of often unpublished materials, not consciously created works with multiple realizations. He also acknowledges the attempt of FRAD to engage more deeply with archives and considers other cooperative efforts between the archives and library sectors. In Chapter 9 Murtha Baca and Sherman Clarke address the potential use of FRBR for works of art, architecture, and material culture. They find "areas of potential application, but also several significant points of divergence." They find the relationships part of the entity-attribute-relationship model of FRBR to have the most potential in their realm.

Mary Lynette Larsgaard finds, in Chapter 10, that FRBR's Group 2 and 3 entities fit into the world of cartographic materials quite well but that the Group 1 entities are somewhat problematic. She believes, however, that if FRBR encourages system design that would allow the retrieval of all versions of a given map together, the end result would be salutary. In Chapter 11 Martha M. Yee sets forth the proposition that if FRBR interpretations clearly distinguish "content" from "carrier," then the model works well for moving image materials. She finds, however, that the current work going into the new cataloging rules does not make this distinction in a way that is useful for this realm. She presents an analysis that might be used for a more beneficial approach.

FRBR fits the world of music perhaps the best of any that exists. In fact, music catalogers devised a similar arrangement long before the appearance of the FRBR model. Sherry L. Vellucci explores this fit in Chapter 12, discussing the strengths and potential for improvement of music catalogs. She also finds some weaknesses and some "unresolved issues that have an impact on the conversion of MARC-based records for music entities to the multitiered FRBR model." Finally, in Chapter 13 Steven C. Shadle provides an overview of how serials can be modeled in FRBR, what has been accomplished in the use of FRBR to provide access to serials, and how FRBR has the potential to improve access to the content that is embodied in serially issued resources.

The FRBR model may seem like an abstraction, which in fact it is, but placed in the context of the chapters of this book, it can have some very practical and helpful applications. The major beneficiaries of successful system designs built on interpretations of the model will be the users of the systems, who will be able to see retrieved metadata records displayed in a logical fashion with relationships between and among entities clearly delineated.

Arlene G. Taylor

1

An Introduction to Functional Requirements for Bibliographic Records (FRBR)

Arlene G. Taylor

Remember When?

Readers of a certain age will remember when large dictionary card catalogs had a filing arrangement for the works of prolific authors that enabled users to find everything owned by a particular library that was by or about a particular author together in the card catalog. In addition, one could find everything representing or related to a particular work together under the name of the author of the work. The arrangement was more or less as follows:

- Prolific author
  - titles of works filed alphabetically behind guide card for author's name
    - each work might have a group of cards taking up an inch or more of space

Within a group of cards for a work you often found the following arrangement:

- original publication
- other editions, other formats
- translations (alphabetical by language)
- works in which this work is a subject (criticisms, reviews, etc.)
- related works, e.g.:
  - movie based on book, songs from musical based on book, etc.
    - video versions
    - sound versions
  - adaptation for children
  - text with commentary, etc.

That was Then; this is Now. Online catalogs today give almost no "arrangement" under the name of an author except for allowing choices of arranging in alphabetical order by title (whatever happens to be in the MARC 245 field) or arranging by date of publication (either ascending or descending). The default display is usually the alphabetical order.

In today's online catalog at the Library of Congress (LC) (searched February 17, 2007), an author search for "Ferber, Edna" brings the result of 117 entries to the screen under the controlled form of her name: "Ferber, Edna, 1887–1968." The default display is alphabetical by the title in the 245 field. In the list of 117 entries, numbers 40, 73, 84–93, and 115–116 have something to do with Ferber's novel, *Show boat*. The entries are briefly described as follows:

> #40: "Five complete novels" the second of which is "Show boat."
> #73: "Reminiscence of Show boat"
> #84: title alone (1929 publication)
> #85: microfilm version of the 1928 book, but no date for filming given
> #86–87: title with subtitle "a novel" (2 records: 1981 large print and 1926 publications)
> #88–91: title alone again (4 records: 1943, 1926, 1935, and 2007 publications, in that order)
> #92: another microfilm version of the same 1928 book (filmed in 1974)
> #93: version containing 3 novels: Show boat, So big, and Cimarron (1962)
> #115–116: two sound recordings published in 1988 and 1946

A title search for "Show boat" in the LC online catalog has 91 resulting entries. The default display appears in the following order:

> #1: sound recording of selections from three shows, one of which is "Show boat" (n.d.)
> #2: excerpts from Show boat and No, no, Nanette (1950)
> #3: excerpts from Show boat and Roberta (1960)
> #4: version of the movie (1989)
> #5: selections from Show boat and An American in Paris (1960)
> #6–7: versions of the movie (1951 and 1989)
> #8: show stoppers in dance time [sound rec.] (1942)
> #9: sound recording including "An incident from Show boat" (n.d.)
> #10–15: 6 of the 9 text versions shown under author Ferber
> #16: a "highlights" sound recording (1949)
> #17: themes sound recording (1942)
> #18: vocal score
> #19–20: movie versions (1920 and n.d.)
> #21: sound recording selections (195-)
> #22: sound recording of the movie with additions (1988)
> #23–24: two sound recordings (1942 and 1946)

#25: Theatre Royal Drury Lane production (1928)

#26–27: two bibliographic records for a "highlights" sound recording (1957)

#28: a play version (1934)

#29–30: two more text versions (that were also found under Ferber—1981 and 1926)

#31: sound recording selections (1955)

#32: Show boat cookbook (1996)

etc.

A subject search ("Ferber, Edna, 1887–1968. Show boat") in the LC online catalog results in one entry:

- a sound recording of Ferber reminiscing about Show boat (published 1983, although Ferber died in 1968; so this must be a copy of an earlier recording)

A search in OCLC Connexion for "Ferber" and "Show boat" in subject fields yields five entries:

- a video of a parody of the movie and book (1978)
- a press reel taped at the Gershwin Theater (NY) in 1994
- a thesis on the work as literature and as film (1991)
- a journal review of the controversy around the revival of Show boat (analytical entry—1995)
- the sound recording of Ferber reminiscing mentioned above

If the reader is not yet convinced that the described displays could be greatly improved, I will add that the searches just described do not include searches for "showboat," which retrieve different results from searches for "show boat."

What Can Be Done?

The solution to the lack of order just described, with its attendant effect of making it difficult for users to sort out what is available in the way of versions of a work and other resources related to that work, is, I believe, a combination of three things. We need to accept the principles and the entity-attribute-relationship model espoused by the Functional Requirements for Bibliographic Records (FRBR). We need to construct rules for creating cataloging and other metadata based on this model. And we need to design systems that will display our metadata using the model conceptualized in FRBR.

The next section addresses several points about FRBR: its basics (including entities, attributes, and relationships), what it attempts to accomplish, whom it is for, and how it is being accepted and implemented.

What Is FRBR? (and What Is It Not?)

FRBR is a conceptual model. It is set out in a report composed by the International Federation of Library Institutions and Associations (IFLA) Study Group on the Functional Requirements for Bibliographic Records and was published in 1998.[1] Allyson Carlyle has said, "FRBR is a conceptual model with the primary purpose of improving cataloging records (a product), cataloging (a process), and catalogs (a technology)."[2] She goes on to say:

> Conceptual models (in the systems world, these are sometimes called abstract models) are theoretical models....[A] major strength of conceptual models...is that they facilitate understanding and manipulation of complex entities by rendering them *less* complex. This is also a potential weakness, if critical aspects of what is modeled are somehow assumed away.[3]

A conceptual model, being theoretical, has to be thought about. It cannot be implemented, per se, because it does not cover every possible way that something might appear. It says that *most* of the time, the world covered by this model looks like *this*. So it is important to emphasize that FRBR is *not* a set of rules. It is *not* an international standard. And it is *not* a system design for online catalogs. Those things can be created based on a particular understanding of the model, but FRBR is just the model.

The specific type of conceptual model that is found in FRBR is based on the entity-attribute-relationship model of analysis. An entity is a "thing." An attribute is a characteristic. And a relationship is an interaction. Either entities or relationships can have attributes. In FRBR, *entities* of interest to users of bibliographic systems are identified, *attributes* of interest to users are identified for each entity, and *relationships* that operate between entities are specified.

FRBR Entities

The FRBR entities are divided into three groups:

- Group 1 (products of intellectual or artistic endeavor)
  - Work
  - Expression
  - Manifestation
  - Item
- Group 2 (responsible for content, production, or custodianship of Group 1 entities)
  - Person
  - Corporate body
- Group 3 (may serve as subjects of Group 1 entities)
  - Group 1 and 2 entities
  - Concept
  - Object

- Event
- Place

Group 1 Entities

Let us look at the entities one by one, giving some definitions and examples:

- work
  - distinct intellectual or artistic creation
  - abstract entity with no single material object one can point to
  - recognized through individual *expressions* of the work
  - revisions, updates, abridgements, enlargements, translations, musical arrangements, and dubbed or subtitled versions of a film are considered to be *expressions* of the same *work*
  - paraphrases, rewritings, adaptations from one literary or art form to another, abstracts, digests, and summaries are considered to be *new works*
  - examples of works:
    - Ferber's *Show boat*
    - *Show boat,* the musical
    - Mozart's *The Magic Flute*
    - online journal *D-Lib Magazine*
    - Vincent van Gogh's *Irises*
    - Michelangelo's *David*
- expression
  - realization of a work in alpha-numeric, musical, or choreographic notation, sound, image, object, movement, etc.; or any combination of such forms
  - a new expression excludes aspects of physical form (e.g., typeface) that do not change intellectual or artistic realization of the work
  - a change in form (e.g., change from written word to spoken word or addition of artistic content) or a change in intellectual approach (e.g., translation from one language to another or a revised edition) results in a *new expression*
  - e.g., for Edna Ferber's *Show boat*:
    - e_1—original English language text
    - e_2—the text illustrated with scenes from the movie
    - e_3—version translated into Portuguese
  - e.g., for a work of Franz Schubert:
    - e_1—the composer's score
    - e_2—a performance by the Amadeus Quartet
    - e_3—a performance by the Cleveland Quartet

FRBR is somewhat print oriented. Many of its examples are print or recorded sound resources. We have not quite sorted through what is a *work* or an *expression* in the worlds of museum and art objects, digital objects, cartographic materials, moving image materials, continuing resources, and archives. (Later chapters in this book address some issues involved in identifying *works* and *expressions* in those fields.) But I think that if we look at *work* and *expression* from the viewpoint of an author (rather than from the viewpoint of a cataloger), we might be able to make some interesting observations. As an author I start with a work in my head, and I think about it for months or years before expressing it. Take for example my book *The Organization of Information.*[4] It began life as lectures to my "beginning cataloging" classes. It seemed to me that the required course for everyone, including those who would never be catalogers, should be broader than just opening the cataloging rules on day one and starting to discuss rules. As I successfully broadened it, I began to think about how to share it with other teachers. I could have written a series of articles (one expression of the work). And, in fact, the subject analysis chapter made its first appearance as a chapter in *Guide to Indexing and Cataloging with the Art & Architecture Thesaurus.*[5] Or I could have published my series of PowerPoint presentations, which would have been a different work. In FRBR terms, the PowerPoint presentations are a different work because the extent of intellectual content is quite different. The intellectual content for the book is greatly expanded from the outline form of the presentations. These were originally printed as overhead transparencies—another expression of the work as a presentation. Transparencies versus electronic files are, I think, different expressions, since the electronic files could contain notes not present on the transparencies. And the presentations were updated every year, so the intellectual content of the latest presentations would be different from that printed on the transparencies. I settled on *publishing* my "work" as a book. Had I first written all the chapters as separate articles and then collected them as a book, these would have been two expressions of that work.

- manifestation
  - physical embodiment of an expression of a work
  - when production involves changes in the physical form (or format), it results in a *new manifestation*
    - changes in physical form include changes in display characteristics (e.g., font size, page layout), changes in physical medium (e.g., change from paper to microfilm), or changes in container (e.g., change from videocassette to DVD [but with no additions, modifications, etc.])
    - changes in production signaled by a change in publisher, etc., also result in new manifestations
  - e.g., Ferber's *Show boat*
    - e_1—original text document
      - m_1—Grosset & Dunlap (N.Y.) 1926 publication
      - m_2—archival photocopy of m_1
      - m_3—Heinemann (London) 1926 publication
  - e.g., The New York Times

- e_1—paper (vs. Web) version
  - m_1—print-on-paper format
  - m_2—microfilm format

Manifestations are what we traditionally catalog, describe, and provide subject analysis for.

- item
  - a single exemplar of a manifestation; although in some instances an "item" may consist of more than one physical object (e.g., a two-volume monograph, or a three-disk recording)
  - normally the same as the manifestation itself
  - variations external to the intent of the producer of the manifestation can occur in individual items (e.g., damaged copy, copy autographed by author, copy bound by a library, etc.)

Items are what we collect, house, and provide physical and/or intellectual access to.

Group 1 is the set of entities that you've probably heard the most about, and these entities are the ones that are being used in "FRBRization" projects (i.e., projects attempting to implement an understanding of the FRBR model). Note that the entities are named in FRBR "top down" (i.e., work to item), although cataloging is done "bottom up" (i.e., item to work). A cataloger has an item at hand and uses it to represent all the items that make up that particular manifestation. How can a cataloger know all of the other manifestations and expressions that exist or will exist, especially for a new item? But the "top down" approach seems to make much more sense for display purposes, even though FRBR says there's nothing "tangible" at either the work or the expression level. Naming of the abstract work entity can be followed hierarchically by names for the abstract expression entities, which can then be followed by descriptions of actual manifestations of the expressions. Continuing with the previous example:

w_1—Arlene G. Taylor's *The Organization of Information*—classroom presentation

e_1—overhead transparencies

m_1—collection of celluloid transparencies in file folders

e_2—PowerPoint presentations

m_1—digital files on CD-ROM

w_2—Arlene G. Taylor's *The Organization of Information*—text

e_1—1st ed.

m_1—published by Libraries Unlimited in 1999

e_2—2nd ed.

m_1—published by Libraries Unlimited in 2004

e_3—translation into Chinese

m_1—published by Ji xie gong ye chu ban she in 2006

Group 2 Entities

Group 2 entities are the entities responsible for the existence and/or care of the Group 1 entities:

- person—an individual, living or deceased
- corporate body—an organization or group of individuals and/or organizations acting as a unit

A person and/or a corporate body is a FRBR entity only if involved in the creation or realization of a *work*, or is the subject of a *work*. Descriptions of these entities in their own right are discussed in the new document on authority data (soon to be published by IFLA, and discussed in Chapter 2 of this book). In that document "family" is added as a third Group 2 entity, in cooperation with the field of archives where families are often responsible for the existence of collections.

Group 3 Entities

Any Group 1 or 2 entity may be the subject of any Group 1 entity. There are also four additional entities in Group 3 that may be the subject of any Group 1 entity (i.e., what the entity is "about"):

- concept—an abstract notion or idea—encompasses a comprehensive range of abstractions and may be broad in nature or narrowly defined and precise
- object—a material thing, including animate and inanimate objects occurring in nature; fixed, movable, and moving objects that are products of human creation; objects that no longer exist
- event—an action or occurrence (e.g., historical event, epoch, period of time)
- place—a location, from one of a comprehensive range of locations: terrestrial and extraterrestrial; historical and contemporary; geographic features and geopolitical jurisdictions[6]

Various communities have different definitions of these entities. For example, *Cataloging Cultural Objects* (CCO)[7] has "concept" as a separate entity from "subject." "Concept" contains generic terms, style terms, and the like. I think the difference relates to what a work is "of" versus what it is "about." For example, a work may be a picture "of" a female human figure. Or it may be a picture "of" Lucretia. It may have been determined by art specialists to be a work "about" virtuousness. If I have this somewhat correct, then "concept" in

CCO is rather different from "concept" in FRBR. We always have to be sure we are using terminology as defined in the context of the conceptual model we are working with.

It should be remembered that a concept, an object, an event, or a place is treated as a FRBR entity only if it is the subject of a Group 1 entity. These are not FRBR entities in the sense that a person or corporate body is a FRBR entity. That is, a concept, object, event, or place cannot be responsible for the existence or care of a work, expression, manifestation, or item.

Aggregate and Component Entities

The FRBR model allows us to represent aggregate entities as one work (e.g., several works brought together by an editor in an anthology, monographs brought together by a publisher in a series, collection of private papers organized by an archive as a single fond). Or, we may treat a component of a larger work (e.g., chapter, map segment, journal article) as a work itself. Aggregates and component entities are treated as whole/part relationships.

FRBR Attributes

Attributes are properties or characteristics. They are included in the model to give users the means to find various entities. Users can formulate queries by asking for certain attributes, and they can interpret responses to their queries by looking at the attributes listed for the entities that are retrieved.

Attributes for Group 1

FRBR contains detailed lists of attributes for each Group 1 entity along with definitions of each attribute. For example, the list of attributes that FRBR gives for the entity *work* are:

> title of the *work*
> form of the *work*
> date of the *work*
> other distinguishing characteristic
> intended termination
> intended audience
> context for the *work*
> medium of performance (musical work)
> numeric designation (musical work)
> key (musical work)
> coordinates (cartographic work)
> equinox (cartographic work)[8]

Some of the attributes are included to accommodate particular subtypes of the entity. That is, "musical work" and "cartographic work" are *work* subtypes that would exhibit the attributes designated for them.

The words or character strings used for a particular attribute are the "value" of that attribute. For example, the words "Show boat" represent the value of the attribute "title of the *work*." The values for most attributes are "inherent" in an entity, although some are found only by reference to an external source (e.g., a thematic catalog number for music). Most attributes have only one value, although it is possible to have more than one (e.g., a particular manifestation might show both an original title and a translated title). In addition, an entity might not have any value for one or more of the attributes listed for that entity. For example, "series statement" is an attribute listed for *manifestation,* but many manifestations will have no series statements.

There is no attribute listed under *work* for "creator" or equivalent because that particular characteristic is represented in the FRBR model by a relationship between entities. That is, a person or corporate body entity or entities will be in a "created by" relationship with the *work* entity. Some attributes may appear to be the same as entities, but they are different in FRBR. For example, the *manifestation* attribute "statement of responsibility" and the entity "person" may both be represented by the identical character string "Edna Ferber." The statement of responsibility, however, reflects the labeling information found in the manifestation itself, whereas the entity *person* is a representation of a "created by" relationship.

It is instructive to observe some attributes that *work* and *expression* have in common:

- title
- form
- date
- other distinguishing characteristic
- context
- medium of performance (musical work) [under *expression* the parenthetical part is (musical notation or recorded sound)]

However, these would not necessarily have identical character strings (e.g., *Show boat* for the *work,* but *Teatro flutuante* for an *expression* that is a Portuguese translation; *symphony* for form of *work,* but *musical notation* or *sound* for forms of *expressions*).

The lists of attributes for *expression* and *manifestation* are lengthy. The list for *item* is short but includes very specific attributes, for example, provenance of the *item.* These lists and definitions should be consulted in the *FRBR Report* as needed.[9]

Attributes for Groups 2 and 3

Attributes for Groups 2 and 3 are only minimally specified in FRBR. Group 2 entities, attributes, and relationships are being worked on by the IFLA Working Group on Functional Requirements and Numbering for Authority Records (FRANAR), which will soon issue its report: Functional Requirements for Authority Data (FRAD).[10] Group 3 entities, attributes, and relationships are being worked on by the IFLA Working Group on Functional Requirements for Subject Authority Records: FRSAR.[11]

FRBR Relationships

High-level Relationships

In the FRBR model, relationships are used to show the link between one entity and another. It is through such links that users of bibliographic systems can navigate a system to find connections between one entity that has been found and all the other entities that are related to it. Figures 1.1–1.3, reproduced from the *FRBR Report,* show the high-level entity-relationship diagrams from FRBR that indicate at a generalized level how the entities are connected with one another.

Relationships can be reflected in a number of ways. They are often reflected by including attributes of one entity with those of a related entity in a single record. It is common to include with the attributes of a *manifestation* the attributes of the *work* and the *expression* that are embodied in that *manifestation.* Implied relationships with a *person* or *corporate body* may be shown by the creation of a heading or access point in a bibliographic record. Such a heading is usually meant to identify a person or body that is responsible for the existence of the entity described in the record. A heading for another *work* may indicate a relationship between the works. Or the heading may be a subject heading, implying that the entity represented by the bibliographic record has the entity in the heading as a subject of its intellectual content. Explicit relationships can be shown through use of notes in the bibliographic record that state the nature of a relationship (e.g., "Translation of: The organization of information, 2nd ed.").

Additional Relationships

In addition to the high-level relationships, FRBR identifies major types of relationships that operate between instances of the same entity type and between instances of different entity types. In some of the FRBR tables, related works or expressions are identified as being "referential" or "autonomous." Referential works require an understanding of another work in order to be understood on their own (e.g., a concordance). Autonomous works can be used or understood without reference to another work (e.g., a dramatization).

Relationship types for work-to-work and expression-to-work are almost identical and therefore are listed together here:

- successor (sequel, succeeding work)
- supplement (index, concordance, teacher's guide, gloss, supplement, appendix)
- complement (cadenza, libretto, choreography, ending for unfinished work, incidental music)
- summarization (digest, abstract)

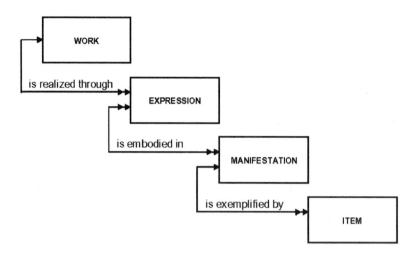

Figure 1.1. Group 1 Entities and Primary Relationships (source: *FRBR Report,* p. 13).

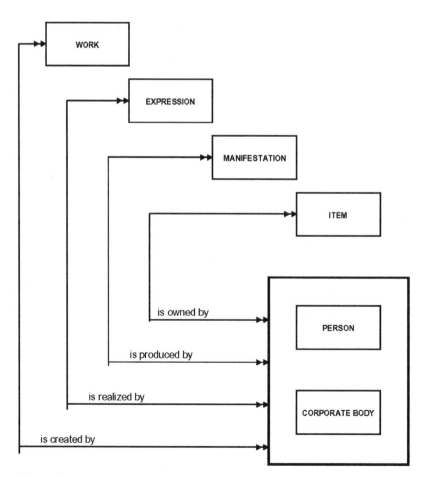

Figure 1.2. Group 2 Entities and "Responsibility" Relationships (source: *FRBR Report,* p. 14).

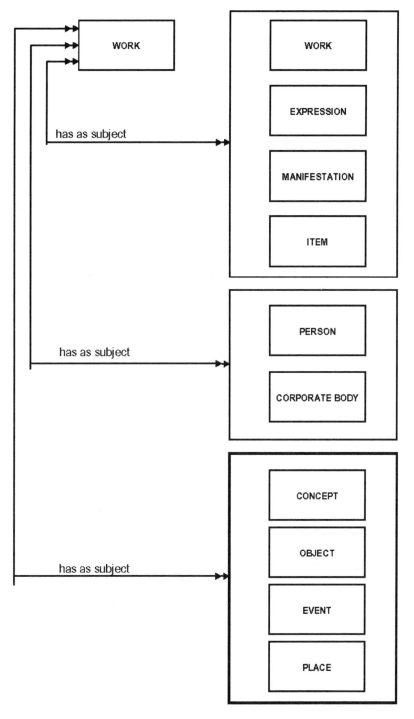

Figure 1.3. Group 3 Entities and "Subject" Relationships (source: *FRBR Report*, p. 15).

- adaptation (adaptation, paraphrase, free translation, musical variation, harmonization, musical fantasy)
- transformation (dramatization, novelization, versification, screenplay)
- imitation (parody, imitation, travesty)

In addition, there are whole/part relationships at the work-to-work level:

- whole/part (chapter, section, part, volume/issue, illustration for a text, sound aspect of a film, monograph in a series, journal article)

These examples are fairly text oriented. Music is also represented. Text orientation is also true of the *Anglo-American Cataloguing Rules Second Edition (AACR2R)*,[12] which is why it is so important to have cataloging manuals specifically oriented to different communities: for example, *Cataloging Cultural Objects* (CCO)[13] for museums and special collections; *Describing Archives: A Content Standard* (DACS)[14] for archives. Also, because of the text orientation of FRBR, it is more challenging to apply the model to works that are basically nontextual.

The list of relationship types for expression-to-expression has a few relationships in addition to the work-to-work and expression-to-work relationships:

- abridgment (abridgment, condensation, expurgation)
- revision (revised edition, enlarged edition, state (graphic))
- translation (literal translation, transcription (music))
- arrangement (music)
- successor [and the rest of the same list under "work-to-work relationships"]

Whole/part relationships for expression-to-expression relations are much the same as those for work-to-work, although the specific kinds of parts are somewhat different:

- whole/part (table of contents, volume/issue, illustration for a text, sound aspect of a film, amendment, monograph in a series, journal article, intellectual part of a multipart work)

Manifestation-to-manifestation relationships involve manifestations of the same expression, so there is no manifestation-to-expression or manifestation-to-work table.

The relationship types for manifestation-to-manifestation relationships are called "Reproduction" and "Alternate."

- The kinds of reproduction listed are reproduction, microreproduction, macroreproduction, reprint, photo-offset reprint, facsimile, and mirror site.

- The kinds of alternates listed are alternate format and simultaneously released edition.

Whole/part relationships at the manifestation level are given as volume of a multivolume manifestation, soundtrack for a film on separate medium, and soundtrack for a film embedded in film.

Tables are also given for a manifestation-to-item relationship (reproduction) and item-to-item relationships (reconfiguration and reproduction). Such a relationship would be expressed when the reproduction or reconfiguration results in only one specific item.

User Tasks

Finally, FRBR maps the attributes and relationships to user tasks:

- to *find* entities that correspond to the user's stated search criteria
- to *identify* an entity
- to *select* an entity that is appropriate to the user's needs
- to acquire or *obtain* access to the entity described

One can see some evolution of these from Cutter's "Objects" and from the purposes of a catalog in the Paris Principles. Charles A. Cutter stated his functions for catalogs in his *Rules for a Dictionary Catalog* in 1904:

Objects

1. To enable a person to find a book of which either
   (A) the author   ⎫
   (B) the title   ⎬ is known.
   (C) the subject   ⎭
2. To show what the library has
   (D) by a given author
   (E) on a given subject
   (F) in a given kind of literature.
3. To assist in the choice of a book
   (G) as to its edition (bibliographically).
   (H) as to its character (literary or topical).[15]

The Paris Principles (1961) state that the catalog should be an efficient instrument for ascertaining:

1) whether the library contains a particular book specified by:
   a) its author and title, *or*
   b) if no author is named in the book, its title alone, *or*
   c) if author and title are inappropriate or insufficient for identification, a suitable substitute for the title,

and   2) a) which works by a particular author *and*
            b) which editions of a particular work are in the library.[16]

In FRBR, the user tasks are plotted into tables with the entities, attributes, and relationships. Symbols are used to indicate the relative importance of each attribute or relationship in supporting a specific user task with respect to each entity. These tables should be of most use to system designers in identifying ways to allow searching and to display records so that users can find, identify, select, and obtain what they need.

Practical Applications

Several countries have already moved to implement systems based on FRBR; the United States is somewhat slow in this regard. *AACR2R* is being revised (as *RDA: Resource Description and Access*) to explain rules in the context of entities, attributes, relationships, and user tasks. RDA will not change the creation of records at the manifestation level, but the structure of the new code will be affected by the FRBR user tasks and the FRBR attributes.

On the other hand, system design may be profoundly affected. OCLC (Online Computer Library Center) is using the FRBR model to plan and design future systems. VTLS Inc.'s Virtua system[17] is modeled on FRBR. People have been writing articles that address FRBR and system design. For example, Martha Yee analyzed work and expression identifiers in existing bibliographic and authority records and made recommendations for better indexing and display of works, expressions, and manifestations.[18] According to Jennifer Bowen, "Most FRBR entities and attributes are already present in library catalog records, and the influence of FRBR can also be seen in existing library activities. FRBR is thus not something totally foreign, but a fresh, more rigorous way of thinking about what libraries already do that provides a basis for designing new ways to improve users' access to library resources."[19]

Model for Organizing Web Resources

The Resource Description Framework (RDF) is an infrastructure that enables the encoding, exchange, and reuse of structured metadata in an online environment. It uses XML as the means for exchanging and processing the metadata based on the premise that resources have properties (or attributes), properties have values, some values can be other resources with their own properties and values, and all these relationships can be linked within the framework (illustrated in Figure 1.4). This is quite similar to FRBR, making a comparison instructive. In FRBR, entities have attributes and attributes have values. In RDF, resources have properties and properties have values. Some of the RDF

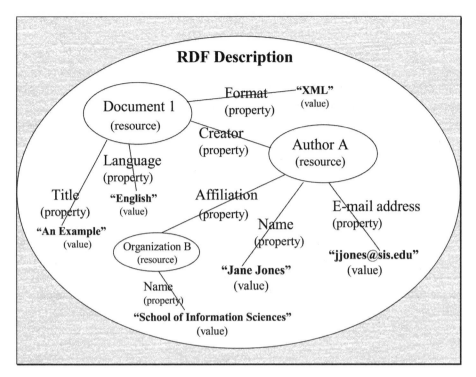

Figure 1.4. Illustration of RDF model.

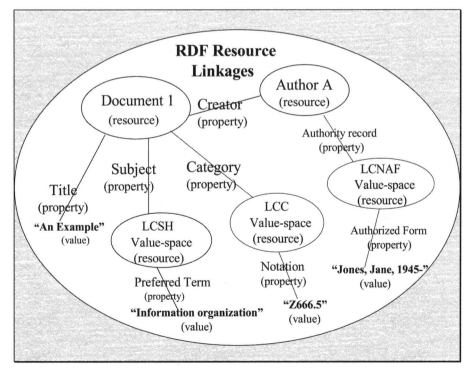

Figure 1.5. Illustration of RDF "authority" linkages.

values come from "value-spaces," the equivalent of authority files, ontologies, classification schemes, or taxonomies in the FRBR realm. These are illustrated in Figure 1.5, where the value-spaces of Library of Congress Subject Headings, Library of Congress Classification, and the Library of Congress Name Authority File are depicted as the sources of values assigned to the properties of "subject," "category," and "author." The work being done by the IFLA groups working on authority data for names and subjects (FRANAR and FRSAR) will model "authority spaces" that are similar to RDF's value-spaces.

Conclusion

This chapter has introduced FRBR as a conceptual model based on entities, attributes, and relationships. The entities have been identified, and examples of attributes and relationships have been given. All of these are important so that users can easily accomplish their tasks of finding, identifying, selecting, and obtaining entities they need from the bibliographic universe. The following chapters address the past, present, and future of FRBR; its related frameworks for authority data; and the issues it raises with respect to retrieval tools in various environments.

Notes

1. *Functional Requirements for Bibliographic Records: Final Report,* IFLA Study Group on the Functional Requirements for Bibliographic Records (Munchen: Saur, 1998). Also available: http://www.ifla.org/VII/s13/frbr/frbr.pdf.

2. Allyson Carlyle, "Understanding FRBR as a Conceptual Model: FRBR and the Bibliographic Universe," *Library Resources & Technical Services* 50, no. 4 (October 2006): 264–273.

3. Ibid., p. 265.

4. Arlene G. Taylor, *The Organization of Information.* Englewood, CO: Libraries Unlimited, 1999; *The Organization of Information,* 2nd ed. Westport, CT: Libraries Unlimited, 2004.

5. Arlene G. Taylor, "Books and Other Bibliographic Materials," in *Guide to Indexing and Cataloging with the Art and Architecture Thesaurus,* ed. Toni Petersen and Patricia J. Barnett (New York: Oxford University Press, 1994), pp. 101–119.

6. *FRBR Report,* pp. 25–27.

7. M. Baca et al., *Cataloging Cultural Objects: A Guide to Describing Cultural Works and Their Images* (Chicago: American Library Association, 2006).

8. *FRBR Report,* pp. 32–33.

9. *FRBR Report,* pp. 35–50.

10. IFLA Working Group on Functional Requirements and Numbering of Authority Records (FRANAR). http://www.ifla.org/VII/d4/wg-franar.htm.

11. IFLA Working Group on Functional Requirements of Subject Authority Records (FRSAR). http://www.ifla.org/VII/s29/wgfrsar.htm.

12. *Anglo-American Cataloguing Rules, Second Edition, 2002 Revision,* prepared under the direction of the Joint Steering Committee for Revision of AACR (Chicago: American Library Association, 2002).

13. M. Baca et al., *Cataloging Cultural Objects,* 2006.

14. *Describing Archives: A Content Standard* (Chicago: The Society of American Archivists, 2004).

15. Charles A. Cutter, *Rules for a Dictionary Catalog,* 4th ed. (Washington, D.C.: GPO, 1904), p. 12.

16. International Conference on Cataloguing Principles. *Paris, 9th–18th October, 1961, Report* (London: International Federation of Library Associations, 1963), p. 26.

17. http://www.vtls.com.

18. Martha M. Yee, "FRBRization: A Method for Turning Online Public Finding Lists into Online Public Catalogs," *Information Technology and Libraries* 24, no. 2 (June 2005): 77–95.

19. Jennifer Bowen, "FRBR: Coming Soon to Your Library?," *Library Resources & Technical Services* 49, no. 3 (July 2005): 175–188.

2

An Introduction to Functional Requirements for Authority Data (FRAD)

Glenn E. Patton

In 1998, the International Federation of Library Institutions and Associations (IFLA) Division of Bibliographic Control and the Universal Bibliographic Control and International MARC Program appointed the IFLA Working Group on Functional Requirements and Numbering of Authority Records (FRANAR). One of the Working Group's three charges was "to define functional requirements of authority records, continuing the work that the *Functional Requirements for Bibliographic Records* [FRBR] initiated."[1] The Working Group has prepared several drafts of a conceptual model that defines those functional requirements. Early drafts had the title, *Functional Requirements for Authority Records,* and thus became known by the acronym *FRAR;* the current draft, which at this writing has been submitted for worldwide review and approval for publication, has been retitled *Functional Requirements for Authority Data,* with the acronym *FRAD.*

In developing functional requirements for authority records, the group has been guided by these two objectives:

- To provide an understanding of how authority files function currently
- To clarify the underlying concepts to provide a basis for refining and improving on current practice in the future

These are similar to the FRBR model objectives of understanding *what* catalogers do and *how* the bibliographic information that is recorded as part of the cataloging process is actually used by users of online catalogs, and to provide a rational basis for improving the cataloging process.

As a step toward understanding how authority files are used currently in the library context, the group has identified five functions of an authority file:

First, the authority file documents decisions made by the cataloger when choosing the appropriate controlled access points for a new bibliographic record and when formulating new access points.

Second, information in an authority file serves as a reference tool for those same two functions and provides information that can be used in distinguishing one person, corporate body, or work from another. It may also help the cataloger determine that none of the controlled access points in the authority file is appropriate and that a new controlled access point is needed. It can also serve a broader reference function for other library staff.

Third, the authority file can be used to control the forms of controlled access points in bibliographic records and, in an automated environment, change those access points when the authority record itself is changed.

Fourth, an authority file supports access to bibliographic records by leading the user from the form of name as searched to the form of name used in the bibliographic file.

Finally, an authority file can be used to link bibliographic and authority files in ways that, for example, allow the conversion of data elements into languages and scripts most appropriate to the user's needs.

The model also defines user tasks and maps the entities, attributes, and relationships to those user tasks. In considering the user tasks, Working Group members first defined two groups of users:

- authority record creators who create and maintain authority files
- users who use authority information either through direct access to authority files or indirectly through the controlled access points (authorized forms, references, etc.) in catalogs, national bibliographies, other similar databases, etc.

The group has also defined a list of User Tasks. These are related to the FRBR user tasks but are specific to what catalogers do in working with authority data. The first three tasks relate to both groups of users; the fourth task relates solely to catalogers.

Find: Find an entity or set of entities corresponding to stated criteria (i.e., to find either a single entity or a set of entities using an attribute or relationship of the entity as the search criteria).

Identify: Identify an entity (i.e., to confirm that the entity represented corresponds to the entity sought, to distinguish between two or more entities with similar characteristics).

Contextualize: Place a person, corporate body, work, etc. in context; clarify the relationship between two or more persons, corporate bodies, works, etc.; or clarify the relationship between a person, corporate body, etc. and a name by which that person, corporate body, etc. is known.

Justify: Document the authority record creator's reason for choosing the name or form of name on which a controlled access point is based.

The conceptual model, which the Working Group has developed, can be most simply described as follows: Entities in the bibliographic universe (such as those identified in FRBR) are known by names and/or identifiers. In the cataloguing process (whether it happens in libraries, museums, or archives), those names and identifiers are used as the basis for constructing controlled access points. Fundamental to the model is a diagram that represents the entity-relationship model that is central to the Working Group's activity (Figure 2.1).[2]

Depicted in the upper half of the diagram are the entities on which authority records are focused (that is, the 10 entities defined in FRBR—*person, corporate body, work, expression, manifestation, item, concept, object, event,*

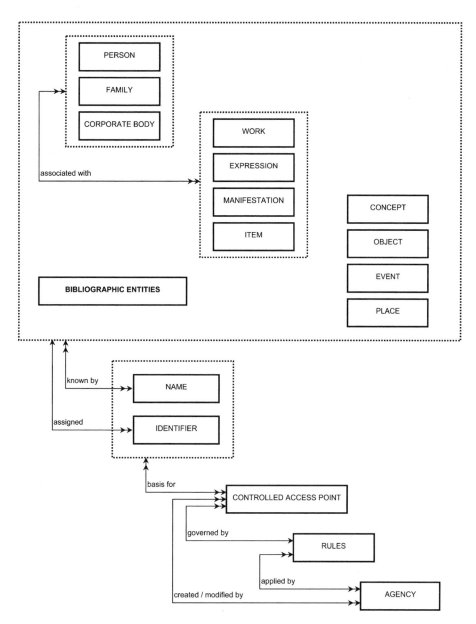

Figure 2.1. Conceptual Model for Authority Data.

and *place*—plus one additional entity—*family,* which came out of the group's involvement with the archival community).[3]

The lower half of the diagram depicts the *names* by which those entities are known, the *identifiers* assigned to the entities, and the *controlled access points* based on those names and identifiers that are registered in authority files. The diagram also highlights two entities that are instrumental in determining the content and form of controlled access points—*rules* and *agency.*

The relationships depicted in the diagram reflect the inherent associations between the various entity types. The lines and arrows connecting the entities in the upper half of the diagram with those in the lower half represent the relationships between *name* and *identifier* and the bibliographic entities with which they are associated. A specific instance of any of those bibliographic entities may be "known by" one or more *names,* and conversely any *name* may be associated with one or more specific instances of any of the bibliographic entities. Similarly, a specific instance of any one of the bibliographic entities may be "assigned" one or more *identifiers,* but an *identifier* may be assigned to only one specific instance of a bibliographic entity.

The relationships depicted in the lower half of the diagram represent the associations between the entities *name* and *identifier* and the formal or structural entity *controlled access point,* and the association between that entity and the entities *rules* and *agency.* A specific *name* or *identifier* may be the "basis for" a *controlled access point,* and conversely a *controlled access point* may be based on a *name* or *identifier.* A *controlled access point* may also be based on a combination of two *names* and/or *identifiers,* as in the case of a name/title access point representing a *work* that combines the name of the author with the name (i.e., the title) of the work. *Controlled access points* may be "governed by" *rules,* and those *rules* in turn may be "applied by" one or more *agencies.* Likewise, *controlled access points* may be "created by" or "modified by" one or more *agencies.*

It should be emphasized that the Working Group is consciously using the more general term *controlled access point,* rather than more specific terms such as *authorized form of name* and *variant form of name,* which might be used more traditionally to describe data elements found in an authority record. The Working Group has defined the term *controlled access point* as "A name, term, code, etc. under which a bibliographic or authority record or reference will be found" and has noted that the term "includes access points designated as authorized or preferred forms as well as those designated as variant forms." The Working Group agreed to this terminology in recognition of authority files in which all forms of name recorded in the authority record are treated as a cluster with none of the forms being designated as an *authorized form of name.*

To relate the general form of the model to one that is aligned more closely with traditional library authority files and to the IFLA *Guidelines for Authority Records and References,* the group has included a pair of diagrams (and accompanying text) as an Appendix.

The first diagram (Figure 2.2A) is the equivalent of the upper portion of the more general model. The second diagram (Figure 2.2B) expands the lower portion of the more general model and focuses on the formal or structural entities that come into play when a *name* or *identifier* is used to formulate an *access point* and the access point is subsequently registered in an authority file as an *authorized heading* or a *variant heading* in an *authority record* or *reference record,* or as an *explanatory heading* in a *general explanatory record.* Also included in this second diagram are the two entities that are instrumental in determining the content and form of headings, references, and records—*rules* and *agency.*

At the time of the writing of this chapter, the Working Group continues its work on a final draft of the *Functional Requirements for Authority Data,* which will be made available, following approval, on the IFLA Web site.

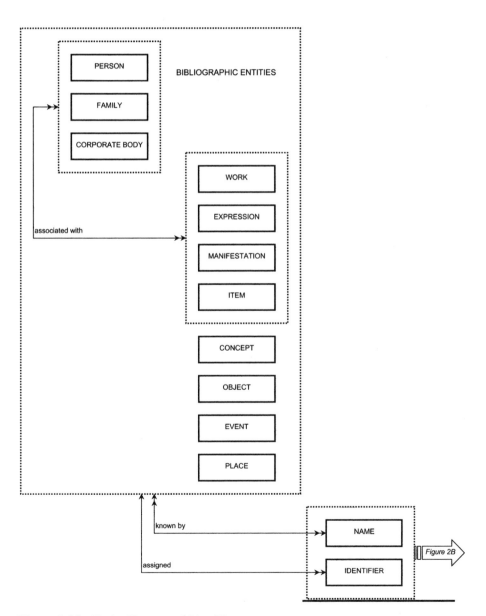

Figure 2.2A. Entity Names and Identifiers.

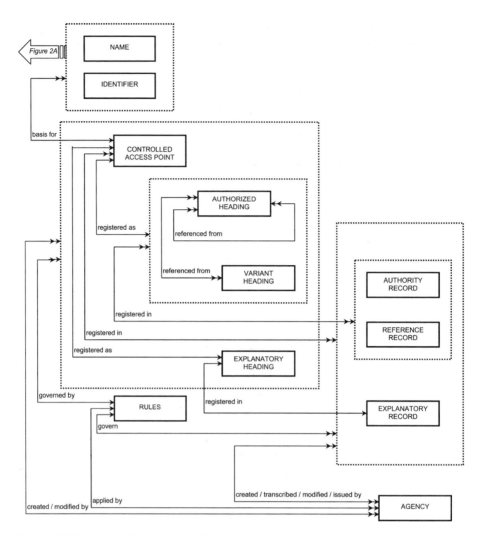

Figure 2.2B. Access Points and Authority Records in a Library Context.

Also at the time of this writing, another IFLA Working Group, the Working Group on Functional Requirements of Subject Authority Records (FRSAR),[4] has begun work to build a conceptual model of Group 3 entities within the FRBR framework as they relate to the aboutness of works. This group's work will further extend the FRAD model to cover both subject authority data and classification data. More information will become available as the group's work progresses.

Notes

1. IFLA, Working Group on Functional Requirements and Numbering of Authority Records (FRANAR), available: http://www.ifla.org/VII/d4/wg-franar.htm.

2. For further discussion of previous versions of the FRAR entity relationship model, see: Glenn Patton, "FRANAR: A Conceptual Model for Authority Data," *Cataloging & Classification Quarterly* 38, no. 3/4 (2004), pp. 91–104; Glenn Patton, "Extending FRBR to Authorities," *Cataloging & Classification Quarterly,* 39, no. 3/4 (2005), p. 39–48.

3. The description of the entity-relationship model is adapted from text prepared for the Working Group by Tom Delsey.

4. IFLA, Working Group, Functional Requirements for Subject Authority Records, available: http://www.ifla.org/VII/s29/wgfrsar.htm.

3

Understanding the Relationship between FRBR and FRAD

Glenn E. Patton

In their final report, the International Federation of Library Institutions and Associations (IFLA) Study Group on Functional Requirements for Bibliographic Records (FRBR) included some suggestions for further study and noted that, "[The model] is intended to provide a base for common understanding and further dialogue, but it does not presume to be the last word on the issues it addresses."[1] The report goes on to suggest, "The model could be extended to cover the additional data that are normally recorded in authority records."[2] The result of that suggestion was the creation of the IFLA Working Group on Functional Requirements and Numbering of Authority Records (FRANAR),[3] which has, as one of its charges, to define functional requirements for authority records. The Working Group has prepared several drafts of a conceptual model that defines those functional requirements. Early drafts had the title, *Functional Requirements for Authority Records,* and thus became known by the acronym *FRAR;* the current draft, which at this writing has been submitted for worldwide review and approval for publication, has been retitled as *Functional Requirements for Authority Data* with the acronym *FRAD.*

What does it mean to extend the FRBR model to cover the data that catalogers record in authority records? How does the model that the FRANAR Working Group is developing relate to and interact with the FRBR model?

Extending FRBR

The FRBR model defines the 10 bibliographic entities that are of most interest to users of bibliographic information: work, expression, manifestation, item, person, corporate body, concept, object, event, and place. It also lays out a number of types of relationships that exist between and/or among those entities. For example, the entities *person* and *corporate body* have "responsibility" relationships with the entities *work, expression, manifestation,* and *item.*

29

The relationship between the FRBR model and authority data was reinforced by early experiments in applying the principles of the FRBR model to existing bibliographic data.[4] These experiments demonstrated that bibliographic records under authority control could be manipulated more easily and accurately into work clusters than was true for records with uncontrolled headings and that the cross-reference structures that appear in authority records assisted in pulling together work clusters.

The FRBR model does not, however, describe how those entities and relationships are reflected in access points that are used in bibliographic records. Nor does it account for how catalogers determine the form of name to be used in those access points.

To help fill that gap, the FRANAR Working Group has laid out a model that is, in its simplest form, described as follows:

> Entities in the bibliographic universe (such as those identified in the *Functional Requirements for Bibliographic Records*) are known by names and/or identifiers. In the cataloging process (whether it happens in libraries, museums or archives), those names and identifiers are used as the basis for constructing controlled access points.

This extends the FRBR model to cover the process in which a cataloger evaluates the information available on the item to be cataloged, compares that information to what is already available in the catalog and related authority files, and determines how access points for the entities associated with the item should be constructed according to whatever cataloging rules and practices are being used.

An Additional Entity

The FRANAR Working Group, as part of one of its charges, has maintained liaison relationships with a number of other organizations that are concerned with authority files. Among those is the International Council on Archives Committee on Descriptive Standards (ICA/CDS). A joint meeting of IFLA and ICA members in Beijing in 1995 laid the groundwork for a mutual liaison relationship, which has continued during that group's work on revisions to the *International Standard Archival Authority Record for Corporate Bodies, Persons, and Families (ISAAR/CPF)*. The FRANAR Working Group had the opportunity to review and offer comments on the draft 2nd edition of the ISAAR/CPF, and it became clear from that review that, in the archival community, the family is recognized as an entity around which archival collections may be collocated. The FRANAR Working Group has, therefore, included *family* as one of the bibliographic entities in its model and is recommending its addition to the FRBR model.

Additional Attributes

The FRBR model defines a selected set of attributes for each of the bibliographic entities. For example, *Person* has these attributes: name of *person,* dates of *person,* title of *person,* and other designation associated with the *person. Corporate body* has these attributes: name of the *corporate body,* number associated with the *corporate body,* place associated with the *corporate body,* date associated with the *corporate body,* and other designation associated with the *corporate body.* Although these attributes are the most prominent of those associated with each of the entities in the context of bibliographic data, the Working Group recognized that each entity has a variety of other attributes that are part of the processes of determining the names by which an entity is known and of constructing access points based on those names.

The Working Group also determined that, for the purposes of modeling authority data, it would be more appropriate to define the entity *Name* as an entity on its own, rather than as an attribute of each of the entities. This approach allows the model, for example, to make it clearer that an instance of one of the entities may be known by multiple names, one of which may, in traditional library practice, be chosen as the *authorized heading,* with the other names serving as *variant headings.*

In the model then, the entities *Person* and *Corporate body* have the following attributes:

Person	**Corporate body**
Dates associated with the *person*	Place associated with the *corporate body*
Title of *person*	Date associated with the *corporate body*
Other designation associated with the *person*	Other designation associated with the *corporate body*
Gender	Type of *corporate body*
Place of birth	Language of the *corporate body*
Place of death	Address
Country	Field of activity
Place of residence	History
Affiliation	
Address	
Language of *person*	
Field of activity	
Profession/occupation	
Biography/history	

If one considers each of these attributes in relation to the processes that a cataloger goes through in identifying an author, determining whether that author is already represented in the authority file and, if not, constructing the appropriate access points for an authority record for that author, one can recognize that these attributes may influence the form of the access point and may also be recorded as part of the authority record.

Additional Relationships

As noted previously, the FRBR model defines basic relationships that exist between and/or among the bibliographic entities. The FRAR model adds the relationships that exist between and/or among the names of those entities and between and/or among the access points based on those names.

Examples of relationships, which have traditionally been expressed in authority records, are those that exist:

- between Persons, Families, Corporate bodies, and Works
- between Names and Persons, Families, Corporate Bodies, and Works
- between Controlled Access Points

Some examples of Person-to-Person relationships include "pseudonymous" relationships in which a "real" person is related to a "persona" adopted by that person; an "attributive" relationship in which one person and another person to whom a work by the former has been attributed, either erroneously or falsely; and, "collaborative" relationships in which two or more persons collaborate in intellectual or artistic endeavors using a single identity.

Some examples of Corporate Body-to-Corporate Body relationships include a "hierarchical" relationship in which one corporate body is subordinate to the other (within, for example, a corporate hierarchy); and, a "sequential" relationship in which two or more corporate bodies are related in order or time, including predecessor/successor relationships, mergers, splits, etc.

Some examples of Name-to-Person relationships include "earlier" and "later" name relationships, in which the name by which a person is known changes over time because of marriage, divorce, adoption of a religious name, etc.; and, "official name" relationships in which a person is known both by his or her own name and by the name assigned to that person in an official capacity.

Some examples of Name-to-Work relationships include an "alternative linguistic form" relationship which exists between a work and the various names by which a work is known in other languages; and, a "conventional name" relationship between a work and other names by which it may be commonly known.

Examples of Controlled Access Point-to-Controlled Access Point relationships include "alternate script" relationships in which two or more access points for the same entity are expressed in different scripts (Latin script and Chinese script, for example) and "different rules" relationship in which two or more access points for the same entity have been established according to different sets of cataloging rules.

More Work to Be Done

The work to extend the FRBR model to cover authority data will not be complete when the FRANAR Working Group completes its model, because the FRAD model touches only the surface of subject-related authority data. The Working Group initially intended to cover subject aspects more thoroughly but quickly realized that the membership of the group did not contain sufficient depth of knowledge in the areas of classification and indexing to accomplish that goal. In 2005, the IFLA Division Classification and Indexing Section established a new Working Group on Functional Requirements of Subject Authority Records (FRSAR)[5] whose task is to extend the FRBR model more fully into all aspects of the aboutness of works, including both subject headings and classification data.

Notes

1. IFLA Study Group on the Functional Requirements for Bibliographic Records. *Functional Requirements for Bibliographic Records: Final Report* (München: K. G. Saur, 1998), p. 5.

2. *FRBR Report,* p. 5.

3. http://www.ifla.org/VII/d4/wg-franar.htm

For further discussion of previous versions of the FRAD entity relationship model, see Glenn E. Patton. "FRANAR: A Conceptual Model for Authority Data," *Cataloging & Classification Quarterly* 38, no. 3/4, (2004): 91–104; Glenn E. Patton. "Extending FRBR to Authorities," *Cataloging & Classification Quarterly,* 39, no. 3/4, (2005): pp. 39–48. For more information about the other aspects of the Working Group's charge, see Glenn E. Patton. "FRAR: Extending FRBR Concepts to Authority Data," *International Cataloguing and Bibliographic Control* 35, no. 2 (2006): 41–45.

4. See, for example, Knut Henga and Eeva Murtomaa. 2002. *Data mining to find FRBR?* Available online at: http://folk.uio.no/knuthe/dok/frbr/datamining.pdf (Accessed September 21, 2006) and Thomas B. Hickey, Edward T. O'Neill, and Jenny Toves. 2002. "Experiments with the IFLA Functional Requirements for Bibliographic Records (FRBR)." D-Lib Magazine 8, 9 (September). Available online at: http://www.dlib.org/dlib/september02/hickey/09hickey.html (accessed September 21, 2006).

5. http://www.ifla.org/VII/s29/wgfrsar.htm (accessed September 21, 2006).

4

FRBR and the History of Cataloging

William Denton

Functional Requirements for Bibliographic Records, FRBR, is an end point of almost 175 years of thinking about what catalogs are for and how they should work—*an* end point, not *the* end point. There is no *the* end point to how libraries should make their collections available to people. That changes all the time, and lately it's been changing quickly. That's one of the reasons we have FRBR.

In this chapter I explain where FRBR comes from. I know that many of you have a horror of cataloging, and the thought of it brings back bad memories of obscure rules about spaces, colons, and dashes. Even strong-willed catalogers may blanch at the thought of a history of cataloging, but it's not as bad as you think. No special knowledge of cataloging is required. I won't go into details about main entries or who disagreed with whom about how works of corporate authorship should be handled. No actual cataloging rules are quoted and no MARC fields are shown.

We'll follow these four ideas through modern Anglo-American library history and see how they lead up to FRBR: the use of axioms to explain the purpose of catalogs, the importance of user needs, the idea of the "work," and standardization and internationalization.

The last three ideas are fairly simple. Library users are important people and wherever they are, whatever they want, serving them is the basis of what we do. "Work" has quotes around it to make it clear that under discussion is the abstract notion of a work, not the FRBR entity. (The idea goes beyond just FRBR—different people have different definitions of what a "work" is, but they're all generally the same.) As a librarian, you know all about standards and the international sharing of information.

By axioms explaining the purpose of catalogs, I mean a core set of simple, fundamental principles that form the basis for complete cataloging codes such as *Anglo-American Cataloguing Rules.* In mathematics, Euclid set out five simple axioms and from them, by proof and deduction, built up all of geometry (a simplification, but true enough). Cataloging isn't like mathematics, and it isn't a science, but it has lots of complicated rules. They weren't invented willy-nilly.

There's a reason for each of them, and the reasons, if you follow them back, come from some simple ideas. *Principles* and *rules* are common terms in cataloging so I've borrowed *axiom* from mathematics and logic.[1] When we get to the first set of axioms, I'll show what I mean about how they can be used to build up a cataloging code.

These four ideas—axioms, user needs, "work," standardization—run through our history in varying strengths, usually growing, sometimes fading. The idea of the "work" is a more modern one, and standardization and internationalization are easier and more necessary now than a century ago. The axiomatic approach goes back to the end of the nineteenth century. The importance of user needs has the longest history. All these ideas move through library work and thought, joining and rejoining, showing up here and there like threads in a quilt or red hair in a family. Unlike those, the ideas are growing in force and they've become stronger over the decades. One of the results of that is FRBR.

Chapter 1 explained FRBR: the three groups of entities; their attributes; their relationships; and the four user tasks of finding, identifying, selecting, and obtaining (plus the fifth task, relating, not officially defined but still important). Keep them in mind as the destination for this trip through the history of cataloging. We'll see where FRBR comes from and, along the way, meet some of the greatest librarians that have lived.

A Little Background

Before we get to modern cataloging, a bit of background will help set the scene.[2] We know libraries have been around for about 4,000 years, going back to Sumerian and Babylonian times. The first libraries were collections of stone tablets, and even they had catalogs. As history went along there were many different kinds of catalogs, some very good and others just inventory lists. Any way you can think of to list books was probably used, including by size, color, or the name of the person who donated them. Some catalogs were just an unorganized jumble.

Classed catalogs were common. They organize books by subject. Because there were no modern standards such as *Sears List of Subject Headings,* people made up their own subject arrangements. They usually had top-level headings (for example history, law, and rhetoric), then subheadings with narrower topics, and under those they would list books by author, title, acquisition date, size, or some other feature. In a catalog like this, it could be very hard to find everything written by a given author.

Author catalogs, listing items by author and then title, fixed this problem. These catalogs bring together all the books by the same person, and it is there that we see the first glimmerings of the "work" idea. How are two different editions of the same book different, and how are they the same?

All catalogers ran into the same problems, and there were no agreed ways to solve them. How to handle variant spellings of names and titles? How to list anonymous or pseudonymous books? Books by many people? Several books bound together into one volume? Series? Each cataloger would decide individually what to do.

Early catalogs were written out by hand, but in the 1600s printed catalogs started to be made. By the mid-1900s catalogs in book form were the most common. For a large library, they would run to many thick volumes. Printed catalogs were hard to organize, with all the cataloging, typesetting, proofreading, and printing, and they were out of date before they were published. New books had to be added by hand. Card catalogs were developed later in that century and were easier to keep up to date, but large card catalogs were unwieldy and hard to manage. Cards reigned for about a century. Now we are in the era of the online catalog.

Three of the four ideas we're following were not much in evidence through most of library history. We know of no axioms set down before the 1900s, and standardization and internationalization played small roles (except, perhaps, at places like the Library of Alexandria, an enormous library with an international clientele). The idea of the "work" has been fleshed out only in the last 70 years.

Devotion to users has been an important thread through all of library history, regardless of whether the library was small or large and whether its books were on stone or paper. Thomas Hyde, a librarian at the Bodleian Library at Oxford University in the seventeenth century, worked for nine hard years on an author catalog. In its preface in 1674 he wrote, "For though I was exhausted, I did not think I should complain or withdraw my neck from the yoke, but labored stubbornly, neglecting even my health, so that I might draw the matter as rapidly as possible to a successful close." He finished by saying, "In this work I have given students a tool to enable each of them to construct for himself and with ease out of this forest of materials an index of selected books that will serve to advance in no small measure his private studies."[3]

Sir Anthony Panizzi

The four ideas—axioms, user needs, the "work," and internationalization—really start to gain force in early Victorian England with an Italian refugee who began the era of modern cataloging. Antonio Panizzi (later Sir Anthony) (1797–1879) was born in the Duchy of Modena in what would become Italy. Politics were lively there during the Napoleonic wars and after, and although Panizzi was a lawyer he was involved with revolutionary secret societies. He had to flee for his safety, and in 1823 he arrived in England. In 1831, he was hired at the British Museum and began a long and prosperous, although not always calm, career. The full story of his life is told in Edward Miller's *Prince of Librarians: The Life and Times of Antonio Panizzi of the British Museum,*[4] and his work at the British Museum is entertainingly described in Dorothy Norris's *A History of Cataloguing and Cataloguing Methods,*[5] both of which I draw on here.[6]

The British Museum was founded in 1753 and when Panizzi arrived almost eighty years later its library was a mess. Michael Gorman described it as "a disorganized and random collection of books cataloged by indigent clergymen and other part-time drudges."[7] In 1825, the Rev. T. Hartwell Horne had presented a classification scheme and a brief set of cataloging rules, both of his own making; the next year he and two assistants were hired to build a classed catalog. In 1834 the trustees wanted a progress report. The assistants had disappeared, and after eight years and £8,000, Horne had "got as far as arranging the titles under the heading, Medical and Chemical Philosophy, with such obscure subdivisions as to be almost useless."[8] The trustees stopped the work.

Over the next few years there was much debate about what to do. By the mid-1830s, a Select Committee of the House of Commons was looking into how the museum was run, in part because of the catalog problems. In 1836 Panizzi made the case that, instead of a classed catalog, they should use an author catalog with a subject index. The next year he was made Keeper of the Printed Books, a sort of second-in-command.[9]

Now Panizzi could take charge of building the catalog he wanted. To do so, he needed a new cataloging code. With Edward Edwards, J. Winter Jones, J. H. Parry, and Thomas Watts (names now usually lost to history), and after interference from the trustees, he drew up the now famous 91 rules, *Rules for the Compilation of the Catalogue.*[10] It defined how to record author names and titles, what to do about anonymous works, and so on. The trustees sanctioned the rules in 1839; they were printed in 1841 and immediately acclaimed. Norris said, "It was believed that with the publication of the ninety-one rules, all cataloging controversies would be laid to rest for ever."[11]

Although the rules ensured the quality of the descriptions of each book, the idea of printing a catalog of the whole collection was a failure. In 1841 an incomplete volume A was printed; no others followed. The trustees had said the entire catalog would be available by 1844. In that year they asked Panizzi how it was coming along, and he said it wouldn't be done before 1854. In 1847 a royal commission was struck to look at the management of the museum and it spent most of its time on the catalog.[12] Panizzi told them that the best that could be done was to have a complete catalog of the holdings up to 1854 in print in 1895.

Many people were against Panizzi and his approach to cataloging, and the commission attracted a remarkable amount of attention. He fought his case well. "Armed with a superior knowledge of libraries and catalogs, trained in law, and possessing an instinct for verbal combat, he subjected his critics' arguments to withering attack. He analyzed their testimony point by point with great success, for 'he was a man with the annoying habit of not only being right, but of being able to prove it.'"[13] He was vindicated when the commission decided he was right and his numerous opponents, including interfering trustees, were wrong.[14]

The writer Thomas Carlyle was one of the opponents. He and others thought that building a catalog was a simple matter of writing down a list of titles, but Panizzi was after much bigger game, involving the "work" and a better sense of user needs:

> Panizzi's response was, in effect: Yes, I require the reader to look in two places
> for the information he wants, because I want to tell him much more than merely

whether or not the library has a particular book; yes, my rules are complicated, but that is because my rules are concerned not only with the book as a single and separate item, but also as a complex of editions and translations of potential interest to an acquiring reader…In Panizzi's own words, "a reader may know the *work* he requires; but he cannot be expected to know all the peculiarities of different *editions,* and this information he has a right to expect from the catalogues." So here we have two individuals looking at the same object—the book—but seeing different things. Carlyle saw the book as a material object, a separate entity unrelated to any other book in the library, and he did not see why it should not be so represented in the catalog. Panizzi saw the book as an edition of a particular work that is intimately related to the other editions and translations of the work that the library may have, and thought that it should therefore be *integrated* with them.[15]

Seymour Lubetzky also put it another way: "[A]n adequate catalog, concerned about the actual *needs* of a reader, must be designed to tell one not only whether the particular book he or she seeks is in the library but also what other editions of the work and what other works of the author the library has. That was the object of Panizzi's rules."[16]

Panizzi's career at the British Museum was filled with controversy and argument, but he emerged blameless from both the investigations during his time there and was responsible for turning the library into the great institution it became—and for the Round Reading Room. He was made Principal Librarian in 1856, retired in 1866, and was knighted (on the instigation of his friend, Prime Minister William Gladstone) in 1869.[17]

Panizzi's rules are the wellspring of modern cataloging for several reasons: they were developed by a group and not just one man (although certainly Panizzi was the primary force); they were subject to intense debate, scrutiny, and justification; they were approved by government bodies; they were used at a major library; they received international attention; and, at root, they were good rules made by a great librarian and gave a better catalog than any that had come before. Panizzi did not set down any axioms, but user needs, the idea of the "work" (although he did not think of it that way), and standardization are all part of his legacy.

Charles Cutter

Charles Ammi Cutter (1837–1903) is now the second most famous nineteenth-century American librarian, overshadowed by Melvil Dewey. Cutter was an important figure in his time: a leading librarian; one of the founders (with Dewey and others) of the American Library Association and *Library Journal;* the creator of the Expansive Classification; the first man to put slips into library books to make it easier to track what was checked out; and a cataloger whose work has affected all of cataloging to this day. Anyone interested in learning more about him should read the source of this biographical information, Francis L. Miksa's *Charles Ammi Cutter: Library Systematizer,*[18] which goes into detail about Cutter's work and influence and collects his important writings.

Cutter was born in Boston and lived there almost his entire life. He went to Harvard College, then Harvard Divinity School, and at 21 was ready to become a Unitarian minister. He had worked at the divinity school's library during his time there, however, and was drawn to librarianship instead of preaching. In 1860 he was hired at the Harvard College library, and in 1869, at age 31, he became librarian at the Boston Athenaeum, a library and art gallery that was at the heart of Boston intellectual life. He was there for 23 years. He kept working—at other libraries, on his classification system, and with American and international library groups—until his death at 65.

Cutter is best known today because of Cutter numbers, which help form unique call numbers for different books about the same subject. Cutter's classification scheme, the Expansive Classification, was advanced and flexible but never completed. It lives on today only in the Library of Congress Classification, whose creators used it as a basis for their work.

Most important to us, tracing FRBR's development, is Cutter's cataloging code *Rules for a Dictionary Catalog.* It was first published in 1876, in the same report that unveiled Dewey's classification scheme, as *Rules for a Printed Dictionary Catalogue.* (Cutter published a five-volume dictionary catalog of the Athenaeum's holdings.) It drew on earlier codes, including Panizzi's, and the preface even mentions "the famous 91 rules of the British Museum."[19] A slightly revised edition in 1889 was called *Rules for a Dictionary Catalogue,* with "printed" dropped because card catalogs were becoming popular. The third edition was identical but for the addition of an index. The fourth edition[20] was published posthumously in 1904, and the change to *Rules for a Dictionary Catalog* reflected Cutter's desire for simplified spelling.[21]

A dictionary catalog was a new development. Instead of just listing items by author, it listed them by author, title, and subject, all together in one alphabetically sorted list. In a card catalog system this meant all of the cards would be filed in the same set of drawers. A dictionary catalog brings together, for example, all of the books both *by* and *about* a person. If you're old enough to have used a card catalog, it probably worked this way.

Cutter[22] opens *Rules* with some brief general remarks and then explains, in some of the most quoted words in library history, what a catalog is for and how it should work.

Objects

1. To enable a person to find a book of which either
    - (A) the author
    - (B) the title   } is known.
    - (C) the subject
2. To show what a library has
    - (D) by a given author

(E) on a given subject

(F) in a given kind of literature.

3. To assist in the choice of a book

    (G) as to its edition (bibliographically).

    (H) as to its character (literary or topical).

Means

1. Author-entry with the necessary references (for A and D).
2. Title-entry or title-reference (for B).
3. Subject-entry, cross-references, and classed subject table (for C and E).
4. Form-entry and language-entry (for F).
5. Giving edition and imprint, with notes when necessary (for G).
6. Notes (for H).

Cutter added a wry footnote to the second edition: "This statement of Object and Means has been criticized; but it has also been frequently quoted, usually without change or credit, in the prefaces of catalogs and elsewhere. I suppose it has on the whole been approved."[23] "In a given kind of literature" (2F) means that users should be able to see what novels the library has, or what plays, what poetry, etc. Cutter says the form of a book may be either "Practical, as in Almanacs, Dictionaries, Encyclopaedias" (the same books that have a topical character) and the like, or "Literary, as Fiction, Plays, Comedies, Farces" and so on.[24]

    These Objects are the first set of axioms made in cataloging. They are the foundation on which Cutter built a full set of rules, covering all a cataloger would need to do to make a dictionary catalog. Let's take the author as an example. Cutter says the user should be able to find a book if the author is known. The most basic implication of this is that when cataloging a book, the name of the author must be recorded and made part of the description. But some books don't just have one author; they have two, or three, or an editor, or annotator, or illustrator, and the different roles may need to be handled specially. Should all of the authors in an anthology be listed? If 15 people collaborate, should they all be listed, or just the first few? How should pseudonyms be handled?

    Next, how should the names be written down? If the name is spelled differently in different books, which is the proper version? How should names from other alphabets be transliterated? Should Ovid go under his real name, Publius Ovidius Naso? Should John Buchan be listed as 1st Baron Tweedsmuir? The names will be sorted into alphabetical order, which works easily for people with simple First-name Last-name names, but what about Hildegard of Bingen? Does Leonardo da Vinci go under L or D or V? What about languages where the name is Family-name Personal-name? Corporate authorship (many people working together under one name) is often a problem. If a commission of a government ministry writes a report, does it go under the commission's name, or the ministry's, or the country's, or the name of the head of state, or something else? What if the commission or the ministry changes its name, then issues an updated version of the report?

Those are just some of the problems that cataloging rules need to settle. On top of all that, there's the problem of providing cross-references so that if the user looks up a name but the catalog lists that person under another name, the user is directed to the right place. To meet the other Objects, similar rules are needed for titles, subjects (which need to be chosen by the cataloger), and the rest. By the time all of the rules have been decided, there will be scores of them, and they all arise from those few axioms.

Unlike mathematics, there are different ways to decide those rules. Pythagoras's theorem about right-angled triangles follows directly from Euclid's rules, but one can't always use pure logic and deduction to decide the best way to write down a name. It's possible for someone to start with Cutter's axioms and build up a different set of rules. That's a problem: the two sets of catalog records can't be shared. If one rule puts Sir Arthur Conan Doyle under C (for Conan Doyle) and the other uses D (for Doyle), when the catalogs are melded, the same writer would appear in two places and Cutter's Objects would not be met nor the user's needs served.

FRBR's user tasks are descended from Cutter's Objects. For example, "to find a book of which the author is known" becomes to "[f]ind all manifestations embodying the works for which a given person or corporate body is responsible" and to "[f]ind a particular manifestation when the name(s) of the person(s) and/or corporate body(ies) responsible for the work(s) embodied in the manifestation is (are) known."[25]

In FRBR the full set of possible tasks is far more broad and inclusive than Cutter specified and allows users much more freedom. Author becomes "any Group 2 entity," book becomes "any Group 1 entity," subject becomes "any Group 1, 2, or 3 entity," and the Means open up to allow searching and browsing by any attribute of any entity. FRBR doesn't say that "find X when Y is known" is necessary, it says that any user tasks can be performed on any combination of entities. The user could search for all books by a given author, but could also search for any manifestation of a set of related works where the expressions have attributes A and B, the manifestations have attributes C and D, the producer of the manifestations has attribute E, and the relation between the expressions and the works is one of F, G, or H. FRBR even sets requirements for *acquiring* items that exemplify these manifestations, which goes beyond anything Cutter said. Acquiring is not a part of cataloging, but it is part of the whole system of making information available. FRBR's more demanding user tasks reflect the changes in libraries between Cutter and now.

In Cutter's *Rules* we see the very strong presence of two of the ideas we're following: a set of axioms and a profound concern for user needs. Standardization and internationalization were also a part of Cutter's life and work. What we don't see is the idea of the "work." When Lubetzky later discussed "work," he dismissed "Cutter's vague *what the library has by a given author.* Cutter's unqualified *what* is expressive of the failure to distinguish clearly and consistently between the book and the work in his rules."[26]

S. R. Ranganathan, the next librarian we will meet, summed up the importance of Cutter's work:

> None of the above drafts [that is, Panizzi's 91 rules and some Germanic codes] set forth cataloguing rules in a systematic or exhaustive way. Nor was there much evidence of their roots stemming from some kind of first principles. Nor again was any of them from a general code and not particularly conditioned by the practice of a single library. *Rdc* [*Rules for a Dictionary Catalog*] was the first code to reach beyond those limitations. Its limitation was only in the linguistic context. The library profession has been fortunate in the author of this code. He was a genius. This is seen in the ring of certitude and the profoundness of penetration found in the rules and the commentaries of *Rdc*. They are like the eternal epigrams of a sage. *Rdc* is indeed a classic. It is immortal. Its influence has been overpowering. It inhibits free re-thinking even to-day. It appears to have been the chief source of later codes in the English language. Being a one man's creation, it has been largely apprehended intuitively. It has been later chiseled to a slight degree. That is why *Rdc* is whole as an egg.[27]

The Early Twentieth Century

The year 1908 was important in cataloging: the American Library Association and the Library Association of the United Kingdom published a set of common cataloging rules. They did not agree on absolutely everything, so separate American and British editions were made, but this was the first set of Anglo-American cataloging rules. Standardization and internationalization were running strong.[28] Michael Gorman called this the start of the Second Age of descriptive cataloging, "the era of the committee code, the increasingly loose, baggy monsters" that lasted to 1967. The First Age began with Panizzi and included Cutter, "the age of the single-author code."[29]

Cutter had published his *Rules* in 1876, and soon after the ALA was working on a standard cataloging code. It didn't get far the first time. The same movement was on in Britain, and in 1877 Cutter and some other Americans went to a conference there to talk about cooperative cataloging. The British made new cataloging rules, and in the United States, the ALA made rules, the Library of Congress made rules for the cards it started to sell, and Dewey made rules. There were no clear standards, and without everyone using the same rules they could not share their work. In 1900 the ALA started working on standardization again—Cutter was actively involved in this up to his death—and in 1902, Dewey asked the British to get involved. They did. In 1908 the results were published; *Catalog Rules: Author and Title Entries* was "very much in the Panizzi-Cutter mold."[30] It also referred to the *Prussian Instructions,* a set of German cataloging rules in use there and in some Scandinavian countries. The internationalization idea was getting stronger.

"Sixty-nine years after Panizzi's ninety-one rules, the Anglo-American cataloging alliance had been forged," as Blake put it.[31] The rules weren't kept up to date, however, and problems arose. Work on revisions began and internationalization suffered as the Americans went their own way,[32] but axioms were about to return and the "work" was finally going to get serious attention.

Interlude: S. R. Ranganathan

Before getting to that development, let's take a step sideways toward the great Indian librarian S. R. Ranganathan (1892–1972). Ranganathan devoted his life to librarianship and wrote on every possible aspect of the field, from philosophizing about theories of classification to giving practical advice on where to place rat traps when closing a library for the night.[33] He is most famous for inventing faceted classification, and he created the faceted Colon Classification, so named because the colon was the first of the punctuation marks he used to make classification numbers like L,45;421:6;253:f.44'N5. His body of work and influence on librarianship is enormous. Ranganathan studied mathematics before turning to librarianship, and he had a mathematician's love of logic, deduction, and inference. His books are filled with principles, laws, and canons the way math textbooks are filled with theorems and corollaries. Don't let that discourage you from reading them, because they are profound and delightful. The best one to start with is *The Five Laws of Library Science,* first published in 1931. The laws are:

- Books are for use.
- Every reader his book.
- Every book its reader.
- Save the time of the reader.
- Library is a growing organism.[34]

These were the building blocks of all of his work and they are as valid today as they were in 1931. The laws are important examples of the ideas of axioms and user needs, and FRBR, rich with those ideas, fulfills the laws. Where Ranganathan says "book," for FRBR we can say any kind of work, expression, manifestation, or item: music is also for use, and movies, and Web sites. A catalog that uses FRBR will make a library's collection more open to users ("books are for use") by increasing the numbers of ways in which people can use the catalog. Readers will have more ways to find the entity they need ("every reader his book"), and entities will be exposed to more interested readers ("every book its reader"). A good implementation of the user tasks will save the user's time. The "growing organism" refers not only to floor space and shelves, but also means libraries must adapt and change as the world does, using new ideas and technologies. FRBR is one of the ways libraries will grow.

Ranganathan combined the Five Laws with Cutter's rules (we saw above how greatly he admired Cutter) in his own books about cataloging. In *Classified Catalogue Code* he said:

[A] Library Catalogue should be so designed as to:
  1. Disclose to every reader his or her document;
  2. Secure for every document its reader;
  3. Save the time of the reader; and for this purpose
  4. Save the time of the staff.[35]

Those first two tasks are mixes of Cutter's "find" and "show" with Ranganathan's second and third laws.

The Five Laws are a solid basis for all library work, but they are not explicit in FRBR. In our discussion of the main stream of ideas flowing through FRBR history, we are up to World War II.

Back to Basics with Seymour Lubetzky

The reemergence of cataloging axioms and the idea of the "work" both involve Seymour Lubetzky (1898–2003), the greatest cataloger of the twentieth century. Elaine Svenonius and Dorothy McGarry compiled his papers in *Seymour Lubetzky: Writings on the Classical Art of Cataloging* (also the source for the biographical information here), and I recommend it to anyone interested in pursuing in depth any of the ideas I discuss briefly.[36] Among Lubetzky's many fine traits, he was a good writer.

Lubetzky was born in what is now Belarus and taught school before moving to Los Angeles in 1927. He earned teaching credentials and a master's degree in German at Berkeley, but with the Depression (and being Jewish) he could not find work. He went back to school to become a librarian, graduating in 1934. He worked at the University of California, Los Angeles (UCLA), then in 1943 moved to the Library of Congress, where he stayed until 1960 when he returned to UCLA as a professor. He taught for nine years, then retired but did not stop working.

Lubetzky worked mightily to simplify cataloging rules and build on first principles. Since the 1908 rules, cataloging had been getting difficult. Things were a quagmire of complicated, sometimes contradictory, often confusing rules made up to patch over problems as they appeared. The Library of Congress had an enormous backlog of books, and it seemed unlikely they could ever catch up—and they were the ones making the catalog cards other libraries used! In 1941, Andrew Osborn wrote a paper about this called "The Crisis in Cataloging." He described different approaches to cataloging, and attacked what he called the "legalistic" method used by the draft revision of the ALA rules then underway. "According to it, there must be rules and definitions to govern every point that arises; there must be an authority to settle questions at issue. So the reviser sits in judgment on the cataloger, and the head cataloger is the supreme court for his particular library...Debate, discussion, and decision eat up a surprising amount of time. Hence the demand in some quarters for a cataloging code that will define or rule on all debatable points."[37]

The Library of Congress had Lubetzky investigate. His work was key to the 1949 *Rules for Descriptive Cataloging in the Library of Congress Adopted by the American Library Association*. That same year *A.L.A. Cataloging Rules for Author and Title Entries* came out. The two were meant to be used together to cover different parts of a cataloger's job. The Library of Congress rules were simple and straightforward; the ALA's were complicated and legalistic. Lubetzky tackled them next. "He moved his residence from his office at the Library of Congress to the stacks, where he spent whole days, from morning to evening, studying the history of cataloging. He wanted to begin at the beginning, to understand the thinking of the visionaries of the golden age of cataloging, Panizzi, Jewett, and Cutter."[38] The result was 1953's *Cataloging Rules and Principles*.

"Is this rule necessary?" Chapter 1 famously asks. The first line harks back to Panizzi and admires "the broad knowledge, keen thinking, and fruitful imagination which the founders of the rules have brought to the profession of cataloging." But what about the newer complicated rules? "One is impelled to ask: Are all these rules necessary? Are all the complexities inevitable? Is there an underlying design which gives our code unity and purpose?"[39] He carefully analyzed cataloging rules such as one about names of married women—that they're women, or married, isn't the cause of the rule; it's that their names changed. There were already rules about how to handle name changes, so there was no need to create a special case.

Later Lubetzky says a "complete reconstruction" of the rules is necessary, one built on "deliberately adopted objectives" and "well considered principles."

> The objectives implicit in our rules for entry are two. The first objective is to enable the user of the catalog to determine readily whether or not the library has the book he wants. The catalog is constantly searched by many readers and members of the staff, and the quicker this information can be found the better the catalog. The second objective is to reveal to the user of the catalog, under one form of the author's name, what works the library has by a given author and what editions or translations of a given work.[40]

This is an axiomatic approach, drawing on Cutter's rules, with some "save the time of the reader." Notice how Cutter's "to enable a person to find a book of which either the author, the title, or the subject is known" has become "to determine whether or not the library has the book he wants," with no restrictions on attribute details, and how closely this matches FRBR's "to find entities that correspond to the user's stated search criteria."[41] The second objective seems like the basic "find by author" Cutter rule, but notice how Lubetzky says "work" and "editions or translations of a given work." We will come back to this.

Lubetzky's work was key to the wording of the Paris Principles, the common name for the *Statement of Principles* passed at the International

Conference on Cataloguing Principles in that city in 1961. A total of 53 countries and 12 international organizations were there. They were ready to build common principles on which national cataloging codes could be based. Increasing internationalization meant that more countries wanted to share cataloging records, if the other systems were similar enough to permit it. German librarians, who had a strong cataloging tradition, had found problems with their rules, and the wartime destruction of their libraries meant they could start fresh.[42] The result was the Paris Principles, just 12 points on five pages.

Principle #2, "Functions of the Catalogue," says:

> The catalogue should be an efficient instrument for ascertaining
>   2.1 whether the library contains a particular book specified by
>
>   (a) its author and title, or
>   (b) if the author is not named in the book, its title alone, or
>   (c) if author and title are inappropriate or insufficient for identification, a suitable substitute for the title; and
>
>   2.2 (a) which works by a particular author and
>   (b) which editions of a particular work are in the library[43]

These axioms are clearly descended from Cutter's Objects, and Lubetzky said the first objective was "substantially identical" to Cutter's.[44] You'll notice also the use of the word "work." This fixed the "failure" Lubetzky saw in how Cutter's Objects confused the book and the "work."

As with Cutter's *Rules,* the axioms can be used to generate a large set of detailed rules. The rest of the Paris Principles sketch out some of those rules but stop well short of a full code. Also as before, the axioms don't lead inevitably to one set of cataloging rules. They were built up over the next few years into *Anglo-American Cataloguing Rules* (*AACR*) and also form the basis of other national codes.

FRBR's user tasks descend from Cutter through the Paris Principles, but they expand and broaden Principle #2 to give users more scope and power. With some rewording, 2.1 (a) becomes "ascertain whether the library contains a particular manifestation when the name(s) of the person(s) and/or corporate body(ies) responsible for the work(s) embodied in the manifestation, and the title of the manifestation and/or expression and/or work, is (are) known."

The creation of the Paris Principles was a major event in cataloging history. All four of the ideas are here: an axiomatic approach, user needs, the "work," and standardization and internationalization. The Paris Principles are an important part of FRBR's history, and, as we will see, FRBR has shaped the wording of the revision of the principles. Next, however, we go back to look at the "work."

The "Work"

You know what a FRBR work is; we've seen that the idea of the "work" was part of Panizzi's thinking but not Cutter's; and we saw that through Lubetzky it was fundamental to the Paris Principles.[45] Lubetzky was influenced by a 1936 paper by Julia Pettee, "The Development of Authorship Entry and the Formulation of Authorship Rules as Found in the Anglo-American Code."[46] She surveyed cataloging history—going back to Thomas Hyde at the Bodleian Library in 1674, as well as Panizzi and Cutter—and exposed an adumbrated idea:

> The attribution of authorship is a first principle of American catalogers. But why this tireless search? A second principle, even more fundamental, which necessitates the search, emerges. The book in hand is considered not as a single item but as a representative of a literary unit. It is the province of the catalog to assemble these literary units, issued in various forms, under a single caption. Pope's translation of Homer's *Odyssey* does not stand by itself. It is a version of the original Greek.[47]

The axiom idea is there. But "literary units"—what are they? They're not exactly "works" (as de Rijk shows[48]), but they're close. Lubetzky began the full development of the idea of the "work." I quoted him talking about Panizzi and the idea, and I quoted him talking about objectives of the catalog.[49] Here is a bit more about that:

> The need for the second objective [to show all works by a given author, and bring together all editions and translations] arises from the fact that the works of an author may be issued under different names as a result of a change, translation, transliteration, or even misprint of the author's name, and the editions of a work may be issued under different titles for similar reasons, and could, therefore, be separated in the catalog.[50]

This is almost pure FRBR talk about works, expressions, and manifestations. Lubetzky kept advocating this way of thinking up to and during the creation of the Paris Principles, and although it was not without argument, they refer to "works." This terminology is standard now, has been the subject of much research, and is a key part of the FRBR model. In fact, the four-level hierarchy of work, expression, manifestation, and item is probably the most well-known thing about it.

Here's one last quote from Lubetzky, which ties together the idea of the "work" with cataloging history and the importance of user needs:

> The book, it should be noted, comes into being as a dichotomic product—as a *material* object or medium used to convey the *intellectual* work of an author. Because the material *book* embodies and represents the intellectual work, the two have come to be confused, and the terms are synonymously used not only by the layman but also by the cataloger himself. Thus catalogers refer to *the author and title of a book* instead of, more accurately, to *the author of the work and the title of the book embodying it,* and the inquirer searching the catalog for a *particular book* is more often than not after *the work* embodied in it, although he is very likely unaware of the distinction between the two . . . The question that must then be faced

at the outset—and that has been faced since Panizzi, though beclouded by the failure to distinguish clearly and consistently between the *book* and the *work*—is whether the objective of the catalog should be merely to tell an inquirer whether or not the library has the *particular book* he is looking for, or whether it should go beyond that and tell him also what other editions and translations—or other representations—of the *work* the library has so as to help him more effectively determine whether the library has what he needs and to select what might best serve his purposes.[51]

FRBR uses its four-level hierarchy to move from an abstract work to an item one can hold in one's hand, but other people have other arrangements, such as work, version, adaptation; work, text, edition, printing, book; work, document, text; work, derivations, item;[52] or work, edition, subedition, version, document.[53] They can all more or less be mapped to each other. There are ranges of thought about the *expression* entity—when something is a new expression of an existing work and when it is sufficiently different to be a new work—and what it means for a work to contain other works.

The four entities have been the subject of much debate and thought. FRBR has an axiomatic approach, but we've seen how a small set of axioms can generate complex systems. FRBR's axioms are not simple so there is even more to consider about their implications. A work is more complicated than a circle, and the concept of an expression is harder to grasp than that of a straight line. The entire bibliographic universe is grander even than three-dimensional geometry.

More and More of More and More

The Paris Principles brought us up to 1961, almost half a century ago now. It was a culmination (*a* culmination, not *the* culmination) of most of the major ideas we've followed: an axiomatic approach, user needs, and standardization and internationalization. The "work" was still in its early stages.

There are two ways I could continue now. I went into some detail about Cutter and Lubetzky, and I could do the same for contemporary cataloging. I won't, because it would take the rest of the book and you'll find the other chapters far more interesting. I'll summarize where we are now, some problems we face, and how FRBR was made to help fix them.

Cataloging as it stands today has been built up in earnest since 1967—the dawn of the Third Age, as Michael Gorman puts it.[54] That year *Anglo-American Cataloguing Rules* was released; it was an international (American, Australian, British, Canadian) standardization of descriptive cataloging rules, with a philosophy based on the Paris Principles. (As in 1908, the British and Americans didn't agree on everything, so there were two editions.) By 1968 the Machine Readable Cataloging (MARC) format had passed its trials and electronic sharing of cataloging records was here to stay. In 1971 the International Federation of Library Institutions and Associations (IFLA) published the International

Standard Bibliographic Description (ISBD) specification, which got folded into the major 1978 *AACR* revision (on which the British and Americans did agree).

Catalogers use these and many other standards in their daily work. There are classification schemes and subject heading systems. There are thick manuals on how to catalog serials. There are thick manuals on library software that implements the standards. There are thick manuals on *everything*. Special fields like medical or legal librarianship have their own rules. Every standard has books explaining how to use it. Everything is under regular maintenance and revision.

It's hard to keep up with all that, but the real problem is that all those rules cannot keep up with what is happening around us. Cutter saw the invention of the telephone, the phonograph, and the moving picture in his lifetime. There must have been libraries where users came in wanting to borrow wax cylinders holding recorded sound, but the library wasn't ready for the new 1880s technology. Today things are vastly more complicated:

- Cataloging costs money and takes time. Sharing cataloging records will save both, if everyone can agree on how to catalog things the same way.
- Electronic resources (on computers) are hard to catalog and manage, and not always easy to make available.
- Everything comes in many formats, and they're hard to catalog, manage, and make available, too.
- There's more of everything.
- Technology is changing how libraries work, what they have in their collections, and what users need and expect.

This probably describes the situation in your library today, but it's not new. In fact, almost two decades ago, these problems were the subject of a two-day conference, the Seminar on Bibliographic Records, held in Stockholm in 1990.[55] One of the resolutions passed at the end was: "That a study be commissioned to define the functional requirements for bibliographic records in relation to the variety of user needs and the variety of media."[56] Functional requirements for bibliographic records!

FRBR Is Born and Grows Up

The resolution was honored. In 1991, a group was formed by IFLA, which has a division for international cataloging issues, to do the study. Olivia M. A. Madison was chair and wrote the full history of FRBR's creation in "The Origins of the IFLA Study on Functional Requirements for Bibliographic Records."[57]

The group worked for six years, with some members and consultants coming and going. Terms of reference were set at the start and followed closely.

They soon decided on using an entity-relationship model, and then had to figure out what the entities were and how they would all relate. In dealing with user needs, they had to decide whether or not to start with fresh research. To save time, they decided to rely on their own knowledge and that of reviewers and experts in different fields.

> The needs of researchers, students, librarians, library staff, publishers, vendors, retailers, systems designers, and users of information services, etc., in and outside traditional library environments, were considered and evaluated within the context of tasks such as finding information, verifying citations, determining display and information retrieval functions, purchasing, selling, managing acquisitions information, cataloging, indexing and abstracting, managing inventories, circulation, interlibrary loan, preservation, reference, etc.[58]

The work was presented at IFLA conferences in 1993 and 1994, and the group used the comments to help with their work. A draft of the final report was sent out and made available on the Web in 1996, resulting in 40 comments (7 negative) from 16 countries. More revisions were made. Madison said, "I believe that the worldwide review process and resulting feedback were clearly reflected in the proposed final report, and played a large part in the ease of approval that followed."[59]

The report was approved in 1997 and published in 1998. The Study Group became a Working Group, then finally a Review Group as FRBR became part of the international library establishment. Subgroups were established to look into particular issues and their work may result in a revision of FRBR.

FRBR, which builds on so much previous work, is now a basis for other work. Foremost are two other IFLA projects, Functional Requirements for Authority Data (FRAD) and Functional Requirements for Subject Authority Records (FRSAR), which will work intimately with FRBR and support its implementation. Another is IFLA's *Guidelines for Online Public Access Catalogue (OPAC) Displays,*[60] which says the four FRBR user tasks are also the four functions of an OPAC. One of its guidelines is that catalogs should show a "FRBRized" view of search results, and it includes an example of how that might look.

We've been looking at FRBR as a set of axioms that can underlie a cataloging code without defining exactly how it should work. This is explicitly stated. "The model developed for this study represents, as far as possible, a 'generalized' view of the bibliographic universe; it is intended to be independent of any particular cataloging code or implementation of the concepts it represents."[61] Barbara Tillett's chapter explains one example of this: how *AACR* is being rebuilt with a FRBR foundation.

FRBR builds on the Paris Principles, and in turn it is feeding back and helping to improve their revision. As of mid-2007, *Statement of International Cataloguing Principles* (an IFLA project) is still in draft and receiving international scrutiny. It says it is meant to "adapt the Paris Principles to objectives that are applicable to online library catalogues and beyond. The first of these objectives is to serve the convenience of the users of the catalogue."[62] "The new principles build on the great cataloging traditions of the world:" Cutter, Ranganathan, and Lubetzky. FRBR's entities are the basis of cataloging records, it says, and catalogs exist so that users can perform five basic tasks: find, identify, select, obtain, and navigate (i.e., the unofficial fifth FRBR task, relate).

We have followed four ideas—the use of axioms, the importance of user needs, the "work," and standardization and internationalization—through some of the history of cataloging, and have seen how they have appeared with growing force since Panizzi in the 1840s. Cutter's *Rules* gave a basic set of Objects and Means that have guided cataloging ever since, including the Paris Principles. Ranganathan's Five Laws of Library Science give a basis for all library work, including cataloging. English-speaking countries have collaborated on cataloging for over a century, and with IFLA's support there is a worldwide movement for universal bibliographic control. Underpinning all of this is the idea of the "work."

All four of the ideas are showing strongly now, and one of the outcomes is FRBR. It will be interesting to watch how FRBR and the ideas continue on from here, and to see—and help shape—what comes next.

Bibliography

Battles, Matthew. 2003. *Library: An Unquiet History.* New York: W. W. Norton.

Blake, Virgil L. P. 2002. Forging the Anglo-American Cataloging Alliance: Descriptive Cataloging, 1830–1908. *Cataloging & Classification Quarterly* 35 (1/2): 3–22.

Bourne, Ross, ed. 1992. *Seminar on Bibliographic Records: Proceedings of the Seminar Held in Stockholm, 15–16 August 1990, and Sponsored by the IFLA UBCIM Programme and the IFLA Division of the Bibliographic Control.* Munich: K. G. Saur.

Brault, Nancy. 1972. *The Great Debate on Panizzi's Rules in 1847–1849: The Issues Discussed.* Los Angeles: The School of Library Service & The University Library, University of California.

British Museum. 1841. *Rules for the Compilation of a Catalogue.* In Carpenter and Svenonius 1985, 3–14.

Carpenter, Michael. 1994. Catalogs and Cataloging. In *Encyclopedia of Library History,* ed. Wayne A. Wiegand and Donald G. Davis, Jr., 107–117. New York: Garland.

———. 2002. "The Original 73 Rules of the British Museum: A Preliminary Analysis." *Cataloging & Classification Quarterly* 35 (1-2): 23–36.

Carpenter, Michael, and Elaine Svenonius, eds. 1985. *Foundations of Cataloging: A Sourcebook.* Littleton, CO: Libraries Unlimited.

Connell, Tschera Harkness, and Robert L. Maxwell, eds. 2000. *The Future of Cataloging: Insights from the Lubetzky Symposium; April 18, 1988, University of California, Los Angeles.* Chicago: American Library Association.

Cutter, Charles A. 1904. *Rules for a Dictionary Catalog,* 4th ed. Washington, DC: Government Printing Office.

De Rijk, Elisabeth. 1991. "Thomas Hyde, Julia Pettee and the Development of Cataloging Principles: With a Translation of Hyde's 1674 Preface to the Reader. *Cataloging & Classification Quarterly* 14 (2): 31–62.

De Rijk Spanhoff, Elisabeth. 2002. Principle Issues: Catalog Paradigms, Old and New. *Cataloging & Classification Quarterly* 35 (1-2): 37–59.

Gladstone, William Ewart. n.d. On Books and the Housing of Them. http://www.gutenberg.org/dirs/etext02/obhot10.txt

Gorman, Michael. 1980. "Let Us Now Praise…" *American Libraries,* April: 201–203.

———. 2000. Seymour Lubetzky, Man of Principles. In Connell and Maxwell 2000, 12–21.

Hanson, Eugene R., and Jay E. Daily. 2003. Catalogs and Cataloging. In *Encyclopedia of Library and Information Science,* 2nd ed., ed. Miriam A. Drake, 431–468. New York: Marcel Dekker.

ICCP. *See* International Conference on Cataloguing Principles.

IFLA. *See* IFLA Study Group on the Functional Requirements for Bibliographic Records.

IFLA Meeting. *See* IFLA Meeting of Experts on an International Cataloguing Code.

IFLA Meeting of Experts on an International Cataloguing Code. 2007. Statement of International Cataloguing Principles. April 2007 draft. http://www.nl.go.kr/icc/down/070412_2.pdf

IFLA OPAC. *See* IFLA Task Force on Guidelines for OPAC Displays.

IFLA Study Group on the Functional Requirements for Bibliographic Records. *Functional Requirements for Bibliographic Records: Final Report.* Munich: K. G. Saur, 1998. Also available at http://www.ifla.org/VII/s13/frbr/frbr.pdf

IFLA Task Force on Guidelines for OPAC Displays. 2003. *Guidelines for Online Public Access Catalogue (OPAC) Displays.* Draft ed. http://www.ifla.org/VII/s13/guide/opacguide03.pdf

International Conference on Cataloguing Principles. 1961. Statement of Principles. In Carpenter and Svenonius 1985, 179–183.

Lubetzky, Seymour. 1953. Cataloging Rules and Principles. In Svenonius and McGarry 2001, 78–139.

———. 1956. Panizzi vs. the "Finding Catalog." In Svenonius and McGarry 2001, 174–179.

———. 1961. The Function of the Main Entry in the Alphabetical Catalogue—One Approach. In Svenonius and McGarry 2001, 231–237.

———. 1969. Principles of Cataloging. Final Report. Phase I: Descriptive Cataloging. 1969. In Svenonius and McGarry 2001, 259–341.

———. 1979. The Fundamentals of Bibliographic Cataloging and AACR2. In Svenonius and McGarry 2001, 369–378.

Lubetzky, Seymour, and Elaine Svenonius. 2000. The Vicissitudes of Ideology and Technology in Anglo-American Cataloging Since Panizzi and a Prospective Reformation of the Catalog for the Next Century. In Svenonius and McGarry 2001, 421–429.

Madison, Olivia M. A. 2005. The Origins of the IFLA Study on Functional Requirements for Bibliographic Records. *Cataloging & Classification Quarterly* 39 (3-4): 1–13.

Miksa, Francis L., ed. 1977. *Charles Ammi Cutter: Library Systematizer.* Littleton, CO: Libraries Unlimited.

Miller, Edward. 1967. *Prince of Librarians: The Life and Times of Antonio Panizzi of the British Museum.* London: Andre Deutsch.

Norris, Dorothy May. 1939. *A History of Cataloguing and Cataloguing Methods, 1100–1850: With an Introductory Survey of Ancient Times.* London: Grafton, 1939.

Osborn, Andrew D. 1941. The Crisis in Cataloging. In Carpenter and Svenonius 1985, 92–103.

Panizzi, Sir Anthony. 1848. Mr. Panizzi to the Right Hon. the Earl of Ellesmere.—British Museum, January 29, 1848. In Carpenter and Svenonius 1985, 18–47.

Pettee, Julia. 1936. The Development of Authorship Entry and the Formulation of Authorship Rules as Found in the Anglo-American Code. In Carpenter and Svenonius 1985, 75–89.

Petroski, Henry. 1999. *The Book on the Bookshelf.* New York: Alfred A. Knopf.

Ranganathan, S. R. 1935. *Library Administration.* Madras: The Madras Library Association.

———. 1955. *Heading and Canons: Comparative Study of Five Catalogue Codes.* Madras: S. Viswanathan.

———. 1963. *The Five Laws of Library Science,* 2nd ed. With amendments. Bombay, India: Asia Publishing House.

———. 1989. *Classified Catalogue Code; With Additional Rules for Dictionary Catalogue Code,* 5th ed. Bangalore, India: Sarada Ranganathan Endowment for Library Science.

Smiraglia, Richard P. 2001. *The Nature of "A Work:" Implications for the Organization of Knowledge.* Lanham, MD: Scarecrow Press, 2001.

Strout, Ruth French. 1956. The development of the catalog and cataloging codes. *The Library Quarterly* 26 (4): 254–275.

Svenonius, Elaine. 2000. *The Intellectual Foundations of Information Organization.* Cambridge, MA: MIT Press.

Svenonius, Elaine, and Dorothy McGarry, eds. 2001. *Seymour Lubetzky: Writings on the Classical Art of Cataloging.* Englewood, CO: Libraries Unlimited.

Taylor, Arlene G. 1993. "Cataloguing." In *World Encyclopedia of Library and Information Services,* ed. Robert Wedgeworth. 3rd ed. Chicago: American Library Association, 177–181.

Tillett, Barbara. 1995. Theoretical and practical foundations. *International Cataloguing and Bibliographic Control* 24: 43–44.

Wilson, Patrick. 1989. The Second Objective. In *The Conceptual Foundations of Descriptive Cataloging,* ed. Elaine Svenonius, 5–16. San Diego: Academic Press.

Notes

1. For more about "principles" see Elisabeth de Rijk Spanhoff, "Principle Issues: Catalog Paradigms, Old and New," *Cataloging & Classification Quarterly* 35, no. 1/2 (2002): 37–59.

2. For a general survey of the history of cataloging, see Norris (1939), Strout (1956), or encyclopedia entries by Carpenter (1994), Hanson and Daily (2003), or Taylor (1993). For a popular history of libraries, see Battles (2003) or Petroski (1999).

3. Elisabeth De Rijk, "Thomas Hyde, Julia Pettee and the Development of Cataloging Principles: With a Translation of Hyde's 1674 Preface to the Reader." *Cataloging & Classification Quarterly* 14, no. 2 (1991): 49.

4. Edward Miller, *Prince of Librarians: The Life and Times of Antonio Panizzi* (London: Andre Deutsch, 1967).

5. Dorothy May Norris, *A History of Cataloguing and Cataloguing Methods, 1100–1850: With an Introductory Survey of Ancient Times* (London: Grafton, 1939).

6. For insight into Panizzi's work, see the writings of Seymour Lubetzky (of whom more later) collected in Svenonius and McGarry (2001).

7. Michael Gorman, "Let Us Now Praise…" *American Libraries* (April 1980): 201.

8. Norris, p. 203.

9. Many were against an Italian taking over the position, and one accusation made was that "Panizzi had been seen in the streets of London selling white mice" (Norris, p. 206).

10. Antonio Panizzi, "Rules for the Compilation of the Catalogue," in British Museum, *The Catalogue of Printed Books in the British Museum* (London, 1841), 1: v–ix. The whole complicated story of how 73 rules became 91 is told in Michael Carpenter's "The Original 73 Rules of the British Museum: A Preliminary Analysis" *Cataloging & Classification Quarterly* 35, no. 1/2 (2002): 23–36.

11. Norris, p. 207.

12. The trustees of the British Museum were headed by the Archbishop of Canterbury, the Lord Chancellor, and the Speaker of the House of Commons. Librarians today who find themselves in a project running late and over budget can be happy that at least they do not have to give progress reports to an archbishop and a royal commission.

13. Nancy Brault, *The Great Debate on Panizzi's Rules in 1847–1849: The Issues Discussed* (Los Angeles: The School of Library Service & The University Library, University of California, 1972), pp. 8–9.

14. During the second investigation Panizzi wrote a long letter to the Earl of Ellesmere, the chair of the commission, explaining the difficulties of building a good catalog. It is still worth reading, and Panizzi (1848) is easy to find in Michael Carpenter and Elaine Svenonius, eds. *Foundations of Cataloging: A Sourcebook* (Littleton, CO: Libraries Unlimited, 1985), pp. 18–47.

15. Seymour Lubetzky and Elaine Svenonius. "The Vicissitudes of Ideology and Technology in Anglo-American Cataloging since Panizzi and a Prospective Reformation of the Catalog for the Next Century," in *Seymour Lubetzky: Writings on the Classical Art of Cataloging,* eds. Elaine Svenonius and Dorothy McGarry (Englewood, CO: Libraries Unlimited, 2001), pp. 421–429.

16. Seymour Lubetzky, "The Fundamentals of Bibliographic Cataloging and AACR2," in Svenonius and McGarry, p. 370.

17. Gladstone was a great reader and also enjoyed sorting and arranging his books. He refers to Panizzi in his essay "On Books and the Housing of Them" (n.d.), available: http://www.gutenberg.org/dirs/etext02/obhot10.txt.

18. Francis L. Miksa, ed., *Charles Ammi Cutter: Library Systematizer* (Littleton, CO: Libraries Unlimited,1977).

19. Charles A. Cutter, *Rules for a Dictionary Catalog,* 4th ed. (Washington, D.C.: Government Printing Office, 1904), p. 3.

20. A digitized version is available online at http://www.hti.umich.edu/cgi/b/bib/bibperm?q1=AEY6826.

21. An interest shared with Dewey, who was born Melville Dewey but preferred Melvil Dui.

22. Cutter, p. 12.

23. Ibid.

24. Ibid., p. 20.

25. IFLA Study Group on the Functional Requirements for Bibliographic Records, *Functional Requirements for Bibliographic Records: Final Report* (Munich: K. G. Saur, 1998), p. 97. Also available at http://www.ifla.org/VII/s13/frbr/frbr.pdf.

26. Seymour Lubetzky, "Principles of Cataloging. Final Report. Phase I: Descriptive Cataloging," in Svenonius and McGarry, p. 273.

27. S. R. Ranganathan, *Heading and Canons: Comparative Study of Five Catalogue Codes* (Madras: S. Viswanathan, 1955), p. 15.

28. For the full story on all this, see Virgil L. P. Blake, "Forging the Anglo-American Cataloging Alliance: Descriptive Cataloging 1830–1908," *Cataloging & Classification Quarterly* 35, no. 1/2 (2002): 3–22.

29. Michael Gorman, "Seymour Lubetzky, Man of Principles," in *The Future of Cataloging: Insights from the Lubetzky Symposium; April 18, 1988, University of California, Los Angeles,* eds. Tschera Harkness Connell and Robert L. Maxwell (Chicago: American Library Association, 2000), p. 13.

30. Blake, "Forging," p. 19.

31. Ibid.

32. "The British committee members were otherwise occupied after September of 1939," as Gorman, "Seymour Lubetzky," p. 14, put it.

33. S. R. Ranganathan, *Library Administration* (Madras: The Madras Library Association, 1935), p. 601.

34. S. R. Ranganathan, *The Five Laws of Library Science,* 2nd ed., with amendments (Bombay, India: Asia Publishing House, 1963), p. 9.

35. S. R. Ranganathan, *Classified Catalogue Code; With Additional Rules for Dictionary Catalogue Code,* 5th ed. (Bangalore, India: Sarada Ranganathan Endowment for Library Science, 1989), p. 77.

36. See also the papers given in honor of Lubetzky's 100th birthday, collected in Connell and Maxwell.

37. Andrew D. Osborn, "The Crisis in Cataloging" (originally written in 1941), In Carpenter and Svenonius, pp. 93–94.

38. Svenonius and McGarry, pp. 75–76.

39. Seymour Lubetzky, "Cataloging Rules and Principles," in Svenonius and McGarry, p. 83.

40. Ibid., p. 113.

41. *FRBR Report,* p. 82

42. Carpenter and Svenonius, *Foundations,* p. 176.

43. International Conference on Cataloguing Principles. "Statement of Principles," in Carpenter and Svenonius, p. 179.

44. Lubetzky, "Principles of Cataloging," p. 273.

45. For a complete look at the "work," see Richard Smiraglia's short and very readable *The Nature of "A Work": Implications for the Organization of Knowledge* (Lanham, MD: Scarecrow Press, 2001).

46. Julia Pettee, "The Development of Authorship Entry and the Formulation of Authorship Rules as Found in the Anglo-American Code," in Carpenter and Svenonius, pp. 75–89. If you read it, follow it with De Rijk, "Thomas Hyde, Julia Pettee" for analysis and background.

47. Pettee, p. 75.

48. De Rijk, "Thomas Hyde, Julia Pettee," pp. 31–62.

49. See Patrick Wilson, "The Second Objective," in *The Conceptual Foundations of Descriptive Cataloging,* ed. Elaine Svenonius (San Diego: Academic Press, 1989), pp. 5–16, named after this Lubetzky snippet, for an important pre-FRBR discussion of the "work."

50. Lubetzky, "Cataloging Rules and Principles," pp. 113–114.

51. Lubetzky, "Principles of Cataloging," pp. 270–271.

52. Smiraglia, *The Nature of "A Work."*

53. Elaine Svenonius, *The Intellectual Foundations of Information Organization* (Cambridge, MA: MIT Press 2000).

54. Gorman, "Seymour Lubetzky," p. 13.

55. Barbara Tillett, "Theoretical and Practical Foundations," *International Cataloguing and Bibliographic Control* 24 (1995): 43–44; Olivia M. A. Madison, "The origins of the IFLA study on Functional Requirements for Bibliographic Records," *Cataloging & Classification Quarterly* 39, no. 3/4 (2005): 1–13.

56. Ross Bourne, ed. *Seminar on Bibliographic Records: Proceedings of the Seminar Held in Stockholm, 15–16 August 1990, and Sponsored by the IFLA UBCIM Programme and the IFLA Division of the Bibliographic Control* (Munich: K. G. Saur, 1992), p. 145.

57. Madison, "The origins of the IFLA study." One wouldn't think reading the history of an international committee on cataloging would be interesting, but it is, because *it's a success story.* Read it to see how six years of committee work made something that will change your world.

58. Ibid., p. 29.

59. Ibid., p. 27.

60. IFLA Task Force on Guidelines for OPAC Displays. 2003. *Guidelines for Online Public Access Catalogue (OPAC) Displays.* Draft ed. http://www.ifla.org/VII/ s13/guide/opacguide03.pdf

61. *FRBR Report,* p. 6.

62. IFLA Meeting of Experts on an International Cataloguing Code, "Statement of International Cataloguing Principles," April 2007 draft, p. 1, available: http://www. nl.go.kr/icc/down/070412_2.pdf

5

The Impact of Research on the
Development of FRBR

Edward T. O'Neill

Background

The Functional Requirements for Bibliographic Records (FRBR) originated with the 57th International Federation of Library Associations and Institutions (IFLA) Council and General Conference when a study group chaired by Olivia M. A. Madison was charged with studying the functional requirements for bibliographic records. Madison[1] provides a detailed history of this effort. Seven years later, the study group issued the *Functional Requirements of Bibliographic Records: Final Report* (FRBR Report)[2]. The FRBR model defines three distinct groups of entities:

1. Publications; the products of intellectual or artistic endeavor
2. Persons or corporate bodies; those responsible for the intellectual or artistic content
3. Concepts, objects, events, and places; those that serve as the subjects of intellectual or artistic endeavor

Much of the report's impact has been on the Group 1 entities. For the Group 1 entities, the study group proposed an entity-relationship model with four primary entities: work, expression, manifestation, and item. Although this is not an entirely new way of viewing these products of intellectual or artistic endeavor, it is different from a traditional cataloging perspective where the focus has been on the manifestation.

The work of the study group built on previous studies. Many of the concepts raised in the *FRBR Report* can be traced to the 1961 Paris Conference on Cataloguing Principles[3] or even earlier work; however, the cataloging environment has changed radically since the Paris Conference. Computers have transformed library catalogs from cards or books to digital records, bibliographic utilities have greatly accelerated shared cataloging, and the Web has accelerated the availability of online information. The impact of these changes is often under-estimated; libraries have gone from being relatively isolated local collections to providing access to virtual global collections. Instead of local collections with thousands of volumes, virtual collections such as OCLC's WorldCat provide access to more than a billion volumes.

In 1959, Verona[4] identified the objectives of the catalog as:

1. The rapid location of a particular book [manifestation];
2. The provision of information concerning all editions, translations etc. [expressions] of a given work as far as they exist in the library;
3. The provision of information concerning all works by a given author as far as they exist in the library.

If the phrase *in the library* is dropped to reflect the ability to access the virtual collection, these objectives are still relevant for author and title searches. Furthermore, at the Paris Conference, Lubetzky and Verona generally accepted these objectives but differed on their importance. Lubetzky[5] argued in favor of the *expression,* whereas Verona[6] emphasized the *manifestation.* This debate focused on the distinction between the physical manifestation and the abstract expression. Lubetzky[7] describes the problem:

> The book, it should be noted, comes into being as a dichotomic product—as a material object or medium used to convey the intellectual work of an author. Because the material book embodies and represents the intellectual work, the two have come to be confused, and the terms are synonymously used

At the time of the Paris Conference, when the catalog reflected the local collection, this distinction itself may have appeared somewhat abstract. In any particular library most works had only a single manifestation, and only a small number of works had more than a few different manifestations. Today multiple-manifestation works are common. Applying the work set algorithm[8] [described later in this chapter] to WorldCat, it was found that more than half of the billion plus holdings are associated with multiple-manifestation works. Hickey and O'Neill[9] provide the distribution of manifestations per work and identify works with the most manifestations.

IFLA's Role

IFLA has played a key role in developing FRBR. The origins of FRBR can be traced to the 1990 Stockholm Seminar on Bibliographic Records, which was jointly sponsored by the IFLA Universal Bibliographic Control and International MARC (UBCIM) Programme and the IFLA Division of Bibliographic Control. One of the resolutions coming out of that seminar called for the creation of a study to define the functional requirements for bibliographic records. The scope of the study was defined as follows:[10]

> The purpose of this study is to delineate in clearly defined terms the functions performed by the bibliographic record with respect to various media, various applications, and various user needs. The study is to cover the full range of functions for the bibliographic record in its widest sense—i.e. a record that encompasses not only descriptive elements, but access points (name, title, subject, etc.), other "organizing" elements (classification, etc.), and annotations.

In 1992, the scope and purpose were approved by the Standing Committee on Cataloguing and the members of the study group were appointed. Their report was approved in 1997. Since its approval, the FRBR model has created considerable interest within the broader library community. The *FRBR Report* stressed that "The model operates at the conceptual level; it does not carry the analysis to the level that would be required for a fully developed data model."[11] While this premise is widely accepted, attempts to apply the model frequently resulted in varying interpretations. FRBR is not a fully developed model but rather a model that requires continuing refinement, interpretation, and development.

To support this ongoing development of the FRBR model, three high-level groups, one for each of the three types of entities, have been established. The FRBR Review Group focuses primarily on the Group 1 entities, the Working Group on Functional Requirements and Numbering of Authority Records (FRANAR) focuses on the Group 2 entities, and the Working Group on Functional Requirements for Subject Authority Records (FRSAR) focuses on the Group 3 entities.

The FRANAR Working Group was the first group to be established. It was formed in April 1999 by the IFLA Division of Bibliographic Control and the IFLA UBCIM and was charged with the following:

1. To define functional requirements of authority records;
2. To study the feasibility of an International Standard Authority Data Number;
3. To serve as the official IFLA liaison to and work with other interested groups concerning authority files.[12]

The FRANAR Working Group produced the second draft of the *Functional Requirements for Authority Records: A Conceptual Model.*[13] This draft was made available for worldwide review and comments in April 2007. An earlier draft was released in 2005 and the second draft of the report reflects the comments received during the initial review period. The second draft is titled *Functional Requirements for Authority Data (FRAD).*

In 2002, the Cataloging Section created the Working Group on FRBR, which was upgraded to a Review Group the next year. The FRBR Review Group has a more formal structure than the working groups. Its members are elected by the Cataloguing Section Standing Committee for fixed terms. The current membership and other details are provided on the IFLA Web site.[14] The FRBR Review Group is charged with updating of the International Standard Bibliographic Descriptions (ISBDs); to assist with proposals for incorporating FRBR terminology and concepts in an international cataloging code; to monitor and assist with the development of FRBR concepts in bibliographic record communication formats; to assist with and encourage continued enhancement of the model; to recommend improvements to existing OPACs; to develop training tools and maintain a bibliography on FRBR; to provide mappings or point to mappings with related models and ontologies; and generally to promote FRBR, notably by explaining it, clarifying its definitions and concepts, and providing guidelines for its implementation in current cataloging practice.[15] Many of these activities are coordinated with other units within IFLA.

Much of the FRBR Review Group activities are carried out by Working Groups charged with narrower charges and with limited duration. Currently, the FRBR Review Group has three working groups described on the Cataloguing Section's Web site as:

1. **Working Group on the Expression entity.** Tasks: "to clarify the Expression entity and provide application guidelines through examples."
2. **Working Group on Aggregates.** Tasks: "to investigate practical solutions to the specific problems encountered in modeling (a) collections, selections, anthologies…, (b) augmentations, (c) series, (d) journals, (e) integrating resources, (f) multipart monographs, all of which are gathered under the generic term "aggregates."
3. **Working Group on FRBR/CRM Dialogue.** Tasks: "in cooperation with the CIDOC CRM SIG, prepare an object-oriented formulation of FRBR (FRBRoo) which is a compatible extension of the CRM conceptual reference model."

The following three earlier working groups have been disbanded. Their mission is described by Žumer[16] or by IFLA[17] as:

1. **Working Group on Continuing Resources.** Task: investigate whether the FRBR model is sufficient to account for all peculiar aspects of continuing resources and to assist the process of revision of the ISSN standard through recommendations.
2. **Working Group on Subject Relationships.** Task: produce a follow-up study that expands FRBR and FRANAR in the fields of subject indexing and classification.
3. **Working Group on Teaching and Training.** Tasks: To compare and assess different methods of teaching FRBR and to produce a "Manual for FRBR Teachers."

The Working Group on Continuing Resources was disbanded when it was "decided that a new Study Group should be formed in order to model the peculiarities of continuing resources, independently from the FRBR conceptual framework, and taking time aspects more into account."[18] Some aspects of the Working Group on Continuing Resources have also been assumed by the Working group on Aggregates. The Working Group on Subject Relationships was superseded by the FRSAR Working Group. The Working Group on Teaching and Training disbanded after concluding that "Those who are actually teaching cataloguing have mastered FRBR and are integrating it into their curriculum."[19]

The newest group is the FRSAR Working Group, which was established in April 2005. Its charge[20] is to:

1. Build a conceptual model of Group 3 entities within the FRBR framework as they relate to the aboutness of works (Entities in Group 1 and Group 2 can be used as the subjects of works but further inclusion of them will depend on the outcomes of the work of the FRANAR Working Group).
2. Provide a clearly defined, structured frame of reference for relating the data that are recorded in subject authority records to the needs of the users of those records.
3. Assist in an assessment of the potential for international sharing and use of subject authority data both within the library sector and beyond.

FRBR Research

In 2005, *Cataloging & Classification Quarterly* released a special theme issue entitled *Functional Requirements for Bibliographic Records (FRBR): Hype or Cure-All?*[21] This publication was not an official publication of IFLA or the FRBR Review Group, but it was promoted and edited by Patrick Le Boeuf, who at the time was the chair the FRBR Review Group, and most of the members of the FRBR Review Group contributed to this special issue.

IFLA and particularly the FRBR Review Group and the various working groups have played a particularly significant role in promoting FRBR research. The group created and continues to support the FRBR Bibliography.[22] The bibliography has more than 500 entries and is updated regularly. Some resources included in the bibliography are only indirectly related to FRBR and others predate FRBR, but most of the resources are directly relevant. The bibliography is comprehensive and is organized by topic (Table 5.1). This topical organization provides much insight into the areas that have been a focus of FRBR researchers.

It is not the purpose of this chapter to review any of these studies individually or even to attempt to identify the more significant studies. The bibliography is well organized and most of the resources are available online so that readers can directly access the resources and make their own judgments. The goal here is limited to broadly describing the major FRBR research areas and the role of research in influencing the development of FRBR.

Table 5.1.
FRBR Research Areas

Research Area	Number of Entries
Theoretical Aspects	119
Impact on Current Standards	68
Application Studies	117
Implementations and Research	98
Relationship to Other Models	41
Teaching FRBR	50
Other FRBR-related Material	28
Total	521

General, introductory, and promotional materials are included under theoretical aspects. This group also includes attempts to clarify, refine, or modify the definitions of works, expressions, and manifestations. In the *FRBR Report,* these entities are defined conceptually; but the *Report* is not a cataloging code, and many of these studies reexamine the Group 1 entities, often focusing on a particular genre such as music or film.

Initially, there was considerable interest in the teaching of FRBR. A lot of the documents in this area address the general question of how to introduce and explain FRBR; others focus more on integrating FRBR into the library education curriculum. As FRBR has become more accepted, however, interest in this area has waned. The consensus of the Working Group on Teaching and Training was that a good set of educational resources had been developed, and FRBR was being integrated successfully into the library education curriculum.

There have been a number of studies exploring the potential impact of FRBR on cataloging rules, as well as on the ISBD. Although FRBR is not a cataloging code, most authors agree that it will have a major impact on them. The Joint Steering Committee for Revision of Anglo-American Cataloguing Rules states "Underlying RDA [Resource Description and Access; previously known as AACR3] are the conceptual models FRBR (*Functional Requirements for Bibliographic Records*) and FRAD (*Functional Requirements for Authority Data*). FRBR is the basis for Part A (Description) of RDA, and FRAD is the basis for Part B (Access Point Control)."[23] IFLA has held a series of meetings of experts on an international cataloging code with the goal to "increase the ability to share cataloguing information worldwide by promoting standards for the content of bibliographic records and authority records used in library catalogues."[24] These meetings of experts are occurring independently of FRBR development but, as with RDA, they are heavily influenced by FRBR. The introduction to the statement of international cataloging principles from the Frankfurt meeting states that "These new principles build on the great cataloguing traditions of the world, and also on the conceptual models of the IFLA documents *Functional Requirements for Bibliographic Records* (FRBR) and *Functional Requirements and Numbering for Authority Records* (FRANAR), which extend the Paris Principles to the realm of subject cataloguing."[25]

The largest single area of study has been FRBR applications and implementations. Although the bibliography treats these as separate topics, they are closely related. Together they account for almost half of the entries. Considerable work has been devoted to the application of the FRBR model, both to general collections and to specialized collections. One common theme in many applications and implementations was identified by Matthew Beacom; "Before this digital divide, we based description on the 'physical' form of the item in hand."[26] In the FRBR model, both works and expressions are abstract entities that lack physical form until embodied in a manifestation.

A number of studies have attempted to apply FRBR to particular domains—electronic resources, continuing resources, music, audiovisual materials, performing arts, rare books, etc. The *FRBR Report* gives only passing attention to the application in these specialized fields, and some of these studies serve as models of the specialized applications, whereas others identify the unique problems encountered in attempting to "FRBRize"—that is, converting from the traditional single bibliographic entity model to the four entity FRBR model—special types of resources.

There also have been a variety of studies that have reported on particular aspects of FRBR applications from a functional perspective. Studies of this type have explored the impact and application in areas such as rights management, authority control, classification and subject indexing, quality control, and the semantic Web. The benefit of FRBR to rights management is fairly obvious; intellectual property rights are more closely linked to works and expressions than to particular manifestations of a work. Therefore FRBR potentially can provide a view of the bibliographic universe that is closer to the rights management view. Other studies have models for organizing or presenting information, including RDA, Conceptual Reference Model (CRM), and Interoperability of Data in E-Commerce Systems (INDECS).

In many ways, FRBR exposes errors and inconsistencies that were previously largely unnoticed. In studying the 179 bibliographic records in OCLC's WorldCat for different manifestations of Tobias Smollett's *The Expedition of Humphry Clinker,* O'Neill[27] found that inconsistencies in the bibliographic records were a serious impediment to identifying expressions. There were a variety of different forms of Smollet's name as a main entry, and a number of bibliographic records did not include *The Expedition of Humphry Clinker* either in the title statement or as a uniform title. The variation in title and main entry makes it extremely difficult to algorithmically identify all of the manifestations of a work. In the *Humphry Clinker* study, many of the manifestations were identified only through a combination of algorithmic and manual searching with extensive manual review. Even with that level of effort, some manifestations may not have been identified. The "FRBRization" challenge is to find an algorithm that is effective with less than perfect data.

There can also be a large variation in subject cataloging for the work. The variation in subject cataloging rarely affects "FRBRization," because the subject attributes are not commonly used in that context. The subject inconsistency, however, does affect retrieval; subject searches involving large works will rarely retrieve all manifestations. FRBR potentially can improve subject cataloging while also increasing cataloging productivity. *Aboutness* is a work property; all expressions and manifestations of a work should share the classification and indexing of the work. In principle, the subject cataloging can be done once for the work rather than being individually done for each manifestation. By viewing the classification and indexing assigned to the various manifestations of a work, an improved set of class numbers and subject headings can be derived for the work as a whole.

There have been a number of large-scale implementations around the world including the AustLit Gateway (Australia),[28] RLG's RedLightGreen (United States),[29] and BIBSYS[30] (Norway). Local systems venders have also been moving to incorporate FRBR into their catalogs. VTLS, Inc. in particular has been a leader in integrating FRBR into their systems.[31] The Library of Congress developed a FRBR display that can "be used to cluster bibliographic records retrieved via a search in more meaningful displays to assist users in selecting items from bibliographic collections."[32] These implementations all have reported that FRBR is a practical and valuable model for displaying and organizing bibliographic data.

The OCLC work-set algorithm is one of the more successful "FRBRization" applications; a detailed description of the algorithm is available online[33] and has proven its effectiveness. The work-set algorithm is an automated method of identifying all manifestations of a work that exist in a bibliographic database. It does not attempt to identify expressions or to associate manifestations with expressions. It is based on the simple concept that all manifestations of a given work share a common author and title; therefore a combination of the author and title should be sufficient to identify all manifestations. The description of the work-set algorithm that follows is greatly simplified and is intended to illustrate the algorithm's principles. Continuing with the *Humphry Clinker* example, the relevant fields from a bibliographic record for a typical manifestation are shown here:

```
100 1 Smollett, Tobias George, $d 1721-1771.
245 14 The expedition of Humphry Clinker / $c with
introduction and notes by L. Rice-Oxley.
260 London: $b Oxford University Press, $c 1960,
c1925.
300 xx, 440 p.; $c 16 cm.
440 4 The World's classics; $v 290
740 01 Humphry Clinker.
```

From the bibliographic record, the author and title can be extracted from the main entry and the title statement (100 and 245 fields, respectively):

```
Author: Smollett, Tobias George, $d 1721-1771
Title: The expedition of Humphry Clinker
```

If the bibliographic record had had a uniform title, it would have been used in preference to the title statement. The second indicator in the title statement is used to indicate that the leading "the" should be ignored. For further standardization, the author and title are normalized using the Name Authority Cooperative Program (NACO) rules[34] and concatenated using a slash as a delimiter to form the author/title key:

```
smollett, tobias george$1721 1771/expedition of
humphry clinker
```

The normalization process eliminates most stylistic variations by dropping diacritics, changing all alphabetic characters to lower case, eliminating most punctuation, and other similar stylistic changes. Ideally, all of the manifestations of *Humphry Clinker* will produce the same key; however, that is true only when both the author and title are controlled. When either is uncontrolled, it is likely to result in a variant author/title key. The 179 manifestations of *Humphry Clinker* produced nine different keys from variant authors:

> Smollett, Tobias George
> Smollett, Tobias, $d1721–1771

and variant titles:

> The expedition of Humphrey Clinker
> Humphrey Clinker
> Humphry Clinker
> Călătoriile lui Humphrey Clinker
> Humphry Klinkers Reisen
> Výprava Humfrida Clinkera
> Výprava Humfrida Clinkers

The last four titles are for the Rumanian, German, and two different Czech translations.

Without further processing, the conclusion would be that each of these nine unique keys represents a distinct work, and it would be assumed that these 179 manifestations were part of nine different works rather than just a single work.

One of the bibliographic records that produced a variant key is:

```
100 1 Smollett, Tobias George, $d 1721–1771.
245 10 Humphry Clinker / $c Tobias George Smol-
lett.
260 New York: $b G. Routledge & Sons, $c c1888.
300 2 v.; $c 17 cm.
```

This resulted in the variant author/title key of:

```
smollett, tobias$1721–1771/humphry clinker
```

To minimize the number of variant keys, the work-set algorithm uses information from authority records to control variant forms of the author name and the title. The cross reference in the following authority record would be used to convert the title from the bibliographic record, *Humphry Clinker,* to *Expedition of Humphry Clinker.*

```
010 n 81116162

040 DLC $b eng $c DLC

100 1 Smollett, Tobias George, $d 1721-1771. $t
Expedition of

Humphry Clinker

400 1 Smollett, Tobias George, $d 1721-1771. $t
Humphry Clinker

670 His Humphry Clinker, c1982.
```

After the title change, the new author/title keys match and this manifestation will be correctly linked to the work. A similar methodology is used to revise the form of the author's name.

In addition to using authority records, the work-set algorithm also uses a variety of other techniques to minimize the number of variant keys, but no other single method has as much impact as authority control. It also includes provisions for processing records with corporate name and conference and meeting name main entries, as well as records without main entries. For the *Humphry Clinker* example, these techniques reduced the number of works by correctly identifying all of the English-language manifestations.

The algorithm did fail to associate four translations of the work. For translations, uniform titles are particularly critical. The bibliographic records for the four translations of *Humphry Clinker* that had uniform titles were successfully matched; the four translations without uniform titles were not matched. If the authority record had included the translated titles as cross references, they also would have been used to link the translations. Experience with the work-set algorithm clearly indicates that the results are significantly improved for records with controlled names and titles or names that can be controlled. Uncontrolled headings were the primary reason that the algorithm failed to identify some of the manifestations.

One area where both researchers and implementers have reported difficulties is related to the definition of the Group 1 entities—particularly the expression entity. The *FRBR Report* specifies that "if a text is revised or modified, the resulting *expression* is considered to be a new *expression,* no matter how minor the modification may be."[35] The phrase *no matter how minor* is widely perceived to be a problem. Strict application requires a detailed character-by-character comparison to ensure that the items are identical. Objections have also been made because distinguishing expressions at this level does not serve the user well—few users are likely to notice very minor changes and even fewer are likely to care.

Another area where there was lack of agreement related to the treatment of augmentations. Augmentations occur when an expression is accompanied with other supplemental material such as illustrations, notes, forewords, or other similar material that is not an integral part of the work. The prevailing view was that augmenting an expression created a new expression. When new illustrations are added, for example, the result was considered to be a new expression even if no changes were made to the original expression itself.

A third area of concern was the treatment of aggregates. Aggregates are manifestations comprised of multiple works. There are two distinct types of aggregates: collections and augmentations. Collections are groups of two or more works that are physically *published* together. The collection may be edited but the individual works were created independently. Collections include selections, anthologies, monographic series, serials, and other similar groups of resources. Initially it was common to treat collections as works in their own right, but that view is not currently universally accepted. Treating augmentations as aggregates is the alternative to treating augmentations as new works.

FRBR, including the *FRBR Report,* is a work in progress that can and should be updated when necessary and justifiable. To that end, the Expression Working Group was formed to attempt to resolve the difficulties reported with expressions. After a careful and detailed review, The Expression Working Group recommended a group of revisions be made to the *FRBR Report.* Included in the recommended revisions was a relaxation of the *no matter how minor* rule to allow for slight variations within an expression and to treat most augmentations as separate expressions of their own separate works. The details on these and other proposed changes relating to the expression are available for review, although the period for comment has passed.[36] In response to the concerns about aggregates, FRBR Review Group formed the Aggregates Working Group to examine the treatment of aggregates and, if necessary, recommend revisions.

Conclusion

Attempting to summarize and draw conclusions from more than 500 FRBR-related documents is a challenging task and likely to misrepresent or ignore some important studies. It certainly appears, however, that FRBR has been widely accepted. The doubters have been few and their reservations have generally been limited to particular aspects of the model rather than the rejection of the model as a whole. It is clearly having a major influence on cataloging codes, although exactly how it will be codified is not yet apparent. Because FRBR is a conceptual model, considerable interpretation will be necessary to incorporate it into cataloging codes. One of the challenges to groups such as the Joint Steering Committee for Revision of Anglo-American Cataloguing Rules is to reap the benefits of FRBR without making the cataloging codes overly complex.

Notes

1. Olivia M. A. Madison, "The Origins of the IFLA Study on the Functional Requirements for Bibliographic Records," *Cataloging & Classification Quarterly* 39, no. 3/4 (2005): 15–37.

2. IFLA Study Group on the Functional Requirements of Bibliographic Records, *Functional Requirements of Bibliographic Records: Final Report* (München: K. G. Saur, 1998). http://www.ifla.org/VII/s13/frbr/frbr.pdf (accessed September 25, 2006).

3. International Conference on Cataloguing Principles, Paris, 1961, *International Conference on Cataloguing Principles: Report* (London, Clive Bingley on behalf of IFLA, 1963).

4. Eva Verona, "Literary Unit Versus Bibliographical Unit," *Libri* 9, no. 2 (1959): p. 79.

5. Seymour Lubetzky, "The Function of the Main Entry in the Alphabetical Catalogue—One Approach," in *International Conference on Cataloguing Principles, Paris*, 1961, pp. 39–143.

6. Eva Verona, "The Function of the Main Entry in the Alphabetical Catalogue—A second Approach," in *International Conference on Cataloguing Principles, Paris*, 1961, pp. 145–157.

7. Seymour Lubetzky, *Principles of Cataloging. Final Report. Phase I: Descriptive Cataloging* (Los Angeles: Institute of Library Research, University of California, 1969), p.11.

8. Thomas B. Hickey and Jenny Toves. *FRBR Work-Set Algorithm*, OCLC, July 2003. http://www.oclc.org/research/software/frbr/frbr_workset_algorithm.pdf (Accessed February 6, 2007).

9. Thomas B. Hickey and Edward T. O'Neill. "FRBRizing OCLC's WorldCat," *Cataloging & Classification Quarterly*, 39, no. 3/4 (2005): 239–251.

10. *FRBR Report*, p. 2.

11. *FRBR Report*, p. 4.

12. IFLA, Division of Bibliographic control, Working Group on FRANAR. http://www.ifla.org/VII/d4/wg-franar.htm (Accessed July 22, 2007).

13. IFLA Working Group on Functional Requirements and Numbering of Authority Records. *Functional Requirements for Authority Data: A Conceptual Model (second draft)*. http://www.ifla.org/VII/d4/FRANAR-Conceptual-2ndReview.pdf (Accessed July 22, 2007).

14. IFLA Cataloguing Section, FRBR Review Group. http://www.ifla.org/VII/s13/wgfrbr/index.htm.

15. Ibid.

16. Maja Žumer, "Implementation of FRBR: European Research Initiative," *Cataloging & Classification Quarterly* 39, no. 3/4 (2005): 233.

17. IFLA Cataloguing Section, FRBR Review Group, IFLA Working Group on Teaching and Training, *Report of the Activities, 2005–2006*. http://www.ifla.org/VII/s13/wgfrbr/WG-TeachingReport_2005-06.pdf, (Accessed February 1, 2007).

18. IFLA Cataloguing Section, FRBR Review Group, "Status Report of Activities, 2004–2005." http://www.ifla.org/VII/s13/wgfrbr/FRBRRG_ActivityReport_2004-05.pdf (Accessed September 28, 2006).

19. Ibid.

20. Working Group [on] Functional Requirements for Subject Authority Records (FRSAR). http://www.ifla.org/VII/s29/wgfrsar.htm.

21. Patrick Le Boeuf, ed. "Functional Requirements for Bibliographic Records (FRBR): Hype or Cure-All?" Special issue of *Cataloging & Classification Quarterly,* 39, nos. 3/4 (2005). Simultaneously issued by Haworth Information Press as a book with the same title, ISBN 0–7890–2798–4.

22. "FRBR Bibliography, version 10.11, Sept. 8, 2006." http://infoserv.inist.fr/ wwsympa.fcgi/d_read/frbr/FRBR_bibliography.rtf (Accessed September 29, 2006). Another version is available on IFLANET at http://www.ifla.org/VII/s13/wgfrbr/ FRBR_bibliography.pdf.

23. Joint Steering Committee for Revision of Anglo-American Cataloguing Rules, *RDA: Resource Description and Access.* http://www.collectionscanada.ca/jsc/rda.html (Accessed February 3, 2007).

24. IFLA, Series on Bibliographic Control, "IFLA Cataloguing Principles Steps towards an International Cataloguing Code." http://www.ifla.org/V/pr/Bibliographic-Control-vol26.htm (Accessed February 3, 2007).

25. IFLA Meeting of Experts on an International Cataloguing Code, "IFLA cataloguing principles: steps towards an international cataloguing code: report from the 1st IFLA Meeting of Experts on an International Cataloguing Code, Frankfurt, 2003." (München, Germany: K. G. Saur, 2004).

26. Matthew Beacom, "Crossing a Digital Divide: AACR2 and Unaddressed Problems of Networked Resources," in *Conference on Bibliographic Control for the New Millennium,* Library of Congress, Washington D.C., 2000. http://www.loc.gov/ catdir/bibcontrol/beacom_paper.html (Accessed February 4, 2007).

27. Edward T. O'Neill, "FRBR (Functional Requirements for Bibliographic Records): Application of the Entity-Relationship Model to Humphry Clinker," *Library Resources and Technical Services* 46, no. 4 (2002): 150–159.

28. Marie-Louise Ayres, Kerry Kilner, Kent Fitch, and Annette Scarvell. "Report on the successful AustLit: Australian Literature Gateway implementation of the FRBR and INDECS event models, and implications for other FRBR implementations," in 68th IFLA General Conference and Council, August 18–24, 2002, Glasgow, Scotland. http:// www.ifla.org/IV/ifla68/papers/054-133e.pdf (Accessed February 11, 2007).

29. Merrilee Proffitt, "RedLightGreen: FRBR between a rock and a hard place," in *Back to the future,* ALCTS Preconference, ALA Annual Meeting, Orlando, June 25, 2004. http://www.ala.org/ala/alcts/alctsconted/presentations/Proffitt.pdf (Accessed February 11, 2007).

30. Trond Aalberg, "From Marc to FRBR: A case study in the use of the FRBR model on the BIBSYS database," in *Bibliotheca Universalis: How to organize chaos?* Finish Library Association, August 11–12, 2005. http://www.fla.fi.frbr05/aalberg2BIB SYSfrbrized.pdf.

31. Vinod Chachra and John Espley. "Differentiating libraries through enriched use searching: FRBR as the next dimension in meaningful information retrieval," in *Back to the Future,* ALCTS Preconference, ALA Annual Meeting, Orlando, June 25, 2004. http://www.ala.org/ala/alcts/alctsconted/presentations/Chachra.pdf (Accessed February 11, 2007).

32. Library of Congress. Network Development and MARC Standards Office, "FRBR Display Tool", Version 2. http://www.loc.gov/marc/marc-functional-analysis/ tool.html (Accessed February 11, 2007).

33. Thomas B. Hickey and Jenny Toves. *FRBR Work-Set Algorithm,* OCLC, July 2003. http://www.oclc.org/research/software/frbr/frbr_workset_algorithm.pdf (Accessed February 6, 2007).

34. NACO. "Authority File Comparison Rules, 9/16/98, revised Feb. 09 2001," http://www.loc.gov/catdir/pcc/naco/normrule.html#a. (Accessed February 12, 2007).

35. *FRBR Report,* p. 19.

36. Cataloguing Section. FRBR Review Group. "Invitation to participate: World-wide review of revisions to FRBR section 3.2.2, definition of the entity expression." http://www.ifla.org/VII/s13/wgfrbr/expression-invitation.htm (Accessed February 12, 2007).

6

Bibliographic Families and Superworks

Richard P. Smiraglia

Perhaps the major contribution of the FRBR model is the separate identification, for the first time in the history of bibliographic control, of "the work" as an essential and distinct bibliographic entity. The result of this isolation of the work entity will lead to a major drop in redundancy in the future catalog and should lead to increasingly sophisticated retrieval of works. To accomplish both goals, catalogs or other retrieval mechanisms using the FRBR model will need to attend to the intricacies of what are sometimes called "bibliographic families"—groups of works that share common intellectual content. The FRBR report itself makes no direct reference to bibliographic families, but their importance is implicit in the emphasis on work-to-work, work-to-expression, and expression-to-expression relationships.[1] Specifically, the report defines the entities "work" and "expression"; thus, a work is an identifiable intellectual or artistic creation,[2] and an expression is the specific form that a work takes when realized. The narrative points out that a work might be realized through one or more expressions, which in turn might be embodied in one or more manifestations.[3] There is, then, a presumption that a work might be the central or anchoring node of a group of realizations that differ from one another in various ways, but that all of them have in common the single, identifiable intellectual or artistic endeavor. Finally, FRBR defines basic bibliographic functionality as the ability to identify and find all manifestations and expressions of a work, as well as to be able to select among them. In this chapter, I look at the nature of works by analyzing the known parameters of bibliographic families. I also consider the concept of instantiation, which is the phenomenon that drives the evolution of bibliographic families, and the notion of the "superwork," which describes an overarching abstract concept.

The Concept of a Bibliographic Family

The "bibliographic family" is a metaphor that seems to have originated with Patrick Wilson. His famous book *Two Kinds of Power* is a landmark work in bibliographic control.[4] He posited the parameters of what he called a bibliographical universe—a universe in which *works* (not books mind you) were the orbiting bodies. There were two domains in Wilson's universe; today we might call them concept-spaces. One was called "exploitative" and this was the more important (or at least the more idealistic). In this domain the scholar sought always the most useful information. Once located, an idea from prior research fed the development of new ideas, which in turn led to new knowledge to be shared with all. It was a very idealistic point of view about human scholarship. But, idealism aside, it was also a way, for the first time, of recognizing some sort of efficacy about the other domain, which he called "descriptive." This was the domain where catalogers and indexers toiled to write down records of all known recorded knowledge. The trick was, since those who have the works do not need to find them, this domain always suffers from the concept of "known-item search." This is the let-them-eat-cake syndrome of bibliographic control—the notion that if you really want something, you ought to know enough about it to track it down. But back in the exploitative domain, how is the scholar to know that what he or she really seeks is not the text of *A Thousand Miles up the Nile,* but instead author Amelia Edwards's nineteenth-century illustrations?

The bibliographic family is part of the answer. Wilson said there were large constellations in the bibliographical universe of what he called texts that were so alike that they seemed to orbit each other with some sort of gravity, just like planets. Specifically, he made a clear distinction between the abstract concept "work," and any semantic instance of it, which he called a "text." He said that "a work simply is a group or family of texts, and . . . for a text to be a text of a particular work is the same thing as for it to be a member of a certain family."[5] Creating a work, Wilson said, was tantamount to starting a family by composing its ancestor. And the family metaphor was also apt because, as it turns out, bibliographic families are a little bit like human families. They have lots of members. Some of the members are practically identical and others have just a name in common and still others have just some atomic matter (which, later, we will call ideational content) in common.

In this chapter we explore the concept of a bibliographic family. Through examples we will see the limits of the metaphor. At the end we will see what this has to do with FRBR in terms of implementing a relational model of a work in the future catalog. And then we will see what science has told us about what we are here calling bibliographic families.

What Does a Bibliographic Family Look Like?

Bibliographic families are all unique in the relationship the members bear to the originating work, called the progenitor; yet distinct patterns occur among the members. These patterns are really names of types of relationships—relationships among works that have a common progenitor (sometimes these are termed "derivative bibliographic relationships."[6] Except where noted, these terms have all been derived from the taxonomy in Smiraglia:

- Simultaneous editions—this relationship holds when editions of a work are published in more than one place at the same time. This category includes Yee's "near equivalent" category for moving-image materials with identical distribution characteristics.[7]
- Successive editions—this is the relationship among editions of a work that appear over time (3rd ed., 4th ed., etc.).
- Predecessors—this relationship holds between progenitor works that are somehow in sequence, such as sequels.
- Amplifications—when a work appears together with additional material, such as an illustrated text, or a text republished with commentary.
- Extractions—this is the relationship between segments of a work that have been separately published.
- Accompanying materials—this relationship holds between works that are intended to be kept together, such as a textbook and a teaching aid published with it.[8]
- Musical presentation—this is the relationship between two different iterations of a musical work, such as a full score and a vocal score of an opera.[9]
- Notational transcription—this relationship holds between two writings, usually in different systems, of the same musical work, such as a work for lute in Renaissance tablature and also in modern notation.[10]
- Persistent works—this term identifies relationships among exemplars of a work that persist over time, such as a one-time bestseller that continues to appear in new editions over time.[11]
- Translations—a complete and deliberate rendering of a work in a language other than that in which it was composed.
- Adaptations—an alteration of the work to make it more accessible to an audience other than that for which it was composed, such as condensed versions of novels, or children's adaptations.
- Performances—a version for live rendering of a work that originated in written form; music, theater, screenplays, etc.

Most of the patterns in this list (all except "predecessor") fall into the category of what FRBR calls "expressions." One can see at once that the concept bears further refinement. In fact, recent research has demonstrated that these patterns represent types rather than categories of relationships. That is, just as a bird might be both male and feathered, so can a work be both a translation and a successive edition. This makes quantification of bibliographic families difficult (one of the problems with the metaphor), yet the categories have been demonstrated to be useful in many studies over the past two decades.

Examples

The best way to understand the concept of a bibliographic family is to consider some examples. We begin with a very simple, and also very typical bibliographic family for a work that exists in several editions. Figure 6.1 contains a brief bibliography of the known editions of Bruce Berg's *Qualitative research methods for the social sciences.*

- Boston: Allyn and Bacon, 1989. viii, 172 p.
- 2nd ed. Boston: Allyn and Bacon, c1995. xiii, 252 p.
- 3rd ed. Boston: Allyn and Bacon, c1998. xiii, 290 p.
- 4th ed. Boston: Allyn and Bacon, c2001. xv, 304 p.
- 5th ed. Boston; London: Pearson/Allyn and Bacon, 2003. 336 p.
  - ➤ Princeton, N.J.: Recording for the Blind & Dyslexic, 2005. 1 CD.mono.
- 6th ed. Boston; London: Pearson/Allyn & Bacon, c2007. xvi, 384 p.

Figure 6.1. Berg's *Qualitative Research Methods.*

Citations for these books came from the OCLC WorldCat. Notice that there are six successive editions, and that each edition is slightly larger than its predecessor. In fact, as the qualitative paradigm has developed, Berg has changed some of the content. For example, early editions had a chapter called "sociometric research," which from the fifth edition on was replaced with a chapter on "action research." So, although much of the content remains stable across all six editions, not all of it does. Notice that the cataloging for editions 5 and 6 indicates that they are simultaneously published in Boston and in London. In fact, all of these editions bear the statement "Boston London Toronto Sydney Tokyo Singapore" on their title pages, so this is a problem with the misrepresentation of knowledge based on interpretation of cataloging rules. There is one performance—a sound recording for the blind and dyslexic. In this simple, linear bibliographic family then, there is only one node, with six branches. The fifth branch itself has one branch, for the content of the recorded performance is presumably the same as that of the fifth edition.

A second example, also fairly typical, involves a musical work. Because of the many musical functions required to mount a performance, a variety of functional documents will arise to assist in conveying the musical work to the listening public. Figure 6.2 is a brief bibliography of printed editions of Shostakovich's 14th string quartet available in the OCLC WorldCat.

Notice that functionally we have three iterations—a score, conveying the entire work; a miniature score, conveying the same image but reduced in size

- Moskva: Muzyka, 1974. miniature score (51 p.); 22 cm. and parts; 29 cm.
- Partitura. Moskva: Izd-vo DSCH; [Milwaukee, WI: Distributed by H. Leonard], c2001. 1 score (44 p.) 29 cm. H. Leonard 073999842747.
- Partitura [i] golosa = Score [and] parts. Moskva: Izd-vo DSCH; [Milwaukee, WI: Distributed by H. Leonard], c2001. Publisher's no.: 50484264 (Score) ; 50484265 (Parts). 073999842647 (Score) 073999292046 (Parts)

Figure 6.2. Shostakovich, Quartets, strings, no. 14, op. 142, F# major.

for use as a study guide; and a set of score and parts, the parts being the music for each instrument alone. Notice that the publication details suggest that we are likely looking at three impressions from the same musical image originated by the Soviet era state music publisher. This is a very simple bibliographic family and also one that occurs typically in all kinds of libraries—one work, one musical image, three functional iterations.

There are two key points to be made at this time in our discussion. The first is that in both cases the members of the bibliographic family would be somewhat indistinct in the catalog, collocating by main entry (or the citation for the progenitor). In fact, brief displays such as are common in online catalogs would likely provide no immediate distinction among the entities in either bibliographic family. The second is that in both cases the catalog is subject to a large amount of redundancy, as each iteration requires the repetition of common bibliographic data. In fact, these examples were deliberately constructed using details of publication to reduce redundancy. In the catalog, the common citations would appear foremost, and they might appear to be indistinguishable at first glance. These two issues are the main reasons bibliographic families are important in the catalog, and the *FRBR* entity-relationship model promises to help with both problems.

What Do We Really Know about Works?

We might now ask what research has demonstrated concerning the real parameters of works, in the library catalog and in the bibliographic universe at large. The answer is that we have actually learned quite a lot in a brace of studies. A meta-analysis brought the evidence together in one place to demonstrate just what we know.[12]

First, we know that the phenomenon of the bibliographic family conforms, more or less, with typical bibliographic distributions. That is, most works exist in only one iteration, the "first" edition. The proportion of works that eventually generate bibliographic families lies somewhere between one-third (the proportion found in studies of bibliographic utilities) and one-half (the proportion found in studies of library collections). The difference between these two figures seems to be attributable to the higher proportion of unique materials that find their way into bibliographic utilities. By the same token, many (if not most) materials acquired by academic libraries are considered to be part of a "canon" of literature. Canonicity seems to be a major factor in determining which works will evolve bibliographic families over time.

As for the types, or patterns, observed in bibliographic families, the majority have simultaneous and successive editions, as well as translations. In other words, the majority of bibliographic families develop from works that were published simultaneously in the beginning, and for which market demand remained sufficient to prompt publication of second editions soon thereafter, to be followed by translations. We also know that older progenitors are associated with larger bibliographic families—the longer the work remains in the public consciousness the more likely it is that new iterations will appear. But we also know that more recent progenitors (those published in approximately the last half-century) tend to generate more complex bibliographic families. That is, very old progenitors anchor large networks of editions and translations and commentaries, but very recent progenitors reside at the core of large galaxies of differing nodes—motion pictures, screenplays, novelizations based on the screenplay, translations, sound recordings, theatrical productions, interactive multimedia, and so forth.

In sum, we know that a large but predictable number of works are to be found in the catalog as members of bibliographic families. We know that there is a long typology of bibliographic relationships that might be found in those bibliographic families, but that most consist of simultaneous, successive, and translation nodes. We know that the reason a bibliographic family develops has something to do with cultural acceptance, which we call canonicity. And we know that the longer the progenitor work remains a part of some canon, the larger the bibliographic family will grow. Thus we have all the more reason to celebrate the relational advantages of a bibliographic retrieval system based on a FRBR-like model.

Other Metaphors: Superworks and Instantiation Networks

To this point we have considered FRBR's definitions of works, expressions, and manifestations, and we have seen how bibliographic families incorporate several types or iterations of works. There are two additional metaphors, both derived from research, that we need to consider to fully comprehend the nature of works. These are the notion of the "superwork" coined by Elaine Svenonius and used in writing by Carlyle among others, and the idea of the phenomenon of "instantiation" that Smiraglia has used to describe and extend the notion of content-based relationships among information resources.[13]

The Superwork

The notion of the superwork describes the abstract intellectual concept of a given work that is the principle node around which all iterations of that work may be collocated. Alyson Carlyle also used the term to describe the concept of a "superwork record set," a collocating device that includes catalog records for all items related to a work that can be linked together with the same author-title heading, whether that heading is in the place of main entry or added entry.[14] A single such set of bibliographic records might include editions, significant derivations, and sequels of a work, as well as works based on the original. This is not unlike the situation in many libraries in the days of card catalogs when there would be one drawer of cards for Shakespeare, and all works related to Shakespeare were collocated in that one drawer. In this case, the unifying element is a given work, say Shakespeare's *Hamlet*.

Svenonius equates the use of the term *superwork* with that of *bibliographic family*, to mean all works and their subsets that descend from a common intellectual origin.[15] She writes, "Identifiers are needed to construct derivative relationships and to collocate the subsets of a superwork. However, there is no need to create special identifiers for superworks; the work identifiers, which they already possess, suffice for the purpose of structuring bibliographic relationships."[16] Svenonius is here referring to the same concept as Carlyle, the superwork record set. The superwork, so defined, is roughly equivalent to the work entity defined by FRBR. That is, it represents the abstract intellectual conception, as the creator might have imagined it, before its realization as text (or music or art, etc.).

As an example of a superwork, we can extend our bibliography of the Shostakovich quartet from Figure 6.2 by adding to it a discography of recordings and the citation for a video performance. Figure 6.3, then, is the superwork set for Shostakovich's 14th string quartet.

Editions in print:

- Moskva: Muzyka, 1974. miniature score (51 p.); 22 cm. and parts; 29 cm.
- Partitura. Moskva: Izd-vo DSCH; [Milwaukee, WI: Distributed by H. Leonard], c2001. 1 score (44 p.) 29 cm. H. Leonard 073999842747.
- Partitura [i] golosa = Score [and] parts. Moskva: Izd-vo DSCH; [Milwaukee, WI: Distributed by H. Leonard], c2001. Publisher's no.: 50484264 (Score) ; 50484265 (Parts). 073999842647 (Score) 073999292046 (Parts)

Recordings by release date:

- Quartet no. 14 in F-sharp major, op. 142; Quartet no. 15 in E-flat minor, op. 144. N.Y., N.Y.: Columbia/Melodiya, **[1977]**, **p1974-75**. 1 stereo LP. **Taneyev Quartet**. Recorded in U.S.S.R. Program notes by R.S. Brown on container. Durations: 002625 003601. Columbia/Melodiya M 34527.
- String quartets nos. 10, 13 & 14. Hayes, Middlesex, England: EMI, **p1987**. 1 CD. **Borodin String Quartet**. Recorded in Moscow. Original analog recording made by Melodiya. ... EMI CDC 7 49269 2.
    - ➢ [Moscow?]: Melodiia; BMG Classics, p1997. 1 CD. **Borodin Quartet**. Recorded in Moscow: 1981 (op. 142); 1978 (op. 144). ... Durations: 002825 003627. Melodiia 74321 40717 2.
- The complete string quartets. Vol. 6. Dobbs Ferry, NY: ESS. A.Y. Recordings, **p1991**. 1 CD. **Manhattan String Quartet**. Recorded June 11 - June 27, 1990 at St. Paul's Evangelical Lutheran Church, Jersey City, NJ. ... String quartet no. 14 in F sharp major, opus 142 (1973) (26:59) ... CD1013
- String quartet no. 14 in F sharp major, op. 142, String quartet no. 15 in E flat minor, op. 144. Praga, **p1994**. 1 CD. **Glinka String Quartet** (1st work); Beethoven Quartet (2nd work). Recorded Aug. 23, 1977 (1st work) and Oct. 18, 1976 (2nd work). ... Praga PR 254043.

Figure 6.3. Superwork set for Shostakovich, Quartets, strings, no. 14, op. 142, F# major (*Continued*)

- Streichquartette nos. 4, 11, 14 Hamburg: Deutsche Grammophon, **p1995**. 1 CD. **Hagen Quartett**. 1st work recorded in the Bibliothekssaal, Polling, Dec. 1993… Deutsche Grammophon 445 864-2.
- String quartet, no. 14 in F sharp major, op. 142, String quartet no. 15, in E flat minor, op. 144. London: Decca, **p1998**. 1 CD. **Fitzwilliam String Quartet**. Produced by Peter Wadland. Recorded at All Saints Church, Petersham, Surrey, 1975-1977. Originally released on analog discs by Decca; previously released in 1982. 455 782-2
- String quartets (complete). Volume 5. [Germany]: Naxos; Unterhaching, Munich, Germany: Distributed by MVD Music and Video Distribution, **p1998**. 1 CD. **Éder Quartet**. Recorded at the Unitarian Church, Budapest, Sept. 1-4, 1996. … No. 14 in F sharp major, op. 142 (26:04) No. 15 in E flat minor, op. 144 (35:49). Naxos 8.550976.
  - ➤ … [Hong Kong]: Naxos Music Library, **[2004]** Streaming audio, mode of access: World Wide Web (viewed Dec. 15, 2004). **Éder Quartet**. Recorded at the Unitarian Church, Budapest, Sept. 1-4, 1996. Contents: No. 14 in F sharp major, op. 142 (26:04) No. 15 in E flat minor, op. 144 (35:49). Naxos Music Library 8.550976.
- String quartet no. 12 in D-flat major, op. 133, String quartet no. 14 in F sharp major, op. 142, String quartet no. 10 in A flat major, op. 118. London: Hyperion, **p2003**. 1 CD.
- **St. Petersburg String Quartet**. Recorded Dec. 2002 and Jan. 2003, St. Petersburg Recording Studio. … Hyperion CDA67156.

Video Recording of Performance:

- The quartets of Shostakovich: odyssey of a man and of a nation, developed by F. Ellsworth Peterson. Brown Symposium XVII, Southwestern University, Georgetown, Tex.), **1995**. 10 videocassettes … Shostakovich, quartets 13, 14 and 15 / **Manhattan String Quartet**.

Figure 6.3. *(Continued)*

In this set we have eight audio recordings set as nodes and one video-recording node, as well as the three printed editions we observed before. Within the eight recording nodes we find two re-releases, one of which is streaming audio rather than a physical item. The different recordings are denoted by giving the release dates and the performers' names in bold type. Notice that in order to track one work, the 14th string quartet, we need to have access to the contents of 11 different catalog records, all of which contain other works as well. In fact, it is an interesting discographical observation to note the different combinations that producers used in different formats. That is, we find quartets 14 and 15 coupled on LP recordings, but more often other combinations occur on compact discs. At any rate, the issue of content versus carrier is well known among music catalogers. Almost all musical sound recordings are anthologies of some sort; the problem always has been how to provide both intellectual access to the contents and physical access to the carriers. The FRBR relational design should help alleviate this problem.

A second superwork example is much more complex. Here the progenitor work is Annie Proulx's story "Brokeback Mountain," which appeared originally in *The New Yorker* in 1997. The original magazine short story, cited here in brackets, would not have been separately cataloged as a monograph before it drew fame as the source of the motion picture screenplay. Here in Figure 6.4 is the bibliographic family, or the Superwork set, drawn from OCLC WorldCat (the article citation was located in ProQuest™).

Node 1: The Story

- [*The New Yorker* v.73, issue 31 (Oct 13, 1997): 74-84.]
- London: Fourth Estate, 1998. 58 p.; 19 cm
- London : Harper Perennial, 2005. 300 p.; 20 cm.
- New York: Scribner, 2005. 55 p.; 19 cm.
- New York: Scribner; [distributed by Simon & Schuster], c2005. 55 p.; 22 cm.
- New York: Simon & Schuster Audio, c2005, p1999. 1 CD (ca. 1 hr.) Simon & Schuster Audio 0-7435-5010-2. Read by Campbell Scott.
  - ➤ ... Prince Frederick, MD: Repackaged and distributed by Recorded Books, [2005], p1999. 1 CD (ca. 1 hr.) Recorded Books CB343.
  - ➤ ... New York: Simon and Schuster Audio; Wayne, N.J.: Distributed by Audible, p2005. [electronic resource]
- traduit ... par Anne Damour. Paris: Editions Grasset & Fasquelle, c2005. 93 p. 19 cm.
- Burōkubakku Maunten ... Yonezuka Shinji yaku. Tōkyō: Shūeisha, 2006. 95 p. 16 cm.
- Tajemnica Brokeback Mountain ... przekł. Konrad Majchrzak; przekł. eseju Katarzyna Karłowska. Poznań: Dom Wydawniczy Rebis, 2006. 73 p. 20 cm.
  - ➤ Tajemnica Brokeback Mountain ... Poznań: Dom Wydawniczy Rebis, 2006. 73 p. 20 cm.

Node 2: The story Amplified

- Story to screenplay ... Annie Proulx, Larry McMurtry, and Diana Ossana. 1st Scribner trade pbk. ed. New York: Scribner, 2005. 166 p., [8] p. of plates: ill.; 23 cm.
  - ➤ New York: Scribner, 2006, c2005 166 p., [8] p. of plates: ill.; 23 cm.
  - ➤ London: Harper Perennial, 2006. 166 p., [8] p. of plates: ill.; 23 cm

Node 3: The Screenplay (unpublished)

- McMurtry, Larry. Brokeback Mountain: a screenplay adapted from an Annie Proulx story by Larry McMurtry and Diana Ossana. [2003?] 162 p.; 28 cm.
  - ➤ McMurtry, Larry. Brokeback mountain: a screenplay by Larry McMurtry and Diana Ossana. [2005?] 97 p. 21 cm.

Node 4: The Motion Picture (Videorecordings)

- Brokeback Mountain, Focus Features and River Road Entertainment; directed by Ang Lee, screenplay by Larry McMurtry & Diana Ossana, producers Diana Ossana, James Schamus. Entertainment in Video, 2005. 1 DVD (129 min.)
  - ➤ ... Entertainment in Video, c2005. 1 DVD (PAL region 2)
  - ➤ ... Universal City, CA: Focus Features: Distributed by Universal Studios Home Entertainment, c2006. 1 DVD (2 hrs., 15 min.)

Figure 6.4. *Superwork set for* Annie Proulx's *Brokeback Mountain* (*Continued*)

Node 5?: Included in an Anthology *Close Range, Wyoming Stories*

- Close range, Wyoming stories, watercolors by William Matthews. New York, NY: Scribner, c1999. 283 p. 25 cm. A collection of stories set in Wyoming: The half-skinned steer, The mud below, Job history, The blood bay, People in hell just want a drink of water, The bunchgrass edge of the world, Pair of spurs, A lonely coast, The governors of Wyoming, 55 miles to the gas pump, Brokeback Mountain.
  - ➤ … London: Fourth Estate, 1999. 318 p. 20 cm.
  - ➤ … Thorndike, Me.: GK Hall, 1999. 359 p. (large print) 24 cm.
  - ➤ … "First Scribner Paperback Fiction International Edition". New York: Scribner, c1999. 335 p. 17 cm.
  - ➤ … 1st Scribner Paperback Fiction ed. New York: Scribner Paperback Fiction, 2000. 285 p. 21 cm.
  - ➤ … London: Fourth Estate, 2000. 320 p. 20 cm.
- Lyhyt kantama, kertomuksia Wyomingista … suomentanut Marja Alopaeus. Helsingissä: Otava, 2001. 317 p. 22 cm.
- Les pieds dans la boue, nouvelles … traduites de l'anglais (Etats-Unis) par Anne Damour. Paris: Rivages, 2001. 295 p. 22 cm.
- Sipure Vayoming … tirgmah me-Anglit ve-hosifah aharit davar, Śarah P. Fridman. Lod: Zemorah-Bitan, 762, 2001. 255 p. 22 cm.
- Close range, Wyoming stories. 1st Scribner trade paperback ed. New York: Scribner, 2003, c1999. 285 p. 21 cm.
- Duan bei shan, Huaieming zhou gu shi ji, Close range… yi zhe Song Yingtang. Chu ban. Taibei shi: Shi bao wen hua chu ban qi ye gu fen you xian gong si, 2005. 292 p. 21 cm.
- Close range, Brokeback Mountain and other stories. London : Harper Perennial, 2005. 318 p. 20 cm.
  - ➤ … London : Harper Perennial, 2006. 318 p. 20 cm.
- Har Brokbek, sipure Vayoming … tirgemah me-Anglit Śarah P. Fridman. Or Yehudah: Zemorah-Bitan, 2006. 255 p. 21 cm.
- Brokeback Mountain, secreto en la Montaña, historias de Wyoming … traducción de María Corniero. Madrid: Siglo XXI de España Editores, 2006, c2000. 332 p. 22 cm.
  - ➤ … Buenos Aires : Siglo XXI Editoria Iberoamericana, c2006. 332 p. ; 23 cm.
- •Bŭrokŭbaek Mauntin … Cho Tong-sŏp omgim. Chopan. Sŏul-si: Media 2.0, 2006. 366 p. 21 cm.

Sound Recordings

- … [New York]: Scribner, p1999. 4 sound cassettes (6 hrs.) Simon & Schuster Audio 04449-4. Read by Francis Fisher, Bruce Greenwood, and Campbell Scott.
  - ➤ … Hampton, NH: Chivers North America, p1999. 6 sound cassettes (8 hr.) Chivers Sound Library CSL 368.
- … Hampton, NH: BBC Audiobooks America, Sound Library, p2001. 6 compact discs (8 hr.) Sound Library SLD 368. Read by William Dufris.
  - ➤ … Hampton, NH: Chivers North America, p2001. 6 sound cassettes (8 hr.) Sound Library CSL 368.

Figure 6.4.   *(Continued)*

Notice there are four intellectual nodes: (1) successive editions, performances, and translations of the original story; (2) an amplification, *Story to Screenplay,* which is a compilation that includes the original story, the whole screenplay, and a series of other essays; (3) a screenplay adaptation derived from the progenitor; and (4) the motion picture performance produced from the screenplay—in this case video releases (because our source is the OCLC World-Cat, we are looking at iterations held by libraries). The motion picture, then, is two generations removed from the progenitor work.

A possible fifth node exists as well, where we find editions titled *Close range: Wyoming stories*—a collection in which all of Proulx's stories about Wyoming appear (most recent releases have a note on the cover saying "including Brokeback Mountain, now a motion picture"). We list this as a "possible" fifth node, because it is debatable whether to consider the anthology to have been built around *Brokeback Mountain* or whether it simply includes our story at the end. The titles begin to include the words *Brokeback Mountain* in 2005—the year the motion picture was released. In fact, it is true of the entire bibliographic family that, although the story was originally published in 1997, following the demands of the marketplace most iterations appear after the release of the motion picture. This is what we mean when we say the evolution of a work over time seems to depend on canonicity. Once cultural acceptance followed in the wake of the production of the motion picture—the appearance of the motion picture made the original work "canonical" in some way—simultaneous and successive editions of both the story and the picture followed rapidly, as did translations.

Instantiation Networks

So far in this chapter we have seen a typology of patterns that can often be found in bibliographic families, and in FRBR we have several tables that represent a similar (if less clear-cut) typology of literary and bibliographical forms. Smiraglia has used the generic term *instantiation* to describe all of these patterns or types. An instantiation is simply the realization of a phenomenon in time—a concrete exemplar of a work as it has appeared at a specific point in the lifetime of the work. The advantage of this term is its generic simplicity. That is, the phenomenon has been observed to occur among the representations of artifacts in a museum, as well as among the documents in an archives.[17] This means the FRBR entity-relationship model might be useful for the control of inter-repository data, and especially for use in digital libraries. In fact, FRBR is currently being harmonized with the international standard CIDOC Conceptual Reference Model for the representation of artifacts to make "works" language accessible and applicable to artifacts of all kinds (http://cidoc.ics.forth.gr/official_release_cidoc.html).

Thus the term *instantiation network* has been used to describe the bibliographic family in a more generic way. These descriptions rely on Smiraglia's definition of a work:

Work is the intellectual content of a bibliographic entity; any work has two properties: a) the propositions expressed, which form ideational content; and b) the expression of those propositions (usually a particular set of linguistic (musical, etc.) strings), which form semantic content.[18]

The key element here is the recognition that works consist of ideas, as well as their expression. This allows us to make a clear distinction between iterations of a work, in which the ideational content remains the same but the semantic content changes (such as a translation), those in which the ideational and semantic content both remain predominantly unchanged (such as a successive or simultaneous edition), and those in which both ideational content and semantic content change (such as an adaptation). In fact, instantiations can be grouped into two types: derivations, in which the ideational and semantic content remain, and mutations, in which there is great change in either or both ideational and semantic content. Thus we can say that translations, adaptations, and performances are kinds of mutations, whereas editions constitute derivations. In this way we can understand that the entity FRBR calls *expression* in fact has two types that are defined by the degree to which change has taken place in the realization of the content of the work.

Conclusion

There is no doubt that constellations of works exist with abundance in the bibliographic universe. Although this is good news for library users—cultural forces drive the marketplace to see to it that a wide variety of useful instantiations evolves—it presents a challenge for information retrieval. A simple citation for a work might be the anchoring node for a large family of related works. The uniform-title heading was the collocating device preferred by catalogers through most of the twentieth century to cause all elements of a bibliographic family to file together in the catalog. FRBR promises a more sophisticated approach in which the generations and siblings (as it were) are sorted according to the concepts of expression and manifestation.

Research has demonstrated that this phenomenon is actually commonplace among all sorts of informing objects—not just books, but artifacts and archival documents as well. Much more research will be required to understand the phenomenon of instantiation more fully, but the future of sophisticated information retrieval depends on the development of integrated repositories that allow informed selection among the plethora of entities that share intellectual content. Achieving this goal will bring us much closer to Wilson's notion of exploitative control of humankind's store of recorded knowledge.

Bibliography

Carlyle, Allyson. 1996. "Ordering Author and Work Records: An Evaluation of Collocation in Online Catalog Displays." *Journal of the American Society for Information Science* 47: 538–554.

International Federation of Library Associations, Study Group on the Functional Requirements for Bibliographic Records. 1998. *Functional Requirements for Bibliographic Records*. München: K. G. Saur.

Leazer, Gregory H. and Richard P. Smiraglia. 1999. "Bibliographic Families in the Library Catalog: A Qualitative Analysis and Grounded Theory." *Library Resources & Technical Services* 43:191–212.

Smiraglia, Richard P. 1992. Authority Control and the Extent of Derivative Bibliographic Relationships. Ph.D. diss., University of Chicago.

———. 2002. "Further Progress in Theory in Knowledge Organization." *Canadian Journal of Information and Library Science* 26 (2-3): 30–49.

———. 2005. Instantiation: Toward a Theory. In *Data, Information, and Knowledge in a Networked World: Proceedings of the Canadian Association for Information Science Annual Conference June 2–4 2005*, ed. Liwen Vaughan. http://www.cais-acsi.ca/search.asp?year=2005

———. 2005. "The 'Works' Phenomenon and Best Selling Books." *Cataloging & Classification Quarterly* 44, no. 3/4 (2007): 179–195.

———. 2006. Empiricism as the Basis for Metadata Categorisation: Expanding the Case for Instantiation with Archival Documents. In Budin, Gerhard, Christian Swertz, and Konstantin Mitgutsch, eds. *Knowledge Organization for a Global Learning Society: Proceedings of the Ninth International ISKO Conference 4–7 July Vienna, Austria. Advances in Knowledge Organization* vol. 10. Würzburg: Ergon Verlag, pp. 383–88.

Svenonius, Elaine. 2000. *The Intellectual Foundation of Information Organization*. Cambridge: MIT Press.

Vellucci, Sherry Lynn. 1994. Bibliographic Relationships among Musical Bibliographic Entities: a Conceptual Analysis of Music Represented in a Library Catalog with a Taxonomy of the Relationships Discovered. DLS diss., Columbia University.

Yee, Martha M. 1994. "Manifestations and Near-Equivalents: Theory, with Special Attention to Moving-image Materials." *Library Resources & Technical Services* 38: 227–256.

Notes

1. *FRBR* 1998, Tables 5.1–5.7
2. Ibid., p. 16.
3. Ibid., p. 13.
4. Patrick Wilson, *Two Kinds of Power: An Essay on Bibliographical Control* (Berkeley: University of California Press,1968).
5. Ibid., p. 9.
6. Richard P. Smiraglia, "Authority Control and the Extent of Derivative Bibliographic Relationships" (Ph.D. diss., University of Chicago, 1992).
7. Martha M. Yee, "Manifestations and Near-Equivalents: Theory, with Special Attention to Moving-Image Materials," *Library Resources & Technical Services* 38 (1994): 246.

8. Gregory H. Leazer and Richard P. Smiraglia, "Bibliographic Families in the Library Catalog: A Qualitative Analysis and Grounded Theory," *Library Resources & Technical Services* 43 (1999):191–212.

9. Sherry Lynn Vellucci, "Bibliographic Relationships among Musical Bibliographic Entities: A Conceptual Analysis of Music Represented in a Library Catalog with a Taxonomy of the Relationships Discovered" (DLS diss., Columbia University, 1994).

10. Ibid.

11. Richard P. Smiraglia, "The 'Works' Phenomenon and Best Selling Books," *Cataloging & Classification Quarterly* 44, no. 3/4 (2007): 179–195.

12. Richard P. Smiraglia, "Further Progress in Theory in Knowledge Organization," *Canadian Journal Of Information And Library Science* 26 no. 2/3 (2002): 30–49.

13. Elaine Svenonius, *The Intellectual Foundation of Information Organization* (Cambridge: MIT Press. 2000); Allyson Carlyle, "Ordering Author and Work Records: An Evaluation of Collocation in Online Catalog Displays," *Journal of the American Society for Information Science* 47 (1996): 538–554; Richard P. Smiraglia, "The 'Works' Phenomenon and Best Selling Books."

14. Carlyle, p. 540.

15. Svenonius, p. 38.

16. Ibid., p. 98.

17. Richard P. Smiraglia, "instantiation: Toward a Theory," in *Data, Information, and Knowledge in a Networked World: Proceedings of the Canadian Association for Information Science Annual Conference June 2–4 2005,* ed. Vaughan Liwen. http://www. cais-acsi.ca/search.asp?year=2005; Richard P. Smiraglia, "Empiricism as the Basis for Metadata Categorisation: Expanding the Case for Instantiation with Archival Documents," in Budin, Gerhard, Christian Swertz and Konstantin Mitgutsch eds. *Knowledge Organization for a Global Learning Society: Proceedings of the Ninth International ISKO Conference 4–7 July 2006, Vienna, Austria. Advances in Knowledge Organization*, vol. 10 (Würzburg: Ergon Verlag, 2006), pp. 383–388.

18. Smiraglia, "Authority Control and the Extent of Derivative Bibliographic Relationships," p. 9.

7

FRBR and RDA: Resource Description and Access

Barbara B. Tillett

We are now at a point in history where there is a convergence of ideas reflecting the optimism that improvements can be made on the way we describe, organize, and make resources available to users. We now have the ability to use descriptive metadata for direct access to resources. Formerly this descriptive metadata was separated in a bibliographic record that served as a surrogate for the items in our collections. It gave the identifying data and location information to connect our users with where they could obtain those resources in our collections. Now, through the digitizing of resources or having online versions of resources directly accessible to users, that rich descriptive metadata can be used by search engines to provide users with clear pathways to what our libraries hold and what is available to them worldwide. When the resource is available digitally online, that descriptive metadata can be the direct connection to serving the user with the desired resource, while also enabling libraries to inform the user of versions of that resource in multiple languages or editions and providing pathways to related resources—all the works by the same creator(s), all the resources on the same subject, etc. The descriptive metadata also still provide the surrogate to lead users to resources that are not yet available online.

Our cataloging codes provide instructions to catalogers, so they can describe resources in a predictable, consistent way. The codes help us build a database of records that convey to our users the organization that we have provided for them in our library collections, to make it easier for them to find what they are looking for, and to inform them of related resources within our collections and beyond. This service to users is our reason for existence as libraries and builds on a long tradition of organizing information.

FRBR and RDA

Functional Requirements for Bibliographic Records, better known as *FRBR,*[1] is a conceptual model describing the bibliographic universe that we organize and control through cataloging codes. *FRBR* describes the entities in the bibliographic universe, their relationships, and attributes. It describes user tasks that serve as criteria to determine which attributes and relationships are important to include in a bibliographic description. *FRBR* also includes what were considered in the mid-1990s to be the mandatory data elements (attributes) to include in a national bibliographic record.

All of these features of *FRBR* are incorporated into the new cataloging code now being developed, called *RDA: Resource Description and Access.* This is the code that will replace the *Anglo-American Cataloguing Rules (AACR2)* and it is hoped that it will become an international cataloging code, in the vision that the International Federation of Library Associations and Institutions (IFLA) set for itself in the early 2000s. This code is being built on the strong foundations of cataloging tradition as reflected in the work of Panizzi, Cutter, Lubetzky, and Verona;[2] and IFLA standards, such as the International Standard Bibliographic Descriptions *(ISBDs)* and *Names of Persons,* and IFLA's internationally agreed principles and the *FRBR* conceptual model, as well as the extensions of *FRBR* into the realm of authority control, namely the *Functional Requirements for Authority Data (FRAD)* and *Functional Requirements for Subject Authority Records (FRSAR).* Like *FRBR, FRAD* and *FRSAR* are being developed by working groups within IFLA with worldwide review. *FRAD* is expected in 2007. *FRSAR* is expected in 2008.

IME ICC (IFLA Meetings of Experts on an International Cataloging Code)

Another related IFLA initiative is the updating of the underlying principles behind cataloging codes. Currently the Paris Principles, developed through IFLA in 1961, are followed for the most part by all the major cataloging codes used throughout the world.

Since 2001, IFLA has been working on updating the Paris Principles. Natalia Kasparova at the Russian State Library, who was then a member of the IFLA Cataloguing Section, reminded the group that it had been 40 years since the Paris Principles were written, and they were in need of review and updating for today's Web environment. The series of regional meetings then began in 2003 to bring together rule makers and other cataloging experts from each country around the world to discuss and agree on the basic principles to govern cataloging rules. The IME ICC meetings are as follows:

1st for Europe and the Anglo-American countries, held in Frankfurt, Germany, in 2003. The IME ICC1 participants drafted the base set of principles and underlying "Objectives for the Construction of Cataloguing Codes." Eighteen rule making bodies, including the Joint Steering Committee for Revision of AACR2, were represented in addition to national representatives from Europe.

2nd for Latin America and Caribbean countries, held in Buenos Aires, Argentina, in 2004. The countries primarily follow *AACR2* or the French AFNOR rules.[3]

3rd for the Arabic-speaking Middle East, held in Cairo, Egypt, in 2005. The countries primarily follow *AACR2*.

4th for Asian countries, held in Seoul, Korea, in 2006. Three rule-making bodies were represented for China, Japan, and Korea. The other Asian countries primarily use *AACR2,* with a few using the French AFNOR rules or ISBD, and nearly all Asian countries use *AACR2* for cataloging "western" materials.

5th for sub-Saharan Africa, held in Pretoria, South Africa, in August 2007. The countries follow AACR2, the French AFNOR rules, or use ISBD.

The result of these meetings will be international agreement on a set of cataloging principles and the related glossary of terminology. Drafts of the statement of principles and glossary have been translated into 24 languages.[4] The final version of the IFLA principles is expected sometime in 2008.

The principles stress the focus on users and state that a bibliographic description should describe a manifestation and the identifying data as found on the manifestation, while using the language and scripts that the users can read. In the IME ICC "Statement of International Cataloguing Principles," the background "objectives" for cataloging codes follow Ranganathan, Leibniz, and Svenonius. These can also be seen as the underlying principles that guide cataloging rules:

"There are several objectives that direct the construction of cataloguing codes[#]. The highest is the convenience of the user.

* *Convenience of the user* of the catalogue. Decisions taken in the making of descriptions and controlled forms of names for access should be made with the user in mind.
* *Common usage.* Normalized vocabulary used in descriptions and access should be in accord with that of the majority of users.
* *Representation.* Entities in descriptions and controlled forms of names for access should be based on the way an entity describes itself.
* *Accuracy.* The entity described should be faithfully portrayed.
* *Sufficiency and necessity.* Only those elements in descriptions and controlled forms of names for access that are required to fulfill user tasks and are essential to uniquely identify an entity should be included.
* *Significance.* Elements should be bibliographically significant.
* *Economy.* When alternative ways exist to achieve a goal, preference should be given to the way that best furthers overall economy (i.e., the least cost or the simplest approach).

*   *Standardization.* Descriptions and construction of access points should be standardized to the extent and level possible. This enables greater consistency which in turn increases the ability to share bibliographic and authority records.

*   *Integration.* The descriptions for all types of materials and controlled forms of names of entities should be based on a common set of rules, to the extent possible.

The rules in a cataloguing code should be

*   Defensible and not arbitrary.

"It is recognized that at times these objectives may contradict each other and a defensible, practical solution will be taken.

"[With regard to subject thesauri, there are other objectives that apply but are not yet included in this statement.]

#Based on bibliographic literature, especially that of Ranganathan and Leibniz as described in Svenonius, E. *The Intellectual Foundation of Information Organization.* Cambridge, Mass.: MIT Press, 2000, p. 68."[5]

RDA basically follows the draft IFLA Statement of International Cataloguing Principles.

FRBR's Influence

The concepts of *FRBR* are not really new. They are a new view of the traditions of cataloging. They are valuable to remind us of those traditions and of what was valuable about them and worth continuing into the future. They present a new way of looking at the bibliographic universe, a new vocabulary that we hope system designers and future generations of librarians will understand.

FRBR reminds us of user tasks and recasts them as: *find, identify, select,* and *obtain.*[6] This reminds us of the structures behind our catalogs. It also reminds us of the importance of Cutter's objectives for the catalog of enabling the user to find information by a known author, title, or subject, and also to gather together all the materials a library has by an author, on a given subject, or in a given kind of literature.[7] Cutter also added that we should be assisting the user to choose a book (part of *FRBR's* user task: *select*) by identifying the bibliographic edition and the literary or topical character. Especially important are the efforts libraries make to help users find resources by uniquely identifying the resources through bibliographic description and by collocating or gathering together resources that share some common characteristic. These are usually resources in a library's own collections, but sometimes bibliographic descriptions or pointers are provided to resources beyond its collections.

The *FRBR* vocabulary describing entities and relationships and attributes is becoming increasingly the normal terminology for bibliographic resources. The entities within *FRBR* are divided into three groups: Group 1 entities are *work, expression, manifestation,* and *item;* Group 2 entities are *person, corporate body* (and *FRAD* is adding *family* in recognition of the importance of that entity to the archival world); and Group 3 entities are *concept, object, event,* and *place.* It is recognized in *FRBR* that resources can exist as a unit or as aggregates of units or as components of a unit. The primary relationships,[8] as *FRBR* calls them, among the Group 1 entities link the Group 1 entities in a hierarchy:

> a *work* "is realized through" an *expression,*
> an *expression* is "embodied in" a *manifestation,* and
> a *manifestation* "is exemplified by" an *item.*

There are also relationships that present the "role" of the Group 2 entities, *person* or *corporate body,* to the Group 1 entities. *FRBR* categorizes these relationships as:

> a "created by" relationship that links a *person* or a *corporate body* to a
>   *work,*[9] that is, the *person* or *corporate body* plays the role of creator
>   with respect to the *work;*
> a "realized by" relationship to link to the *expression;*
> "produced by" for links to the *manifestation;* and
> "owned by" for links to the *item.*

For the Group 3 entities, there is simply the "subject relationship" to the *work.*

Beyond those primary relationships, *FRBR* identifies other relationships between various pairs of Group 1 entities. The terms used in *FRBR* for the types of relationships reflect what was found in cataloging rules, especially the *Anglo-American Cataloguing Rules* in the late 1990s. The relationship types in *FRBR* are grouped by relationships between *manifestation* to *manifestation, work* to *work, expression* to *expression, expression* to *work, manifestation* to *item,* and *item* to *item.* In addition, there are also compatible categories for relationships of content that have been suggested by others[10] and are being explored now for possible use for *RDA. FRBR* also indicates attributes that translate in *RDA* to the data elements that are important to provide when identifying resources.

RDA

RDA is intended to be a set of instructions for the content of descriptive metadata, whether packaged as a bibliographic record, an authority record, or some other structure. It will be a standard for the Web environment, meaning it is being designed to describe both analog and digital materials, it is intended to be used for access to resources through a Web environment, and it will itself be a Web-based tool (current plans also intend for it to be available as a paper, print-product).

In 1997, the Joint Steering Committee for Revision of AACR (JSC) organized a conference to look at future directions for the *Anglo-American Cataloguing Rules.* This had followed years of criticism about the inconsistencies and inadequate structure of the rules for today's resources that often consist of multiple types of material. Some of the topics under consideration were *FRBR,* content versus carrier, internationalization, seriality (modes of issuance, as we call it now), and principle-based rules. The JSC invited international participants to attend the conference with the hope to move away from the Anglo-American centricity of the rules to develop a code that could be used worldwide. A strategic plan was put in place, and the JSC began the work. A "Format Variations Working Group" was formed to look at *FRBR*'s relationship to the new rules. Jennifer Bowen chaired this group. One member, Pat Riva from Canada, took her sabbatical to analyze where FRBR terminology might be substituted in the AACR2 rules. Among the recommendations was to use the term *resource* to be an overarching word to express the materials in a library's collection or things that would be part of the greater bibliographic universe. Another recommendation was to use only the *FRBR* terms when they accurately reflected the intention of the rule. The Working Group also recommended a structure for uniform titles that builds on the identification of the *work,* then the *expression,* then the *manifestation,* and finally the *item,* through added data elements as needed. If one needs to cite a *work,* then only the *work* elements need be included. If one needs to point to a specific *item,* then the full string including elements to identify the specific *item* are included.

Once the JSC decided to develop a new cataloging code, then called AACR3, Tom Delsey was hired as the editor. The JSC subsequently decided that in order to achieve many of its goals, they must abandon the title *Anglo-American Cataloguing Rules* and take a more global view, which led to the title, *Resource Description and Access.* From the start, it was to build on the great Anglo-American cataloging traditions, the conceptual models of *FRBR* and *FRAD* (called *FRANAR* at the time), and international cataloging principles.

The scope and structure of *RDA* were documented in 2006 to clarify the foundation of *FRBR, FRAD,* and the IME ICC International Statement of Cataloguing Principles. The JSC scope and structure statement and related documents can be found at the JSC Web site for *RDA:* http://www.collectionscanada. ca/jsc/rda.html

The influence of *FRBR* in particular can be seen in the very structure of the new draft code. It addresses the *FRBR* user tasks, starting with data elements for *identify*ing, *select*ing, and *obtain*ing resources; moving on to relationships that are considered significant, and concluding with the structure of access points for *find*ing the resources. As described in the "Prospectus,"[11] *RDA* is to be organized in two parts with several appendices as follows:

Part A—Description

Chapter 1—General guidelines on resource description
Chapter 2—Resource identification (*FRBR* user task: identify)
Chapter 3—Carrier (*FRBR* user task: select)

Chapter 4—Content (*FRBR* user task: select)

Chapter 5—Acquisition and access (*FRBR* user task: obtain)

Chapter 6—Persons, families, and corporate bodies associated with a resource ("role" relationships of the *FRBR* Group 2 entities (*persons, corporate bodies,* and also *families* added per *FRAD*) with respect to the Group 1 entities of *work, expression, manifestation,* and *item*)

Chapter 7—Related resources (relationships among the Group 1 entities) (FRBR user task: find)

Part B—Access Point Control

Chapter 8—General guidelines on access point control (*FRBR* user task: find)

Chapter 9—Persons

Chapter 10—Families

Chapter 11—Corporate bodies

Chapter 12—Places

Chapter 13—Works, expressions, manifestations, and items

Appendices

A—Capitalization

B—Abbreviations

C—Initial articles

D—Record syntaxes for descriptive data (ISBD display, etc.)

E—Record syntaxes for access point control data

Glossary

Index

There may also be a provision for elements that are data about data (e.g., "Description based on…" notes), but it is not yet decided how best to include that—as Part C, an Appendix, or some other means.

Chapters 1–5 will be arranged by data elements—the *FRBR* attributes. These are elements like title, place of publication, and date of publication. *RDA* will describe the source of a data element, how to present it (as transcribed or recorded data), and how to use it for a descriptive element, a note, or an access point. Chapter 1 also will include a listing of the mandatory data elements for bibliographic description, currently including the following (these are expected to change slightly as terminology and agreements are further discussed):

"Title proper

Earlier/later variations in the title proper

Statement of responsibility (person, family, or corporate body with principal responsibility)

Edition statement

Numbering

Publisher, distributor, etc. (if more than one then only the first recorded)

Date of publication, distribution, etc.

Title proper of series

Numbering within series

Resource identifier

Form of carrier

Extent

Scale of cartographic content

Coordinates of cartographic content

"When describing a resource, include as a minimum all the elements listed above that are applicable to that resource.

"*Optionally,* provide a controlled access point... in lieu of the mandatory statement of responsibility.

"Include any additional elements that are required to identify the resource (i.e., to differentiate the resource from one or more other resources bearing similar identifying information).

"When describing a resource more fully, include additional elements in accordance with the policy of the agency preparing the description, or as judged appropriate by the cataloguer."[12]

Chapters 6 and 7 will describe the relationships covered in *FRBR* and indicate the devices to use when presenting relationships. The identification of relationships will enable systems to show users pathways to related resources. By identifying the *works* and *expressions* embodied in *manifestations,* the *RDA* will enable future systems to collocate those *works* and *expressions* following the cataloging principles. In June 2007 the JSC issued a table that provides a mapping between RDA and FRBR.[13]

RDA is expected to be issued in early 2009. There will be much discussion and debate between now and then, and details of the instructions will be adjusted through the JSC process, which includes constituency review. The foundation of *FRBR* and cataloging principles will remain constant. It's a time of great expectations and hopes for improvements. Even more, there is the hope for international acceptance of an international cataloging code.

Notes

1. *Functional Requirements for Bibliographic Records: Final Report,* IFLA Study Group on the Functional Requirements for Bibliographic Records (Consultants: Tom Delsey, Elizabeth Dulabahn, Elaine Svenonius, Barbara Tillett). München: K. G. Saur, 1998. Available at: www.ifla.org/VII/s13/frbr/frbr.pdf or as html: www.ifla.org/VII/s13/frbr/frbr.htm.

2. For example, see the British Museums' 91 rules formulated by Panizzi found in the first (and only) volume of the British Museum's book catalog, and Panizzi's defense of cataloging and cataloging rules to the Board of Trustees: "Mr. Panizzi to the

Right Hon. the Earl of Ellesmere.—British Museum, January 29, 1848" in *Foundations of Cataloging: a Sourcebook,* edited by Michael Carpenter and Elaine Svenonius. (Littleton, CO: Libraries Unlimited), 1985, pp. 18–47; also see Cutter's "objects": Charles A. Cutter, *Rules for a Printed Dictionary Catalogue* (Washington, D.C.: Government Printing Office, 1876), p. 10; also see the Paris Principles that were essentially written by Lubetzky: "Statement of Principles adopted by the International Conference on Cataloguing Principles, Paris, October 1961," in *International Conference on Cataloguing Principles, Paris, 9th–18th October, 1961, Report* (London: International Federation of Library Associations, 1963), pp. 91–96; and the debates on bibliographic unit and literary unit between Lubetzky and Verona: Seymour Lubetzky, "The Function of the Main entry in the Alphabetical Catalogue—One Approach," in ICCP *Report,* pp. 139–143; and Eva Verona, "The Function of the Main Entry in the Alphabetical Catalogue—a Second Approach," in *ICCP Report,* pp. 145–157.

3. The AFNOR rules for cataloging are issued in a series of publications from the Association française de Normalisation, for example: "Documentation—Catalogage des monographies—Texte imprimé—Rédaction de la description bibliographique allégée," Association française de Normalisation (AFNOR), FD Z44-073 (Avril 2005).

4. See the IME ICC Web sites: IME ICC1: http://www.d-nb.de/standardisier ung/afs/imeicc_papers.htm. IME ICC2: http://www.loc.gov/loc/ifla/imeicc/imeicc2/. IME ICC3: http://www.loc.gov/loc/ifla/imeicc/. IME ICC4: http://www.nl.go.kr/icc/ icc/papers.php. IME ICC5: http://www.imeicc5.com/.

5. From the April 2006 draft of the "Statement of International Cataloguing Principles" as found on the IME ICC Web sites noted above.

6. *FRBR Report,* p. 82.

7. Charles A. Cutter, *Rules for a Dictionary Catalogue,* 4th ed., rewritten. (Washington, D.C.: Government Printing Office, 1904), p. 12.

8. *FRBR Report,* p. 58.

9. *FRBR Report,* p. 60.

10. Barbara A. B. Tillett, "Bibliographic Relationships: Toward a Conceptual Structure of Bibliographic Information Used in Cataloging" (Ph.D. diss., University of California at Los Angeles, 1987); Barbara B. Tillett, "Bibliographic Relationships," Chapter 2 in *Relationships in the Organization of Knowledge,* ed. Carol A. Bean and Rebecca Green (Dordrecht, Boston, London: Kluwer Academic Publishers, 2001), pp. 19–35; Barbara B. Tillett, "A Taxonomy of Bibliographic Relationships," *Library Resources & Technical Services,* vol. 35 (1991), pp. 150–158; Richard P. Smiraglia, "Authority Control and the Extent of Derivative Bibliographic Relationships" (Ph.D. diss., University of Chicago, 1992); Richard P. Smiraglia and Leazer, G. H., "Derivative Relationships: The Work Relationship in a Global Bibliographic Database," *Journal of the American Society for Information Science,* 50 (1999): 493–504; Sherry L. Vellucci, "Bibliographic Relationships among Musical Bibliographic Entities: a Conceptual Analysis of Music Represented in a Library Catalog with a Taxonomy of the Relationships Discovered" (D.L.S. diss., Columbia University, 1994); Sherry L. Vellucci, *Bibliographic Relationships in Music Cataloging* (Lanham, MD: Scarecrow Press, 1997).

11. The Prospectus can be found at http://www.collectionscanada.ca/jsc/rdapro spectus.html.

12. See instruction 1.4 in the draft of RDA at http://www.collectionscanada.ca/ jsc/docs/5rda-part1.pdf.

13. "RDA-FRBR Mapping" can be found at http://www.collectionscanada.ca/ jsc/docs/5rda-frbrmapping.pdf.

8

FRBR and Archival Materials: Collections and Context, not Works and Content

---

Alexander C. Thurman

The relevance of the *Functional Requirements for Bibliographic Records* (FRBR) conceptual model to archives is essentially limited to the subset of archival holdings consisting of items not traditionally considered "archival," such as published works. The FRBR model's innovations in bibliographic description help libraries collocate the intellectual or artistic content of a work (usually a published work) as it is variably iterated into different realizations. Published works, however, are much likelier to have multiple versions than conventional archival materials, which are more typically unique, unpublished by-products of the everyday activities of organizations, families, or individuals. An archival collection might contain a manuscript that may be the first expression of a published work. Nevertheless, the research value of traditional archival materials principally derives from their shared context within a hierarchically arranged collection, rather than from their individual content. As a result archival description relies on the finding aid, a format that includes more information about the creator(s) and context of creation of the materials than would typically appear in the bibliographic records for library catalogs that are the focus of FRBR.

If an archival collection includes published works, then conventional library cataloging informed by FRBR might be applicable for those works, as a supplement to the archival control exercised at the collection level. For example, in a case where a scholar's personal papers were housed with copies of her publications and donated to an archive, the archivist might wish to provide separate access to these publications so that they would collocate with other related manifestations in a FRBR-compatible library catalog. Normally, however, archival practice consists of describing traditional archival materials with collection-level finding aids (that may be electronically accessible via Encoded Archival Description (EAD) records[1] or by links in collection-level MARC records). Because the key entity in the FRBR model (i.e., the *work*), cannot adequately represent the central unit of archival organization (i.e., the *collection*), FRBR has little impact on archival control. This assertion is borne out by the lack of literature on the subject; a search of the Library Literature database for articles containing both "FRBR" and "archives" as keywords yielded just 3 hits, none of which were pertinent to archival control (searching "FRBR" alone yielded 88 hits).

Whether or how directly FRBR was intended to apply to archival, as well as library materials, is unclear. One of its authors, Barbara Tillett, describes FRBR as a "conceptual model of the bibliographic universe," adding, "that bibliographic universe includes anything a library might wish to collect or make accessible to its users."[2] But Tillett goes on to class archives as one of several "other knowledge and information providers" that are comparable to but distinct from libraries, indicating perhaps that FRBR's library-centered bibliographic universe was not designed with archival materials foremost in mind.[3] The FRBR report itself does make one passing attempt to include archival materials under its dominion, but this effort (discussed later) lacks sufficient underlying substance to have significant implications for archival control. A draft of *Functional Requirements for Authority Data* (FRAD), a successor document to FRBR, goes slightly further in including archival matters, acknowledging the influence of the archival authority record standard ISAAR(CPF) and adding the entity *family* (long important in archival control).[4] But in its final pages the FRAD draft also firmly reiterates the distinction between the "library sector" and "archives, museums, and rights management organizations," explaining in detail some of the issues making the sharing of authority records between these sectors problematic.[5]

FRBR is an entity-relationship model that revolves around the entity of the *work*. In addition to the work, FRBR defines nine other entities, all inextricably linked to the work. The work stands at the top of the hierarchy of Group 1 entities above *expression, manifestation,* and *item:*

> The entities defined as *work* (a distinct intellectual and artistic creation) and *expression* (the intellectual or artistic realization of a *work*) reflect intellectual or artistic content. The entities defined as *manifestation* (the physical embodiment of an *expression* of a *work*) and *item* (a single exemplar of a *manifestation*), on the other hand, reflect physical form.[6]

The Group 2 entities, *person* and *corporate body,* "are treated as entities only to the extent that they are involved in the creation or realization of a *work*...or are the subject of a *work*."[7] Similarly, the Group 3 entities, *concept, object, event,* and *place,* also are construed strictly in relation to being the "subject of a *work*." Although archival materials also have creators and relate to particular subjects, and some individual pieces in archival collections can be thought of as works, any effort to define archival collections as works in the FRBR sense would be too problematic to be useful. The reasons for this incompatibility derive from archival materials' differences from published bibliographic works in nature, organization, and use.

The *collection,* or *fonds,* is the central unit of archival organization, but neither term appears as an entity in the FRBR model. The term *collection* can refer to a group of archival materials generated organically (according to provenance) or artificially (regardless of provenance); the term *fonds* refers only to organically generated materials. What are these materials? Almost anything can be included in archival holdings, but most archival collections consist of the personal papers of an individual or family or the records of an organization. The common theme is the natural aggregation of everyday materials, as opposed to the conscious shaping implied by the FRBR definition of *work*, "a distinct intellectual and artistic creation."

FRBR doesn't recognize this difference in the nature of archival materials, and instead tries in passing to account for archival materials in Section 3.3 by tucking them under the rubric of "aggregate and component entities," along with anthologies and monographic series:

> The structure of the model, however, permits us to represent aggregate and component entities in the same way as we would represent entities that are viewed as integral units. That is to say that from a logical perspective the entity work, for example, may represent an aggregate of individual works brought together by an editor or compiler in the form of an anthology, a set of individual monographs brought together by a publisher to form a series, or a collection of private papers brought together by an archive as a single fond.[8]

This passage is followed by examples of an anthology and a series represented as "works," with supplied "expression" and/or "manifestation" permutations—but significantly no archival collection example is provided, presumably owing to the unlikelihood of an archival collection having more than one expression or manifestation. It is possible in theory to imagine an archival collection being translated in its entirety, thereby yielding a second expression, for example, or a collection being wholly digitized and thereby reproduced in another manifestation, but real examples of such cases are too few to constitute a need for an organizing scheme like FRBR. Translations or reproductions of individual items within archival collections are much more likely, but cataloging of individual items is not a typical archival practice.

Moreover, this sequence of "aggregate entities" puts increasing strain on the integrity of the concept of the work, with the forced archival example straining it beyond the realm of practical value. An anthology may reasonably be characterized as a work, albeit one wherein the "distinct intellectual and artistic" contribution of its editor or compiler would typically receive either an added entry or no entry in a catalog record rather than "main entry" status. Stretching the category of work to apply to both a series comprised of several monographs (with the publisher as "creator") and to each of its separate component monographs is yet a further diminution of the category's precision. Conceiving of an archival fonds as a work "brought together" by the archive itself, as the FRBR example does, extends the concept of work beyond utility into confusion. An archival collection should be cataloged so that the persons or organizations responsible for generating the collection's materials can be found by an author/creator search—having the archive itself turn up in search results as the creator of all an archive's collections would hamper the ability of users to find and identify materials.

Although the FRBR model itself has little direct relevance to archival control, this doesn't imply that library metadata and archival metadata are intrinsically incommensurable. Efforts to harmonize different types of cultural metadata are well underway, and the draft of FRAD itself considers this topic with regard to authority records. Because many of the individuals or organizations that have generated archival materials may also be creators of bibliographic works, the sharing of authority records between libraries and archives could avoid a lot of duplication of labor. The growing interest in archival authority records spurred by the recent development of the archival authority record standard ISAAR(CPF)[9] and the metadata scheme Encoded Archival Context (EAC)[10] has inspired dreams of a future shared international authority file that might combine the Library of Congress's National Authority File (NAF) and other bibliographic authority files with the more detailed and biographical authority records required by archives.

FRAD contemplates this issue of "cross-sector sharing of authority data," concluding that although desirable, such sharing would still require some reworking of the FRAD model to account for differences of function and practice between libraries, on one hand, and archives, museums and rights management organizations, on the other.[11] Some of these differences are:

> Concepts reflecting the cataloguing practices of libraries, such as "bibliographic identity," are unlikely to have a direct parallel in archival practices. Hence, in an archival context, it is unlikely that one individual would be recognized as two or more persons, as may be the case in a library context. Similarly, in rights management organizations, the entity referred to as a work may be defined quite differently than in a library context, given that the function of the rights management organization relates directly to the work as a legally defined entity associated with copyright law.[12]

So, for example, as the writer Stephen King has published several novels under the alternative "bibliographic identity" of "Richard Bachman," as well as many novels under his own name, the NAF contains separate authority records for King and Bachman; but in an archival context Bachman would not merit a separate authority record, being simply an aspect of the life of Stephen King. Similarly a corporate body that undergoes name changes over time might require multiple library authority records, whereas an archival authority record would more likely represent the entire lifetime of the corporate body. FRAD describes these sorts of mismatches between the library and archives sectors as "asymmetric" relationships,[13] an obvious obstacle to sharing.

Perhaps the furthest advanced current effort to harmonize cultural metadata from the different realms of libraries, archives, and museums is the International Council of Museums' CIDOC Conceptual Reference Model (CRM), which has been accepted as ISO 21127:2006. According to the CIDOC CRM home page, the CRM "is intended to promote a shared understanding of cultural heritage information by providing a common and extensible semantic framework that any cultural heritage information can be mapped to."[14] The CRM has already been mapped to both the FRBR model[15] and the EAD DTD,[16] so there is no doubt that harmonization efforts can provide entities sufficiently inclusive to accommodate both bibliographic works and archival collections (i.e., the CRM element E71, "Man-Made Thing"). In the meantime, archival control will continue to be governed by content standards such as *Describing Archives* (DACS)[17] and format standards such as EAD and EAC, with only little attention to FRBR (and perhaps more attention to forthcoming versions of FRAD).

References

Functional Requirements for Authority Data, a Conceptual Model. IFLA UBCIM Working Group on Functional Requirements and Numbering of Authority Records (FRANAR). Available at http://www.ifla.org/VII/d4/wg-franar.htm.

Functional Requirements for Bibliographic Records, Final Report. IFLA Study Group on the Functional Requirements for Bibliographic Records. Munchen: K. G. Saur, 1998. Also available as http://www.ifla.org/VII/s13/frbr.htm or http://www.ifla.org/VII/s13/frbr/frbr.pdf

International Council of Museums. "The CIDOC Conceptual Reference Model." Available at http://cidoc.ics.forth.gr/

LeBoeuf, Patrick. "Mapping CRM→FRBR." January 2003. Available at http://cidoc.ics.forth.gr/docs/mapping_crm_frbr.doc

Theodoridou, Maria and Martin Doerr. "Mapping of the Encoded Archival Description DTD Element Set to the CIDOC CRM." June 2001. Available at: http://cidoc.ics.forth.gr/docs/ead.doc

Tillett, Barbara B. "FRBR and Cataloging for the Future." *Cataloging & Classification Quarterly* Vol. 39, No. 3/4, 2005, pp. 197–205.

Notes

1. "Encoded Archival Description (EAD): Official EAD Version 2002 Web site." Available: http://lcweb.loc.gov/ead/.

2. Barbara B. Tillett, "FRBR and Cataloging for the Future," *Cataloging & Classification Quarterly* 39, no. 3/4, (2005): 197.

3. Ibid., p. 198.

4. IFLA Working Group on Functional Requirements and Numbering of Authority Records (FRANAR), *Functional Requirements for Authority Data, a Conceptual Model.* Available: http://www.ifla.org/VII/d4/wg-franar.htm.

5. Ibid., p. 64.

6. IFLA Study Group on the Functional Requirements for Bibliographic Records, *Functional Requirements for Bibliographic Records, Final Report* (Munchen: K. G. Saur, 1998), p. 12. Also available as http://www.ifla.org/VII/s13/frbr.htm or http://www.ifla.org/VII/s13/frbr/frbr.pdf.

7. Ibid.

8. Ibid., p. 28.

9. International Council on Archives, *ISAAR(CPF) International Standard Archival Authority Record for Corporate Bodies, Persons and Families,* 2nd ed. (Ottawa: Secretariat of the ICA Ad Hoc Commission on Descriptive Standards, 2004), available: http://www.ica.org/test/biblio/ISAAR2EN.pdf.

10. Ad Hoc EAC Working Group, "Encoded Archival Context," beta version, available: http://www.iath.virginia.edu/eac/.

11. FRAD, p. 64.

12. Ibid., p. 65.

13. Ibid., p. 67.

14. International Council of Museums. "The CIDOC Conceptual Reference Model." Available at http://cidoc.ics.forth.gr/.

15. Patrick LeBoeuf, "Mapping CRM→FRBR." January 2003. Available at http://cidoc.ics.forth.gr/docs/mapping_crm_frbr.doc.

16. Maria Theodoridou and Martin Doerr, "Mapping of the Encoded Archival Description DTD Element Set to the CIDOC CRM." June 2001. Available at: http://cidoc.ics.forth.gr/docs/ead.doc.

17. *Describing Archives: A Content Standard* (Chicago: Society of American Archivists, 2004).

9

FRBR and Works of Art, Architecture, and Material Culture

Murtha Baca and Sherman Clarke

Just as we know that there isn't a "one-size-fits-all" metadata schema or set of controlled vocabularies suitable for all types of resources, neither is there a single conceptual model. For unique cultural works, the FRBR model has some areas of potential application, but also several significant points of divergence.

For many types of works of art, architecture, and material culture, the conceptual model of the FRBR Group 1 entities (*work, expression, manifestation, item*) does not apply. This is due to the very definition of what a *work* is for FRBR, and what *work* means in the realm of unique cultural objects. For FRBR,

> A *work* is an abstract entity; *there is no single material object one can point to as the work*. We recognize the work through individual realizations or expressions of the work, but *the work itself exists only in the commonality of content between and among the various expressions of the work*.[1] [FRBR 3.2.1; authors' italics]

In *Cataloging Cultural Objects* (CCO), we find the following definition of "work":

> [A] work is a distinct intellectual or artistic creation limited primarily to objects and structures made by humans, including built works, visual art works, and cultural artifacts...Visual arts are physical objects meant to be perceived primarily through the sense of sight....Cultural artifacts are physical objects produced or shaped by human craft...A work may be a single item or made up of many physical parts.[2]

Because of this sense of physicality, *work, expression, manifestation,* and *item* are one and the same for many cultural works, which are embodied in a *single material object* and not in an *abstract entity*. In the CCO model, a

103

preliminary drawing by Picasso for a particular painting is not an expression or manifestation of that work—it is a separate and distinct related work. By the same token, a three-dimensional *bozzetto* (preliminary study) by Bernini for a finished sculpture is not considered an expression of the completed work, or vice versa, but rather a related work. A sketch, ground plan, or elevation of a cathedral by Michelangelo is considered to be a related work to the building itself, not an early or preliminary expression of that work. In the very frequent cases of "copies after," or derived works such as Picasso's rendering of Velázquez's famous painting *Las Meninas,* it is clear that we are dealing with related works rather than expressions or manifestations of the same work in the FRBR sense.

Figure 9.1 shows the CCO entity-relationship diagram. As in the FRBR entity-relationship model, for CCO a work and various entities can be linked "verbally"; a work *is created by* a person or corporate body; a work *has as subject* a person, event, object, place, concept, etc. Thus for both FRBR and CCO, the relationships between entities are key.

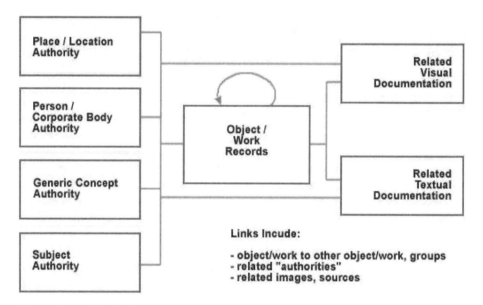

Figure 9.1. CCO Entity-relationship Diagram.

Unlike FRBR, for CCO the main Group 1-type relationship is between a work and another work or works, and/or between a work and a surrogate (often called a "related visual document" in *Categories for the Description of Works of Art* (CDWA)[3] and the *VRA Core Categories* (VRA Core),[4] two of the more well-known data structure standards for art and architecture). A surrogate or related visual document may also be distinguished by its "view type," for example an aerial view of a building, a detail view of a painting, or a lateral view of a sculpture. View type and other data relating to views of a work are clearly delineated metadata elements for both CDWA and VRA Core.

Figure 9.2 adapts the FRBR model to show the relationships between entities in the CCO conceptual model, with specific examples. Here, three of the four FRBR user tasks ("find, identify, select") can be performed on works and related works, and all of the FRBR tasks ("find, identify, select, obtain") can be performed on surrogates. Only in the case of a work of art or material culture actually being purchased can the user obtain it; most users wish to obtain a surrogate of a work by being able to download a digital image, for example, or by ordering a color print or even a poster or other commercial product that is a visual surrogate of a work. Otherwise, the ultimate user task for a work of art or material culture is to *see* it in a museum, archive, or other repository.

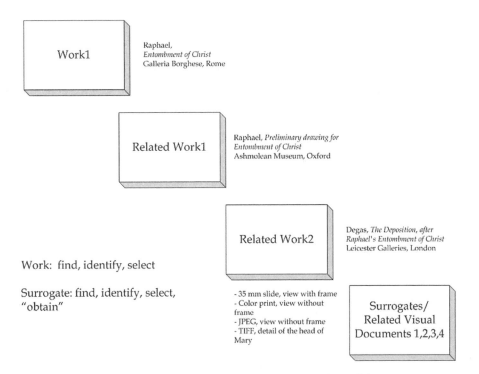

Figure 9.2. Example of Relationships and Tasks in the CCO Model.

The CCO definition of *work* does not include theatrical works, music, or film, for which the FRBR model works quite well. Conceptual art, performance art, and other types of time-based works that are addressed by CCO and CDWA, however, seem to be a possible arena for the application of FRBR to art works and reproductions, unlike works of art that are embodied in a single material object.

By its very nature, a conceptual art work begins with an artist's idea—an abstract entity. Conceptual works may or may not be expressed in verbal instructions, whether written or oral. They may be transcribed or described. The physical or visual results of the concept, such as earthworks or performance art, may be documented via photography, videorecording, or audiorecording. Such documentation may be available in various versions, for example, photographs, DVDs, or audiotapes or videotapes. In the case of earthworks, there is a single material object that embodies the work, but it is subject to change and even to intentional or inevitable deterioration and destruction; in the case of performance art, there is no single immutable material object that embodies the work.

Some works of conceptual art represent projects that have evolved over a long time. For example, during his lifetime, Robert Smithson (1938–1973) made a number of drawings for *Floating Island to Travel around Manhattan Island* (1970). The "island" was not realized until 2005—32 years after Smithson's death, and then by Minetta Brook in collaboration with the Whitney Museum of American Art. On the Web site maintained by the Smithson Estate,[5] there are several photos of the 2005 realization, with the photographer credited. Such a hierarchy—conceptual project, drawings by artist from 1970, the realized island that floated around Manhattan Island in 2005, photographs of the island—may fit the FRBR model of Group 1 entities. The work is *Floating Island* as a project conceived by Robert Smithson; it is expressed as drawings and as a barge-island. The barge is manifested to us through photographs of the 2005 realization. Whether applying the FRBR model to this hierarchy of project—preliminary drawings—realized time-based work makes it any clearer is open to question. The drawings would be considered works of art in their own right by the repositories holding them, and in the CCO model, they are considered "related works" with regard to the realized island. In the CCO/CDWA conceptual model, the photographs of the realized island are "related visual documentation."

The descriptions of these layers of Smithson's *Floating Island* may be hierarchically dependent in the way that a printed work, expression, and manifestation are dependent in the FRBR conceptual model. The access points, however, are significantly different. Although it is always true that an expression may have access points that are not appropriate to the work, and the same for a manifestation, here the difference is even greater. The drawings from Smithson's lifetime are works of individual authorship; the realized "island" from 2005 is still principally a work by Smithson, but could not have been realized without the participation of the artist's widow Nancy Holt, his estate, Minetta Brook, and the Whitney Museum.

Sol LeWitt (1928–2007) is an artist whose wall drawings may fit into the relationship of art works to the FRBR Group 1 entities. LeWitt's earliest wall drawings date from the late 1960s. One such wall drawing, entitled *1 2 3* (1967–2003), is in the collection of the Dia Foundation. In an essay on the Dia Web site,[6] art historian Lynne Cooke states that "*1 2 3* manifests all possible variations on three different kinds of cubes." The use of a FRBR verb ("manifests") might apply in this case. Here again, the work is the idea behind the project, which is expressed in detailed instructions. It was manifested over the years by drawings. Its realization in the Dia:Beacon spaces can be photographed and thereby represented in a visual resources collection.

The various incarnations of the work *1 2 3*—the preparatory drawings, the verbal instructions, the realization at Dia:Beacon—share descriptive elements, but their relationship is not that of work, expression, and manifestation. It is not particularly helpful to apply FRBR Group 1 as a model, even though in this case the access points at each "level" are more similar than they are with Smithson's *Floating Island*. LeWitt is predominantly the creator of the work at each "level," even though others drew the lines on the walls at Dia:Beacon, acting on his very specific instructions. LeWitt's assistants are rarely named.

There are also concepts for works of art that have extended over many years. The Japanese conceptual artist On Kawara (b. 1933) has been creating "date paintings" since 1965. The idea behind the work in Kawara's date paintings, as in other works by this artist, is to use a particular idea and do similar works over time. Kawara's paintings, with accompanying newspaper clippings from the date, have been done in more than 100 cities around the world. In trying to fit these paintings known as the "Today Series" into a FRBR model, the overall conceptual work and the individual paintings push the reasonable and helpful boundaries of work/expression. Together, the paintings are a series of works that have common characteristics that one would describe at the series level. Individual paintings would have characteristics that would be cataloged at the individual painting level, for example, date, measurements, repository.

British artist Damien Hirst garnered considerable notoriety in the 1990s with his art works consisting of dead animals preserved in formaldehyde and displayed in vitrines, such as *The Physical Impossibility of Death in the Mind of Someone Living* (1991), the protagonist of which was a 14-foot dead tiger shark.[7] Here again, the argument could be made that the work was the concept in the artist's mind, although the work does not consist of a performance and is not "time-based" in the sense of the Smithson island, for example. In 2006, when the original shark carcass from this work was in an extreme state of decay, it was replaced with a second dead shark, preserved with more sophisticated methods.[8] The artist seems to have considered this new "manifestation" to be the same work.

In each of these examples of conceptual art, there is some similarity between the concept and its realization that parallels the FRBR idea of work being expressed and manifested in a particular item. The question remains—Does FRBR fit well enough to be a helpful conceptual model for such works?

Another category of the visual arts where it may be useful to apply the FRBR model is performance art. Performance, and the documentation thereof, has been done by visual artists since the early twentieth century; it has significant parallels to the performing arts and theater. The major difference is that most theatrical performances are expressions of a written work. A performance art piece may have a script, but the realization is in the visuals of the performance. Such a performance may be recorded by sound, video/film, or through a transcript. Some performances may include significant props or other visual elements. For example, the work of Nao Bustamante (b. 1963) "encompasses performance art, installation, video, pop music and experimental rips in time."[9] Video recordings of some of Bustamante's performances have been archived by the Hemispheric Institute for Performance and Politics at New York University (NYU). The NYU Libraries are working with the Hemispheric Institute to create preservation digital files of these recordings, as well as DVD and streaming video versions for everyday use. The performance work, its recording (expression) in various versions (manifestation), the artifacts related to the performance (expression), and individual DVDs (item) seem to relate to the FRBR hierarchy of Group 1 entities.

Oskar Schlemmer (1888–1943) created the *Triadisches Ballett* as a symphonically structured "Tanz der Dreiheit" and it premiered in Stuttgart on September 30, 1922, with further performances in Donaueschingen, Frankfurt, and Berlin, 1926, and Paris, 1932. It consisted of 12 scenes performed by one, two, or three dancers, respectively; his fellow performers were the dancers Albert Burger and Elsa Hötzel, with whom he studied choreography. The scenes developed in intensity from lightweight burlesque entertainment to a more solemn adagio and culminated in a mystically heroic mood. With help from his brother Carl, who was a gifted craftsman, Schlemmer designed and made 18 masks and costumes, such as *The Abstract,* which he described as "spatially plastic" because they were like "coloured pieces of sculpture which, when worn by dancers, move in space."[10] In cataloging the works of art (costumes/sculptures) related to this performance, the relationship to the *Triadisches Ballett* is very important; but the sculptures constitute a group of works, not a hierarchy of Group 1 entities in the FRBR sense. Films were made of the early performances of this work. These films have a FRBR relationship to the ballet similar to that of literary works that have been filmed.

Works of performance art are much like works of performing art and theater. Miller and Le Boeuf discuss performing arts relative to FRBR and argue that "there is room in the Anglo-American cataloging tradition to treat *mises-en-scène* and choreographies as autonomous [FRBR] Works."[11] The authors go on to describe how FRBR can be stretched to fit performing arts. Their model is based on the originating creative work of the author or choreographer. This does not hold as strictly in performance art, where there may be no script but merely a space within which the artist performs.

Reproductions of art works are often considered works in themselves. The relationship is somewhat similar to adaptations as described in the *Anglo-American Cataloguing Rules* (AACR). The "main entry" for a reproduction might be the original work if the adaptation is a mere representation of that original. For example, a postcard of the Mona Lisa would probably be cataloged with Leonardo da Vinci as the author. When the reproduction moves beyond the original to supply more context or interpretation, the "main entry" might become the reproduction. To return to our Smithson example, the photographs of the *Floating Island* with significant context of the Hudson River and Jersey City skyline become a work of the photographer. Thinking of the original art work as the subject of the reproduction, however, may make more sense than the idea of an adaptation as in AACR. This is how this type of work/image relationship is handled in the CCO model. For example, in the famous engraving of the Farnese Hercules by Hendrick Goltzius (a Dutch painter of the late sixteenth/early seventeenth century), the work is the engraving, the creator is obviously Goltzius, and the subject is the third-century C.E. statue made by Glykon, which was itself probably an enlarged copy of a Greek statue of the fourth century B.C.E. In the CCO model, the Greek statue, the Roman copy, and the Baroque engraving are all separate but related works; in addition, Goltzius's engraving, which includes the figures of two men gazing up at the monumental statue, has the Roman statue as its subject.

Reproductions appear in generations. For example, an Alinari image of the Coliseum in Rome from the early twentieth century may have been originally issued as a photograph and held in an art history study collection as a mounted photograph.[12] It may also have been used as a lantern slide, which might have been converted in the later twentieth century to a 35-mm slide and now might be digitized. The digitization might even involve several versions. This layering of iterations of the same image is not equivalent to the relationship between work, expression, manifestation, and item as described in FRBR. Editors and trainers for *Cataloging Cultural Objects* are using the term *asset* to distinguish these iterations of a particular image. Although we do not think that *asset* is particularly equivalent to the FRBR manifestation or item, there is value in the FRBR idea of hierarchically arranging a particular work in generations from the original source. The layers for an Alinari image that has gone from photograph to lantern slide to 35-mm slide to JPEG image are generations from the original source image.

In many image collections, all of these generations may be considered subsidiary to the "real" source: the built structure of the Roman Coliseum—that is, the work that is depicted in the images. This determination might be based on the view of the built work. That is, a straightforward image of the Coliseum without showing much of the surrounding area might be cataloged merely for the structure. Even a photograph of the Roman Forum that includes a distinctive view of certain buildings and surroundings would probably be cataloged with "Roman Forum" as the work. A cataloger might record the creator of the original image and subsequent generations in either the descriptive or administrative metadata, but what is being represented is the original built work, not the image of that work.

In the case of art, the principal value of an extended FRBR conceptual model would be to help us determine how groupings of resources, whether the relationship is strictly like that of FRBR Group 1 entities or related in different ways, can be helpful to the user beyond merely sharing access points. AACR and MARC, together, make significant use of uniform titles. Most art collections, including visual resource collections, use other sorts of data models (such as the CCO/CDWA entity-relationship model), which provide a less "flat," more relational structure than MARC/AACR. However it is accomplished, the user is greatly aided by catalogers providing links between resources that are more robust than shared access points. Future generations of online catalogs or other interfaces may be able to build results sets that enhance the prospects of a user finding work clusters and related works; and conceptual models like FRBR and the CCO entity-relationship model may help us to shape that richer universe of information on and access to creative works.

Notes

1. *Functional Requirements for Bibliographic Records: Final Report,* IFLA Study Group on the Functional Requirements for Bibliographic Records (Munchen: Saur, 1998). Also available: http://www.ifla.org/VII/s13/frbr/frbr.pdf.

2. M. Baca et al., *Cataloging Cultural Objects: A Guide to Describing Cultural Works and Their Images* (Chicago: American Library Association, 2006), pp. 4–5.

3. M. Baca and P. Harpring, eds., *Categories for the Description of Works of Art,* http://www.getty.edu/research/conducting_research/standards/cdwa/.

4. *VRA Core Categories*; version 4.0: http://www.vraweb.org/projects/vracore4/.

5. http://www.robertsmithson.com/.

6. http://www.diabeacon.org/exhibs_b/lewitt/essay.html.

7. See http://dh.ryoshuu.com/art/1991physic.html for an image of the 1991 version.

8. Vogel, Carol. "Swimming with Famous Dead Sharks." *The New York Times,* October 1, 2006. Available on line at http://www.nytimes.com/2006/10/01/arts/design/01voge.html?ex=1317355200&en=6fcefeb8359f9748&ei=5088&partner=rssnyt&emc=rss.

9. Quotation from the artist's Web site, http://www.naobustamante.com/.

10. Description of Schlemmer's *Triadisches Ballett* taken from: Karin von Maur, "Schlemmer, Oskar," *Grove Art Online.* Oxford University Press. http://www.groveart.com.

11. Miller, David, and Patrick Le Boeuf, " 'Such Stuff as Dreams are Made On': How Does FRBR Fit Performing Arts?" in *Functional Requirements for Bibliographic Records (FRBR): Hype or Cure-all?* ed. Patrick Le Boeuf (New York: Haworth Information Press, 2005; also published as *Cataloging & Classification Quarterly,* 39, no. 3/4, 2005): 151–178.

12. http://handprints.alinari.it.

10

FRBR and Cartographic Materials: Mapping Out FRBR

Mary Lynette Larsgaard

It is with some feelings of guilt that I contribute my mite to the bibliography of papers, etc., on Functional Requirements for Bibliographic Records (FRBR)—which at the time of writing this chapter (February 2007) is not much less than half as long as is FRBR itself.[1] The object of this chapter is to give an overview of FRBR's influence on the cataloging of cartographic materials (CM) primarily by catalogers in the United States, but at some level by any cartographic-materials catalogers in the Anglo-American cataloging community.

The focus of much of the writing so far is on Group 1 entities. Yes, FRBR's four user tasks—find, identify, select, and obtain—make perfect sense; yes, Group 2 entities (those responsible for intellectual or artistic endeavor—persons and corporate bodies) are correct; and yes, Group 3 entities (subjects of works: concepts, objects, events, places, all of the above) are right on target with "places," which by definition—geographic area—is what CM are all about. But when the map cataloger gets to Group 1 entities, bemusement shading into puzzlement initially occurs.

Group 1 Entities

When FRBR was first issued, portions of it left some catalogers of cartographic materials scratching their heads in puzzlement. One part of it was that in the matter of the Group 1 entities (work, expression, manifestation, item), it reminded me of Alfred North Whitehead using a word and then giving it a definition all his own, or of Humpty Dumpty stating, "When I use a word, it means just what I choose it to mean, neither more nor less."[2] Another part of this was that CM catalogers in some cases—certainly in my case—started out thinking about FRBR as one would think about a set of cataloging rules for placing cataloging information into a structure that bibliographic software can manipulate.

This was not appropriate, given that FRBR is not even a data model, let alone a set of cataloging rules or a machine-readable bibliographic format. Once we realized that FRBR was a conceptual framework rather than a model or rules for the data recorded in bibliographic records, then we could move on to the next step of comprehension and application as appropriate.

The major problem was with two of the Group 1 entities, *work* (a distinct intellectual or artistic creation) and *expression* (the intellectual or artistic realization of a work); *manifestation* and *item* are quite clear. Indeed, for *manifestation* and *item,* I am given the feeling of "old wine, new bottles." Certainly every cataloger must soon recognize that when one is cataloging a printed resource, the piece in one's hand—FRBR's "*item*"—is standing in for all copies of that printed resource—FRBR's "*manifestation,*" in this case being the printed versions of the resource.

Expression—for example, all editions of a given topographic-map sheet, or possibly all digital versions of a given topographic map (that is, one could be raster and the other could be vector; there could be more than one level of resolution of raster and of vector images), and all hard-copy versions of the same topographic map (e.g., paper; microfiche; microfilm)—also fits the methods of issuance of CM. For example, map catalogers would like to see this sort of display in an online catalog, bringing together many versions and editions of the same map (Figure 10.1).

The record in Figure 10.1 is a brief record only; I yearn to add a bit more information, for example, the size of the paper map; height by width; the fact that each map is in color except the 1976 version, which is black and white and instead of being a map is a rectified mosaic of aerial photographs.

But *work* (e.g., the idea of a map of Baltimore), in a content format that has never used uniform titles except for the series entry for monographic series and in a few subject headings, is just not a usable concept. The closest CM cataloging has ever got to a uniform title has been a method of cataloging proposed by the Geography and Map Division of the Special Libraries Association[3] (Special Libraries Association 1956). A standard heading, composed of area, date, subject, scale, and size, was to be placed on the first line of a catalog record; standard cataloging *à la* AACR was to follow (see Figure 10.2). But this would not qualify as a uniform title, as it would be extremely rare for the exact scale, let alone the size, of one map of Baltimore to be the same as another; if the heading had been limited to just area, date, and subject, then a uniform-title situation would be in view.

It could be that there is a deep conceptual reason why not all the Group 1 entities are workable for CM, and perhaps that has to do with the point that, for all its generality, FRBR is fundamentally about literary or fine-art resources, and the full model seems not to apply easily or intuitively even to all text works (e.g., a textbook in physics). The classic example of the full FRBR Group 1 model is a text work such as Shakespeare's Macbeth, which may, for its various *expressions,* be visual (e.g., the presentation of the play; the movie; the ballet). CM are graphic resources that tend to have text on them—but not always; there are remote-sensing images that have no text. Cataloging graphic resources has a good

Geological Survey (U.S.). Goleta quadrangle, California – Santa Barbara Co., 7.5 minute series (topographic).

1950. paper: 3700s VAR .U5 CA 7.5 Goleta Ed.1950
microfilm: 3700s VAR .U5 CA 7.5 Goleta Ed.1950 Film
digital: 3700s_var_u5_ca_75_goleta_ed1950 Available as .jpg ; .tif
(29megabytes)

1951. paper: 3700s VAR .U5 CA 7.5 Goleta Ed.1951
microfilm: 3700s VAR .U5 CA 7.5 Goleta Ed.1951 Film
digital: 3700s_var_u5_ca_75_goleta_ed1951 Available as .jpg ; .tif
(29megabytes)

1967. paper: 3700s VAR .U5 CA 7.5 Goleta Ed.1967
microfilm: 3700s VAR .U5 CA 7.5 Goleta Ed.1967 Film
digital: 3700s_var_u5_ca_75_goleta_ed1967 Available as .jpg ; .tif
(29megabytes)

1976. paper: 3700s VAR .U5 CA 7.5 Goleta Ed.1976
microfilm: 3700s VAR .U5 CA 7.5 Goleta Ed.1976 Film
digital: 3700s_var_u5_ca_75_goleta_ed1976 Available as .jpg ; .tif
(29megabytes)

1982. paper: 3700s VAR .U5 CA 7.5 Goleta Ed.1982
microfilm: 3700s VAR .U5 CA 7.5 Goleta Ed.1982 Film
digital: 3700s_var_u5_ca_75_goleta_ed1982 Available as .jpg ; .tif
(29megabytes)

1995. paper: 3700s VAR .U5 CA 7.5 Goleta Ed.1995
microfilm: 3700s VAR .U5 CA 7.5 Goleta Ed.1995 Film
digital: 3700s_var_u5_ca_75_goleta_ed1995 Available as .jpg ; .tif
(29megabytes)

Figure 10.1. Manifestations described under the title of an expression.

Area. Date. Subject. Scale. Size.

Authority.

Title. Place of publication, publisher if other than authority, date of publication.

Notes.

Tracings

Figure 10.2. Proposed standard for map cataloging.

deal in common with cataloging textual resources (e.g., author, title, issuance information), but cataloging graphic resources requires some different approaches and therefore not just differences in rules but differences in models.

This may be why *AACR2R* Chapter 3[4] stands out as being different from the chapters in *AACR2R* that deal predominantly with textual resources.[5] One of the reasons for this is that for CM there is an emphasis on both content and carrier; however, content is more important than carrier; and content and carrier are clearly separated. The idea that *work* is content, the focus of *expression* is mainly content but also carrier, and the focus of *manifestation* and *item* is carrier[6] is not one with which CM catalogers agree. Content is always primary, and carrier is always secondary.

Conclusion

When FRBR was issued, among the first positive comments that I read were not just by noncatalogers but by nonlibrarians, which made for feelings of caution. There is an overtone of each generation stating its own version of the eternal verities that drive the profession of librarianship. And the overall model is aimed toward those resources that are well served by uniform titles, which are seldom used in CM cataloging—generally only in subject headings, such as those for the Bible. Therefore the immediate influence of FRBR on the processes and procedures of cataloging CM has been slight.

If indeed the cataloging rules that the Anglo-American cataloging community follows, and the MARC21 coding that nearly all of that community uses, allow vendors of ILSs (integrated library systems software) to incorporate FRBR into their software so that a map user could, for example, call up all versions—hardcopy and digital—of a given map, then the influence of FRBR on CM cataloging will become substantial and more positive. At that point, one need not be as harshly to the point as the following statement made in 2003: "The whole range of documents from *Hamlet* to self-published holiday recollections represents a continuum from maximal helpfulness of FRBR to no helpfulness at all."[7]

Bibliography

Baca, Murtha. June 19, 2006. [Personal conversation with Mary Larsgaard]. Los Angeles: Los Angeles International Airport.

"FRBR Bibliography." January 30, 2007 (version 10.11). [Paris, France?] IFLA. http://infoserv.inist.fr/wwsympa.fcgi/d_read/frbr/FRBR_bibliography.rtf (Accessed February 14, 2007).

"Functional Requirements for Bibliographic Records, Final Report." 1998. Munchen: K. G. Saur (UBCIM Publications, New Series, vol. 19). Available

online as htm—http://www.ifla.org/VII/s13/frbr/frbr.htm and as pdf—
http://www.ifla.org/VII/s13/frbr/frbr.pdf (Accessed February 14, 2007).

IFLA. Cataloguing Section—FRBR Review Group. October 12, 2003. "Frequently Asked Questions about FRBR." [Geneva?]: IFLA. http://www.ifla.org/VII/s13/wgfrbr/faq.htm (Accessed February 14, 2007).

Le Boeuf, Patrick. "Brave New FRBR World." 2005. version 3. [Washington, D.C.: Library of Congress] http://www.loc.gov/loc/ifla/imeicc/pdf/papers_leboeuf-eng.pdf (Accessed February 14, 2007).

Special Libraries Association. Geography and Map Division. Committee on Map Cataloging. 1956. "Final Report." Special Libraries Association. Geography and Map Division. *Bulletin* 66:14–19.

Notes

1. "FRBR Bibliography." January 30, 2007 (version 10.11). [Paris, France?] IFLA. http://infoserv.inist.fr/wwsympa.fcgi/d_read/frbr/FRBR_bibliography.rtf. Viewed February 14, 2007; *Functional Requirements for Bibliographic Records: Final Report,* IFLA Study Group on the Functional Requirements for Bibliographic Records (Munchen: Saur, 1998). Also available: http://www.ifla.org/VII/s13/frbr/frbr.pdf.

2. Lewis Carroll, "Through the Looking Glass"; this quote from http://sundials.org/about/humpty.htm (Accessed February 2007).

3. Special Libraries Association. Geography and Map Division. Committee on Map Cataloging. 1956. "Final Report." Special Libraries Association. Geography and Map Division. *Bulletin* 66:14–19.

4. *Anglo-American Cataloguing Rules, Second Edition, 2002 Revision,* prepared under the direction of the Joint Steering Committee for Revision of AACR (Chicago: American Library Association, 2002). Chapter 3: Cartographic Materials.

5. Murtha Baca, Personal conversation, Los Angeles International Airport, June 19, 2006.

6. Patrick Le Boeuf, "Brave New FRBR World," version 3, (Washington, D.C.: Library of Congress, 2005). http://www.loc.gov/loc/ifla/imeicc/pdf/papers_leboeuf-eng.pdf.

7. Last sentence of IFLA Cataloguing Section, FRBR Review Group. October 12, 2003. "Frequently Asked Questions about FRBR." http://www.ifla.org/VII/s13/wgfrbr/faq.htm (Accessed February 14, 2007).

11

FRBR and Moving Image Materials: Content (Work and Expression) versus Carrier (Manifestation)

Martha M. Yee

Some of the major problems with *Anglo-American Cataloguing Rules, Second Edition* (AACR2R) stem from the failure to clearly analyze the FRBR entities *work* and *expression* (content) so as to distinguish them from *manifestation* (carrier) for nonbook materials such as moving image materials. In this chapter, a clearer and more logical analysis of these concepts is attempted, and, at the end of the chapter, the progress made so far in RDA (Resource Description and Access) development is assessed as well.

Moving Image Works and Expressions

FRBR Definition

Let us begin by reminding ourselves of the FRBR definitions of work and expression:

Work (3.2.1): a distinct intellectual or artistic creation.
...Variant texts incorporating revisions or updates to an earlier text are viewed simply as expressions of the same work....Similarly abridgements or enlargements of an existing text, or the addition of parts or an accompaniment to a musical composition are considered to be different expressions of the same work. Translations from one language to another, musical transcriptions and arrangements, and dubbed or subtitled versions of a film are also considered simply as different expressions of the same original work.
...By contrast, when the modification of a work involves a significant degree of independent intellectual or artistic effort, the result is viewed, for the purpose of this study, as a new work. Thus paraphrases, rewritings, adaptations for children,

parodies, musical variations on a theme and free transcriptions of a musical composition are considered to represent new works. Similarly, adaptations of a work from one literary or art form to another (e.g., dramatizations, adaptations from one medium of the graphic arts to another, etc.) are considered to represent new works. Abstracts, digests and summaries are also considered to represent new works.

Examples of new, related works:

w_1 John Bunyan's *The pilgrim's progress*
w_2 an anonymous adaptation of *The pilgrim's progress* for young readers
w_1 William Shakespeare's *Romeo and Juliet*
w_2 Franco Zeffirelli's motion picture *Romeo and Juliet*
w_3 Baz Luhrmann's motion picture *William Shakespeare's Romeo and Juliet*

Expression (3.2.2): the intellectual or artistic realization of a work in the form of alpha-numeric, musical or choreographic notation, sound, image, object, movement, etc., or any combination of such forms.

...The boundaries of the entity expression are defined...so as to exclude aspects of physical form, such as typeface and page layout, that are not integral to the intellectual or artistic realization of the work as such. Inasmuch as the form of expression is an inherent characteristic of the expression, any change in form (e.g., from alpha-numeric notation to spoken word) results in a new expression. Similarly, changes in the intellectual conventions or instruments that are employed to express a work (e.g., translation from one language to another) result in the production of a new expression. Strictly speaking, any change in intellectual or artistic content constitutes a change in expression. Thus, if a text is revised or modified, the resulting expression is considered to be a new expression, no matter how minor the modification may be.

Examples of different expressions of the same work:

w_1 Henry Gray's *Anatomy of the human body*
   e_1 text and illustrations for the first edition
   e_2 text and illustrations for the second edition
   e_3 test and illustrations for the third edition
w_1 J. S. Bach's *The art of the fugue*
   e_1 the composer's score for organ
   e_2 an arrangement for chamber orchestra by Anthony Lewis
w_1 *Jules et Jim* (motion picture)
   e_1 the original French language version
   e_2 the original with English subtitles added[1]

Work/Expression Discussion

Clearly, the FRBR definition of work is in line with the definition of work followed by film catalogers, according to which a filmed version of a previously existing work intended for performance, for example, Shakespeare's *Romeo and Juliet,* is a new work related to the play, not an edition or expression of the play.

By extension, a film of Mozart's *Magic flute* would also be a new work. I have argued elsewhere[2] that moving image works are essentially visual works, not textual or musical works, and that the transformation of a textual or musical work into a visual work necessarily creates a new work. It would appear that FRBR agrees with this analysis.

FRBR examples of different expressions of the same work include a moving image example *(Jules et Jim),* which indicates that any change in the sound, text, music, or image of a moving image work creates a new expression of that work. I have analyzed the various changes in expression that occur with moving image materials elsewhere.[3] Suffice it to say here that any intentional change in *content* of a moving image work (as opposed to changes in *carrier*) creates a new expression of the work, except in the rare cases where the change in content is so substantial as to create a new work. (See the section entitled Manifestation Discussion for a discussion of unintentional/malicious changes in content.)

Work/Expression Summary

Our cataloging rules need considerable work in this area if we are to achieve logically structured cataloging records and resultant logical indexes and displays for our users.

Moving Image Manifestations

FRBR Definition

Let us now remind ourselves of the FRBR definition of manifestation:

Manifestation (3.2.3): As an entity, manifestation represents all the physical objects that bear the same characteristics, in respect to both intellectual content and physical form.... Whether the scope of production is broad (e.g., in the case of publication, etc.) or limited (e.g., in the case of copies made for private study, etc.), the set of copies produced in each case constitutes a manifestation. All copies produced that form part of the same set are considered to be copies of the same manifestation. The boundaries between one manifestation and another are drawn on the basis of both intellectual content and physical form. When the production process involves changes in physical form the resulting product is considered a new manifestation. Changes in physical form include changes affecting display characteristics (e.g., a change in typeface, size of font, page layout, etc.), changes in physical medium (e.g., a change from paper to microfilm as the medium of conveyance), and changes in the container (e.g., a change from cassette to cartridge as the container for a tape). Where the production process involves a publisher, producer, distributor, etc., and there are changes signaled in the product that are related to publication, marketing, etc. (e.g., a change in publisher, repackaging, etc.), the resulting product may be considered a new manifestation. Whenever the production process involves modifications, additions, deletions, etc. that affect the intellectual or artistic content, the result is a new manifestation embodying a new expression of the work.[4]

Manifestation Discussion

Logically, we must necessarily proceed hierarchically. If two changes take place, one of which is a change in expression and the other of which is a change in manifestation, overall, we must consider this a change in expression. If a film is released on DVD, and the underlying content is identical to its original release on 35-mm film, the DVD is merely a new manifestation on a different carrier of exactly the same expression of the same work. If the film is released on DVD with commentary by the director on the sound track, however, the intellectual content is no longer the same as the original release on 35-mm film. The change to the DVD format is a mere change in carrier, but the addition of commentary creates a new expression of the work (a change in content), so overall we must now consider the DVD to be a new expression of the moving image work. Hierarchically, expression trumps manifestation.

Let us proceed through the various elements of the physical description of a moving image to see which are associated with content (work/expression) and which are associated with carrier (manifestation). I propose the following rule of thumb: When one changes the carrier, for example, by copying a 16-mm motion picture onto a VHS videocassette, or by digitizing a 16-mm motion picture, whatever does not change in the course of the copying is not related to the carrier or the manifestation but instead is related to the content. Thus, if one digitizes a 16-mm color film, and the digital copy is also color, that is an indication that color pertains to content, not to carrier. That the carrier is no longer 16 mm wide, however, is an indication that film gauge pertains to carrier, not to content.

Please note that changes in content attributes such as color characteristics, aspect ratio, or projection speed usually represent damage, not the creation of a new expression of the work. When a film is shot, it is shot in color or black and white (b&w) with a particular planned size and shape of image at a particular speed. If that film is presented with the wrong color characteristics (a b&w copy of a color film or a colorized copy of a b&w film), in the wrong aspect ratio (panned and scanned copies that are missing some of the image), or at the wrong projection speed (silent films shown at sound speed so that everything is speeded up too much), it is damaged in the same way that a publication of an Agatha Christie novel missing the last five pages would be considered damaged, not a new edition. There may, in fact, be a gap in the FRBR conceptual model, in that it does not make a distinction between intentional and unintentional/malicious content changes. Unintentional/malicious content changes should not be held to create new expressions. If they are held to create new manifestations, they are a special kind of manifestation that needs a condition note to explain the fact that the manifestation is substandard and undesirable.

General Material Designation (GMD)

The following GMDs are currently available in AACR2R for moving image material:

electronic resource (providing it is moving image)
motion picture
videorecording

These GMDs can change from one to the other without creating a new expression or a new work. Thus change in these GMDs involves mere change in carrier, or manifestation change only. For example, a motion picture can be copied to make a videorecording or digitized to create an electronic resource without any change in intellectual content.

Change from any other GMD, for example, text, music, sound recording, electronic resource, that is not moving image, into the moving image GMD motion picture or videorecording creates a new work by FRBR definition. In other words, it necessarily involves a major change in content, not a mere change in carrier—such a major change in content, in fact, that a new work is created. Music is not a visual medium; if it is transformed into a visual medium in the form of a moving image work, this is necessarily a fundamental change in its underlying content such that a new work has been created. The reverse holds true, as well. Change from a moving image GMD to a nonmoving image GMD necessarily involves the creation of a new work. The change from a moving image to a still image or to a sound recording, for example, is so fundamental that the result has to be considered a new work, for movement and image are fundamental to the nature of moving image works. I have argued elsewhere that changes in fundamental content usually create new works.[5]

One possible exception to this rule might occur when the separate functions that are carried out to create a work of mixed authorship such as a moving image work are split up and separately published. For example, the screenplay for a film can be separately published, as can the sound track recording. These could potentially be conceptualized as parts extracted from the moving image work as a whole, and given whole/part work identifiers (main entries) that begin with the work identifier for the moving image work, followed by an identifier for the part. So far, however, no Anglo-American cataloging rules have conceptualized the situation in this way. Separately published scripts and sound track recordings have traditionally been treated as separate but related works.

It might be instructive to compare the case of moving image works to that of musical works. With musical works, change in GMD from music to sound recording represents a new expression, not a new work, because performances of written music are held to be expressions of same. In other words, it involves a change in content (not a change in carrier), but it is the type of change in content that creates a new expression, not a new work.

Specific Material Designation (SMD)

The following are the current SMDs:

film cartridge
film cassette
film loop
film reel
videocartridge
videocassette
videodisc
videoreel

Any SMD in the moving image family can be copied onto any other SMD as a mere change in carrier. Thus a film on film reels can be copied onto video-cassettes without any change in content. Missing so far are SMDs for electronic resource and DVD. Any SMD in the moving image family can be digitized and/or issued as a DVD as a mere change in carrier.

Physical Description: Extent

Number of SMDs: Change in number of SMD units should be considered to be mere carrier or manifestation change, as it can easily change without any change in intellectual content; examples, film on 8 thousand-foot reels can be moved onto four 2,000-foot reels; videocassette on two one-hour videocassettes can be copied onto one two-hour videocassette.

Playing time: My research shows that change in playing time or footage (or frame count) is the only reliable indicator of expression change from one moving image to another.[6] When multiple copies of the same moving image have been digitized, it is possible that computers will be able to do frame comparisons and reveal differences in intellectual content from one print to another of the same film work. Moving image can be slightly speeded up or slightly slowed down, without the human eye being able to detect it, but not much without ruining the presentation. There can also be variation depending on where someone begins timing the film; for example, do you include entrance music, later distribution credit frames, etc.? The most reliable would be an accurate frame count from the first original release title frame to the last original release title frame, if we could get it. In a way this problem of measuring extent is similar to the one presented by text in which the same number of words or characters can vary in paging without any variation in the intellectual content. Perhaps digitization and computer character counts will eventually provide a solution for that problem as well. It should be noted, though, that one complication is presented by the fact that silent films meant to be projected at a lower fps (frames per second) than standard sound speed (24 fps) are sometimes converted to 24 fps by copying the same frame more than once.

Because of these problems with measuring extent of underlying content, extent can sometimes become caught between content and carrier. Nevertheless, it is still our best hope for tracking changes in underlying content, if we can figure out accurate ways to measure it and report it.

Physical Description: Other Physical Details

Aspect ratio: Aspect ratio refers to the intended proportion of the moving image width to its height. Before the development of the wide-screen film, the standard aspect ratio was 1.33:1, for example. The image was intended to be projected on a screen 1.33 times as wide as it was tall. Wide-screen films were wider; one wide screen aspect ratio, for example, is 2.35:1; such an image is intended to be projected on a screen 2.35 times as wide as it is tall. To fit such a film on a television screen, it can be letterboxed, that is, surrounded on top and bottom with black so as to retain the original image, or it can be panned and scanned, resulting in loss of image content. For example, in a panned and scanned copy of a wide-screen film showing dialogue between two people, the original image showing both people at once is often cropped to show one of them at a time. Aspect ratio should stay the same across carrier change. If it does not, in a panned and scanned copy, for example, it represents a flaw (a condition note for a flawed item), not even a change in manifestation per se. Because there is an aspect ratio associated with a film work on its original release, and manifestations that have cropped this image content in any way should be considered defective, aspect ratio should be considered to pertain to work, not expression.

Sound: In the transition from silent films to sound films, films were sometimes issued in two versions, one a silent version, and one a sound version with either partial or entire music, dialogue, and effects track. Silent films were nearly always intended to be accompanied by music tracks; thus a silent film work can exist in multiple expressions, each of which has a different music track. Therefore silent with music track versus silent with no music track is an expression variation. Sound should stay the same across carrier change, so it is associated with content (expression, as above, or work, when a film does not have different sound expressions), not with manifestation (carrier). If sound does not stay the same across a carrier change, it represents a flaw (a condition note for a flawed item), not even a change in manifestation per se.

Color: Color should stay the same across carrier change, so it is associated with work, not with manifestation. A b&w copy of a color film is a flawed copy, as it lacks a key piece of the image content at the time the work was originally released; thus it rates a condition note for a flawed item, and is not even a change in manifestation per se. A colorized video copy of a film originally issued in b&w is also generally considered a flawed item in film archives, although a media collection might consider it to be a different expression of the work.

Projection speed: Projection speed can vary slightly without humans being able to detect it, but not much. Projection speed should stay the same across carrier change, so it is associated with work, not with manifestation. Too much variation would create a flawed manifestation (condition note for flawed item), not a change in expression (see previous discussion).

Physical Description: Dimensions

Size of SMD (e.g., cassette, reel): Dimensions can vary without affecting intellectual content, so they are associated with manifestation or carrier. For example, a VHS videocassette can be copied onto a 3/4-inch videocassette (in a much larger case) without any change in the underlying content.

Manifestation Summary

The following parts of the physical description of a moving image item pertain to its content (expression or work): the fact that it is a moving image (i.e., that it has one of the moving image GMD's, rather than a nonmoving-image GMD) (work), its extent (playing time or frame count) (expression), its aspect ratio (work), its sound characteristics (expression or work), its color characteristics (work), and its projection speed (work).

The following parts of the physical description of a moving image item pertain to its carrier only (manifestation): its moving image GMD (i.e., the differentiation among "motion picture," "videorecording," and "electronic resource" in AACR2R), its SMD, the number of units or SMDs, and the size or dimensions of the unit(s) or SMDs.

Unfortunately, it looks as if RDA is going to provide only slight clarity or improvement in practice in this area, and only at the GMD level. Users will have to continue to struggle with cluttered displays of multiple manifestations in multiple physical formats in no logical order, and preserving audiovisual archives will have to continue to devise nonstandard solutions to the problem to do their work efficiently.

RDA for Moving Image Materials

One reason that the library world agreed to undergo the trauma of a change in cataloging rules from AACR2R to RDA was that RDA promised to deal with the difficulty caused by differences in the definition of work and expression between the music catalogers and the film catalogers. Film catalogers consider a film of a performed work to be a new work related to the previously existing text for the performed work. Thus a film cataloger considers Bergman's *Magic Flute* to be a new film work, not an edition of Mozart's opera. Music catalogers disagree; to them, Bergman's film is still primarily Mozart's work; that is, not a new work, but a new expression of Mozart's work. AACR2R is structured in such a way that there is an expectation that there will be a general rule to address work identification (creation of main entries) for works of mixed authorship such as these; that is, works that are created by the performance of multiple functions by lots of different people. There is a great gap in AACR2R in this area, however, and the general rule is missing.[7] Now the June, 2006, draft chapter 7 of RDA[8] seems to reveal that mixed authorship has been dropped altogether. Instead we are given the confusing situation of having separate sets of rules for

(1) works with more than one author, (2) works based on previously existing works, and (3) performances. Many moving image works are works of mixed responsibility (with more than one author performing more than one function) which are performances of previously existing works. *Functional Requirements for Bibliographic Records* (FRBR)[9] itself includes the example of a film performance of a Shakespeare play. Now RDA provides three different places to look for a solution to the question of how to enter the film that is a performance of a Shakespeare play, and none of the three places actually has a rule that addresses the situation. We still have not seen RDA Part B, Chapter 13, that will contain the new draft of these RDA rules for identifying works using "primary access points"; perhaps the rules for works of mixed responsibility will improve based on criticisms received in the review process.

Another reason that the library world agreed to undergo the trauma of a change in cataloging rules from AACR2R to RDA was that RDA promised to incorporate FRBR definitions in order to provide a clearer logical framework for the building of catalogs. In the past, the work has been represented by authority records and by main entries (work identifiers) in bibliographic records. The various expressions and manifestations of a work have been represented by bibliographic records, without differentiation between the two entities, *expression* and *manifestation*. In other words, in the past, we have often made a new bibliographic record for a mere change in carrier without any underlying change in intellectual content (i.e., for a mere change in manifestation). It was hoped that RDA would tease out the differences between expression change and manifestation change and help to create catalogs that could group all the manifestations of the same expression of a work together, to help users make better choices more efficiently when seeking a work that exists in multiple expressions, each of which has multiple manifestations (copies of the same intellectual content in different formats or on different carriers).

Drafts of RDA so far demonstrate that RDA is not fulfilling this promise.[10] The FRBR entities are barely referenced in the text, and the status quo is maintained; that is, any change in manifestation (carrier) results in the creation of a new bibliographic record. This is a disaster for catalog users interested in prolific works that exist in multiple expressions and manifestations (and these are the most popular works among users). It is also a disaster for any preserving audiovisual archive that makes multiple copies in multiple physical formats in the course of the preservation process. It appears that we may need to wait for a transformation of the shared cataloging environment before catalog users or preserving audiovisual archives will see any relief for their problems in this area. It is hoped that the analysis in this chapter will help come up with better solutions for moving image materials when we reach that point.

Drafts of RDA so far also lack a clear analysis of content versus carrier in Chapters 3 and 4.[11] Chapter 4 of Part I is called "content description," but content is undefined. Does it refer to work information (form) or expression information (language)? subject information (what the work is about)? relationships between work/expressions? It is unclear why it is necessary to have separate rules for "content description." If content means work/expression information, the following should also be considered "content description": (1) a statement of responsibility concerning translation or illustration, (2) an edition statement about revision of content, or (3) an extent statement that reveals significant differences in length between two different expressions.

The meaning of content seems to have changed completely from the meaning it had in the discussions leading up to RDA, in which content referred to expression and work, as opposed to carrier, the latter standing in for manifestation. Here content seems to refer to what the work is *about*.

It should be noted that as new drafts have come out, the newest being in March 2007,[12] more and more content rules have been moving from Chapter 3 ("Carrier") to Chapter 4 ("Content"). For example, duration is now in Chapter 4, but extent is still in Chapter 3, as are color, sound characteristics, projection characteristics, and film length. However, much content (work and expression) is still being described in earlier RDA chapters.

Given all of the discussion leading up the decision to create a new code that centered around the possibility that reorganization by International Standard Bibliographic Description (ISBD) area might help us deal with new and diverse materials to catalog, one might have expected the rules to be organized by ISBD area. Given all of the discussion leading up the decision to create a new code that centered around the need to analyze the AACR2R class of material concept to determine which categories were actually content categories and which were actually carrier categories, one might have expected the rules to be organized into two parts, one for content and one for carrier.

Instead, the rules in RDA Part 1 are fundamentally organized by FRBR function, as Barbara Tillett explains (see Chapter 7). RDA Chapter 2 concerns identification (of a manifestation?), Chapters 3–4 concern selection (of a manifestation?), Chapter 5 concerns obtaining (a manifestation?), and Part B concerns finding (what? All FRBR entities?). The logic of this principle of organization escapes me, for any given element of the description might be of value for identification or selection of any FRBR entity, depending on the state of knowledge of the catalog user. Consider, for example, the title. When the user is looking for a known item, the title can help the user identify a known work or a known expression. When a user finds the same title in the course of doing a subject search, the title can help to characterize an unknown work—in other words it can help the user make a selection (or rejection) of a work. It would seem that the repetition and redundancy complained of by many RDA commentators may be the result of this faulty logic, as the title needs repetition under each FRBR function and each FRBR entity. Because the desire to reorganize the rules based on either ISBD area or on content versus carrier was behind the decision to create a new code of cataloging rules in the first place, failure to address this issue causes the RDA project to have the appearance of a bait and switch operation.

RDA Chapter 3 ("Carrier") has sections for "media type" (3.2) and "carrier type" (3.3).[13] The definition of *carrier* provided in *RDA: Resource Description and Access: Scope and Structure*[14] indicates that carrier is being defined in such a way that it incorporates both content attributes (for moving image, color) and carrier attributes, and sure enough, the current draft of Chapter 3 has subsequent sections for extent (film length, not playing time, 3.4) and other technical de-tails, including color characteristics (3.12) and sound characteristics (3.17)—all content attributes, not carrier attributes—for moving image material. The *Categorization of Content and Carrier*[15] document, which came out in August 2006 and the subsequent new draft of Chapter 3 in March 2007 are based on the clear analysis of content and carrier contained in the *RDA/ONIX Framework for Resource Categorization.*[16] The latter document did not deal with the problem of assigning attributes such as extent or color characteristics to content or to carrier, however, and in that regard, the RDA draft still muddles content and carrier. It should be noted that the RDA/ONIX framework has had a salutary effect on what used to be called the GMD (a content attribute), in that the new section 4.2 of RDA ("content type") replaces "motion picture," "videorecording," and "electronic resource," with "moving image." The media type (section 3.2) and the carrier type (section 3.3) in conjunction will clarify whether the carrier for the moving image is "computer," "projected," or "video." This is a much cleaner and more logical categorization than we have ever had to work with before, and Tom Delsey is to be commended for this particular improvement in the rules.

Unfortunately, the language in RDA as applied to moving image materials is rather clumsy and arcane. DVDs are called "videodiscs" in rule 3.3 ("carrier type")—very confusing for users because, to them, a videodisc is a different obsolete format; the fact that the "videodisc" is actually a DVD only comes out much further below as an encoding format (rule 3.20.0.5). "Projected" is an odd term to differentiate a motion picture film carrier from a videotape carrier, because video can also be projected. The differentiation between "digital" and "video" in 3.19 and 3.20 reintroduces the cross-classification that was so problematic in AACR2, since most users use the term "digital video" to refer to moving image materials that have been digitized. In the glossary, "Projection" is defined as "media." "Projection" is the process of projecting; it would be better to use the term "Projected media."

"Coloured" is an unfortunate translation of the AACR2R abbreviation "col.," since there are rarely-used color processes that involve coloring black and white film stock in order to create a color film, as opposed to the standard process of using color film stock to create a color film. For moving image users, "coloured" will imply the use of those rare processes. It would be better to use either "colour" or "in colour."

Conclusion

Unfortunately, it appears that the library world is being subjected to all of the trauma involved in changing cataloging rules, without the benefit of the changes recommended in Toronto in 1997. Many in the library world were willing to consider changing the rules only if they could have the improvements promised in Toronto: (1) implementation of FRBR definitions that could underpin more logical indexes and displays in online public access catalogs,

(2) better rules for works intended for performance, (3) a cleaner separation between content and carrier rules, and (4) a rearrangement of the descriptive rules by ISBD area so as to facilitate the cataloging of manifestations of expressions of works that didn't fall cleanly into AACR2R's "classes of materials." Few of these promises have been kept. Instead the rules have been hijacked by those who wish to try to entice other communities (cultural objects, metadata, etc.) into using rules that were originally designed to be used in institutions that are charged with collecting, providing access to, and describing works of prolific authors that are published in multiple expressions and manifestations, thereby creating a permanent cultural record accessible by future generations. It seems highly unlikely that these other communities will actually be interested in spending considerable amounts of money purchasing access to these rules from ALA Publishing. So we may be left with rules that are useful to no one and purchased by no one. They have certainly become no more useful for moving image materials than were the AACR2R rules.

Notes

1. IFLA Study Group on the Functional Requirements for Bibliographic Records. *Functional Requirements for Bibliographic Records: Final Report* (Munich: K. G. Saur, 1998). Also available on the Web at: www.ifla.org/VII/s13/frbr/frbr.pdf.

2. Martha M. Yee. "The Concept of Work for Moving Image Materials." *Cataloging & Classification Quarterly* 18:2 (1993): 33–40.

3. Martha M. Yee. "Manifestations and Near-Equivalents: Theory, with Special Attention to Moving-Image Materials." *Library Resources & Technical Services* 38:3 (July, 1994): 227–256. Note that the term *manifestation* was used in its old, pre-FRBR sense (edition or expression) in this paper published before FRBR had come into existence. Also, see Martha M. Yee. "The Concept of Work for Moving Image Materials."

4. IFLA Study Group on the Functional Requirements for Bibliographic Records. *Functional Requirements for Bibliographic Records: Final Report*.

5. Martha M. Yee. "What is a Work?" In *The Principles and Future of AACR: Proceedings of the International Conference on the Principles and Future Development of AACR, Toronto, Ontario, Canada, October 23–25, 1997,* ed. Jean Weihs. (Chicago: American Library Association, 1998), 68–73.

6. Martha M. Yee. "Manifestations and Near-Equivalents of Moving Image Works: a Research Project." *Library Resources & Technical Services* 38:4 (October, 1994): 355–372.

7. Martha M. Yee. "What is a Work?," pp. 73-74.

8. *RDA Part A, Chapters 6–7, June 2006 Draft.* Available on the Web at: http://www.collectionscanada.ca/jsc/rdadraftch6–7.html.

9. IFLA Study Group on the Functional Requirements for Bibliographic Records. *Functional Requirements for Bibliographic Records: Final Report* (Munich: K. G. Saur, 1998). Also available on the Web at: www.ifla.org/VII/s13/frbr/frbr.pdf.

10. *RDA: Resource Description and Access Part I, December 2005 draft.* Available on the Web at: http://www.collectionscanada.ca/jsc/docs/5rda-part1.pdf; *RDA: Resource Description and Access Part I, January 2006 Draft of Chapter 3.* Available on the

Web at: http://www.collectionscanada.ca/jsc/docs/5rda-part1-ch3.pdf; *RDA Part A, Chapters 6–7, June 2006 Draft*; *RDA: Resource Description and Access Part A, March 2007 Draft of Chapter 3.* Available on the Web at: http://www.collectionscanada.ca/jsc/docs/5rda-parta-ch3rev.pdf; *RDA: Resource Description and Access Part A, June 2007 Draft of Chapters 6-7.* Available on the Web at: http://www.collectionscanada.ca/jsc/docs/5rda-parta-ch6&7rev.pdf.

11. *RDA: Resource Description and Access Part I, December 2005 draft*; *RDA: Resource Description and Access Part I, January 2006 Draft of Chapter 3*; *RDA: Resource Description and Access Part A, March 2007 Draft of Chapter 3.*

12. *RDA: Resource Description and Access Part A, March 2007 Draft of Chapter 3.*

13. Ibid.

14. *RDA: Resource Description and Access: Scope and Structure, June 14, 2007 Draft.* Available on the Web at: http://www.collectionscanada.ca/jsc/docs/5rda-scoperev.pdf.

15. *Categorization of Content and Carrier.* Available on the Web at: http://www.collectionscanada.ca/jsc/docs/5rda-parta-categorization.pdf.

16. *RDA/ONIX Framework for Resource Categorization.* Available on the Web at: http://www.collectionscanada.ca/jsc/docs/5chair10.pdf.

12

FRBR and Music

Sherry L. Vellucci

This chapter examines the complexities of the music bibliographic universe, a subset of the general bibliographic universe, and shows how the FRBR conceptual model is an important step toward meeting the needs of this complexity in a music catalog. It explores the FRBR structure as it relates to musical *works* and *expressions,* and demonstrates FRBR's ability to handle relationships beyond simple hierarchies. The chapter also examines the effect of the cataloging code on the implementation of the FRBR model in music catalogs. Finally, it identifies the strengths and weaknesses of the FRBR conceptual model as it relates to music, and discusses unresolved issues that have an impact on the conversion of MARC-based records for music entities to the multitiered FRBR model.

Music presents distinct challenges for information organization. Musical *works* are frequently issued in many different versions, editions, and formats. Classical music commonly appears as both scores and sound recordings. Music videos and sound recordings in a wide variety of formats permeate the popular music world. Of longstanding concern in information organization is the limited ability of library catalogs to handle the collocation and display of large groups of related resources (i.e., bibliographic families) in a way that is meaningful and easy for users to understand. Nowhere is this challenge more evident than in music catalogs that contain multiple versions of *works* in many different formats. The FRBR model was designed specifically to address these problems by restructuring our approach to the bibliographic universe, and therefore our approach to the structure of bibliographic records. The FRBR model offers an important benefit to music library catalogs, that is, the ability to separate the different states of a *work* into specific entities (*work, expression, manifestation,* and *item*). When applied to bibliographic records in music catalogs, the FRBR structure facilitates the identification, linkage, and grouping of related music resources. This clustering of bibliographic families results in retrieval displays that distinctly identify scores, sound recordings, video recordings, books, electronic resources, etc. The catalog, therefore, can deliver more precise results with simple search queries, render results displays more meaningful, and make navigation through search results easier.

FRBR and the Nature of Music Information

A review of the large and increasing body of literature on FRBR reveals that the majority of writings on this topic use musical works as examples to clarify the conceptual model. Music examples are found in general discussions of FRBR, as well as in writings on FRBR as it relates specifically to music and the arts. Musical works provide excellent FRBR examples because the bibliographic universe of music is often complex. A musical work contains a particular musical idea. This musical idea can be expressed through music notation as a printed score; it can be coupled with textual material that becomes an inherent part of the musical work, such as a song or opera; it can be expressed in sound by performance; and a performance can be captured aurally and visually. Music information, therefore, can be represented as notation-based, text-based, audio-based, or audiovisual-based. Each representational form can be considered a type of music information. Also, a digital music resource may contain all of these forms of music information with additional interactive capabilities, thus representing a microcosm of the music bibliographic universe in one resource.

Just as the representation of music can be complex, each form of music representation can be presented in a variety of ways. Music notation can appear as printed scores (full scores, vocal scores, miniature scores, instrumental parts, etc.), scanned images of music scores, or computer music notation using encoding systems such as *DARMS* or *HyTime*. When the musical work includes text, the words can be integrated beneath the music notation as part of the score, or they may be presented as text separate from the notation. Audio representations can be analog or digital and can come in a variety of "containers" such as LPs, cassettes, CDs, or as MIDI, iPod, or MP3 files. Because of this wealth of possibilities, music presents both theoretical and practical problems for identification, description, and retrieval of music resources. Le Boeuf sums it up well when he states:

> When it comes to music, FRBR recognizes that a given musical *work* can be realized in a virtually infinite number of *expression*s, that can be typified in two broad categories: *expression*s in a notated form … and *expression*s as sound … both of which can be further refined in subcategories that reflect a certain amount of transformation without loss of identity for the initial *work:* transpositions, transcriptions, versions provided with an accompaniment, arrangements.[1]

Additional factors contribute to the development of sizable bibliographic families of musical works, including the existence of multiple formats and versions owing to the intended usage (study, rehearsal, performance, entertainment); the universality of music, which is frequently independent of language; the well-established international scope of the music publishing industry; the cultural importance and popularity of a musical *work* in a particular musical genre; and the age of the *work*.[2] All of these characteristics combined can lead to musical *works* with large bibliographic families consisting of multiple *expressions*, multiple *manifestations*, new *works* derived from the original *work*, and aggregate *works* that include the original or derived *work*. Therefore, unlike many monographic books with a one:one:one relationship between the *work*, the *expression*, and the *manifestation*, a musical *work* frequently has a one:many: many relationship between the *work*, its *expressions*, and *manifestations*. Vocal *works* with music and text and aggregate *works*, such as sound recordings and music anthologies, further complicate these structural relationships. The point is that musical works with multiple relationships have always been a familiar characteristic of the music bibliographic universe.

For many years music catalogers have anticipated the FRBR model at least partially by distinguishing between the *item* and the *work*, a dichotomy described by Lubetzky where the *work* is the intellectual content and the *item* is the physical carrier.[3] The separation of these two concepts was integral to music cataloging, for a musical *work* often appeared in many different *items*. As technology advanced and multiple versions began to proliferate, the question of what is being described became a problem for descriptive cataloging. This became known as the "content versus carrier" issue. The following table demonstrates this dichotomy with three different types of carriers.

Work (Content)	Item (Carrier)
Beethoven's *Symphony No. 9*	Full score (printed music notation) Leipzig: C. F. Peters, 1870.
Beethoven's *Symphony No. 9*	Sound recording (LP) Deutsche Grammophon, 1974.
Beethoven's *Symphony No. 9*	Sound recording (CD) Philips, 1993.

The more fully developed FRBR model, with its four levels of entities rather than two, more closely represents the real-world structural model of the music bibliographic universe. In the older *item/work* model, the *work* was equivalent to the FRBR *work* entity; the *item* incorporated the FRBR *expression, manifestation,* and *item* entities. The following table shows the distinction between the two models for a musical score.

Item/Work Model	FRBR Model	Example
Work	Work	Beethoven's *Symphony No. 9*
Item	Expression	Full score (Music notation)
	Manifestation	Leipzig: C. F. Peters, 1870.
	Item	Copy contains conductor's markings

With its many multiple versions, formats, arrangements, etc., the complex universe of music offers fertile ground for the theoretical and practical application of the FRBR model, and provides optimum examples to clarify the conceptual model.

As noted in earlier chapters, the FRBR model consists of three entity groups. Group 1 is the most frequently discussed entity group (the "things" we catalog), consisting of the *work,* the *expression,* the *manifestation* and the *item.* Group 2 entities (responsible parties) consist of *persons, corporate bodies,* and the recently added *families.* Group 3 entities (subjects) currently consist of *concept, object, event,* and *place,* in addition to the Group 1 and Group 2 entities. When the *FRBR Final Report* was first published, much attention focused on the Group 1 entity concepts and their structural relationships to each other, both of which were new to many catalogers, particularly the *expression* level entity. Because the four entity levels are expressed in the model as a hierarchy, this invariably led to the FRBR model being viewed solely as a hierarchical structure. When all three entity groups and the many possible types of relationships are taken into consideration, however, it becomes evident that FRBR supports a much more complex design structure than those associated with a simple hierarchy. Chapter 5 of the *FRBR Final Report* discusses relationships in detail and outlines many different relationship types that are not limited to hierarchies. The ability to support a complex bibliographic universe, with all its entities and relationships, is especially important to the field of music.

Musical Works

One way to explore the affinity between music and FRBR is by examining the FRBR *entities* in the context of the music bibliographic universe. Each entity in the FRBR model has characteristics, or attributes, associated with it. The attributes defined in FRBR that pertain to *musical works* are listed next. The first seven attributes are general in nature and are applicable to many different types of *work*s. The last three attributes were included specifically as attributes of *musical works.* Each of the work attributes is discussed and an example is given of how it might apply to a *musical work.*

- *Title of the work.* For music, the title can be distinctive, such as *The City Wears a Slouch Hat* by John Cage, or it can be a generic form, such as Joseph Haydn's *String Quartet in C major.* Musical *work*s frequently require uniform titles to distinguish *work*s with generic titles (Haydn wrote nine *Quartets in C Major*), to collocate *work* records when the title has appeared in differed languages (Verdi's *Drinking Song*), to collocate component parts of *work*s with the complete *work* (Verdi's *Traviata. Libiamo ne' lieti calici*), and to help identify the *work.* Title alone is not enough to identify a *work,* however, and it is usually combined with an entity from FRBR Group 2 (person or corporate body) to complete the citation for the *work*. Parallel titles are also common when the title of a vocal *work* has text in more than one language, such as J. S. Bach's Cantata *Ein feste Burg ist unser Gott*, for which several different editions of the score have the parallel English title *A mighty fortress is our God.* Variant titles are also common in the music world, especially when a composer's *work* becomes known by a popular title. For example, Beethoven's *Piano Sonata no. 14, C minor, op. 21, no. 2* is popularly known as the *Moonlight Sonata*, and Mozart's *Symphony no. 41 in C major, K. 551* is often called the *Jupiter Symphony.*

- *Form of work.* For music the form of *work* includes both the musical form of the composition, for example, sonata, concerto, symphony, etc., and the genre to which the *work* belongs. For musical *work*s without distinctive titles, the generic title is usually the *form* of the *work*, to which is added identifying characteristics such as key, opus number, etc. For *work*s with distinctive titles, form may include genres such as jazz, folk music, or hymns. Form may also be used as a qualifier when a work has the same title as another work. It is not uncommon for a composer to write works for different genres based on the same tune. For example, J. S. Bach wrote *Christ lag in Todes Banden* as a cantata, a chorale for four voices, and as several chorale preludes for organ. In these cases the form can be used as a distinguishing characteristic.

- *Date of the work.* This refers to the date of the original composition only. Other dates are associated with the entities *expression* and *manifestation.*

- *Other distinguishing characteristics.* As seen previously, form is often used as a distinguishing characteristic. In other cases the additional attributes of "medium of performance," "numeric designation," and "key" are used to distinguish one *work* from another. Other attributes such as duration (short version) may be used to help distinguish two works with the same title.

- *Intended termination.* This attribute applies particularly to sequentially issued volumes such as the complete *work*s sets of composers. It could also apply to music education songbook sets appropriate for a specific range of grades if the volumes are published sequentially.

- *Intended audience.* FRBR defines this attribute by age of the user, education level, or other categorization. The first two examples given in the FRBR report can certainly apply to musical *work*s, especially for *work*s intended for study or music education (Mozart's *Twelve Variations on Ah! Vous Dirai-je, Maman (Twinkle Variations) K. 265,* or *Hal Leonard Piano Methods Book 1*), but for the majority of musical *work*s it is difficult to define a particular audience. This becomes easier at the *expression* and *manifestation* levels where we find such examples as different presentation formats for scores, or sound recordings directed toward a particular audience (*Tumble Tots Action Songs* for children).

- *Context for the work.* FRBR defines this attribute as the "context within which the *work* was conceived."[4] Musical *work*s may have a variety of contexts, most of which are brought out through controlled vocabularies and notes in the bibliographic record. For example, the historical context for Beethoven's *Symphony No. 3 (Eroica)* is the Napoleonic wars, and the historical/social context for *I-Feel-Like-I'm-Fixin'-To-Die-Rag* by Country Joe and the Fish is the Vietnam War. Other contexts might include a chronological context, (the Baroque era), or the particular ballet company (Ballets Russes) and its collaborating choreographer (Diaghilev) for which a musical *work* was composed.

- *Medium of performance.* This is one of three important *work* attributes identified specifically for music in the FRBR model and refers to the performing forces for which the original *work* was written. *Works* with a generic title generally include the medium of performance as part of the uniform title, for example, Brahms' *Quartets, piano, strings, no. 3, op. 60, C minor.* The medium of performance is also used as a subject string for both generic and distinctive titles. With generic titles the *Library of Congress Subject Heading* (LCSH) may duplicate the information in the uniform title in a somewhat different form. The *LCSH* assigned to this *work* by Brahms is "Piano quartets."

- *Numeric designation.* This is another *work* attribute identified specifically for music in the FRBR model. Numeric designations may refer to numbers assigned to a particular *work* by the composer, a publisher or musicologist. Opus numbers are generally listed in chronological order of their composition, and the number is often assigned by the composer (Beethoven's *String Quartets,* Opus 59, Nos. 1–3). Publishers frequently assign their own serial numbering systems. For example, these same quartets are numbered *String Quartets* Nos. 7–9, which would be the consecutive numbers following the first group of *String Quartets,* Opus 18, Nos. 1–6. Thematic index numbers are assigned by musicologists compiling information about the entire corpus of *works* by a particular composer. These numbers are a way of *classifying* the *work*s by genre. J. S. Bach's *work*s, for example, were assigned BWV (Bach Werke Verzeichnis) numbers by W. Schmieder and are periodically updated. Bach's Cantatas are grouped together in the catalog with the BWV numbers 1–224.

- *Key.* This *work* attribute refers to the key of the original *work*. The key represents the tonal center of the *work* (if it has one) and is frequently added to uniform titles as an additional way of identifying *work*s, such as *Preludes, piano, op. 45, C# minor.*

Definition and Primacy of the Work

Two issues associated with the FRBR *work* entity are of particular concern with musical *work*s. These include (1) defining the *work* and (2) determining *work* primacy when a *work* contains more that one type of semantic content. The undercurrent (perhaps undertow!) of these difficulties is closely related to the issue of main entry, especially for complex *work*s with many different *expressions,* and *work*s that aggregate or integrate two or more *work*s.

Finding consensus on the definition of "the *work*" has been an ongoing challenge for cataloging theoreticians.[5] The FRBR definition states that a *work* is "a distinct intellectual or artistic creation" and goes on to state that "a *work* is an abstract entity."[6] The developers of the FRBR model acknowledged that the definition and the parameters of a *work* may vary according to the culture in which the term is used.[7] Cultures may have different parameters when it comes to deciding when an original work has been modified to the extent that a new derived *work* is created. Different cultures may also entertain different views on primacy and main entry decisions for a work. Culture applies not only to national identity but to the culture of a particular community of users. The music community, for example, might perceive the movie of Mozart's *Die Zauberflöte* as a film version of the opera, and would most probably search under the composer and/or the title to retrieve the *musical work*. The film community, on the other hand, might consider Bergman as the primary creator of the film and would likely search under Bergman and/or the title to retrieve the *film work*. Complicating the problem further, many individuals contributed to the performance of Mozart's musical *work* and the creation of Bergman's film *work*. In fact, with so many people contributing to the musical performance and the making of the film, no one person is given the main entry and the *work* is entered under title according to AACR2R. This does not negate the fact that these two cultures perceive the work differently and therefore perceive primacy differently, but it does eliminate the cataloger's need to decide primacy. Complex situations such as this lead to the fundamental questions: what is the *work,* how do we define it, and can it be different based on the cultural norms of a particular community? As it relates to the FRBR model, does a main entry serve or hinder the ability to identify a work? If a complex work is approached as a single, one-dimensional entity, problems like this will continue to perplex us.

Anticipating the conversion of library catalogs to the FRBR model, researchers at OCLC examined the *WorldCat* database to determine the proportion of *work*s that would benefit from conversion to the FRBR model.[8] To help analyze their data, Bennett, Lavoie, and O'Neill defined three classes of *work*s. An *elemental work* is a *work* with a single *expression* and a single *manifestation* and is very common in the book world, although less so in the music world. A *simple work* is a *work* with a single *expression* but multiple *manifestation*s. In the music world this could be a musical work represented by notation (a score) that had been published by different publishers but never recorded as a performance. It could also be a work that was performed and recorded several times, but without a published score. A *complex work* is a *work* with multiple *expression*s, or realizations, of its intellectual or artistic content. This class of *work* is well represented by any of the voluminous composers or popular music groups, where scores, sound recordings, and videos abound.

The findings of OCLC's researchers indicate that the FRBR model is most useful when applied to catalogs that contain *work*s that have multiple *expressions* and/or *manifestations*. Bennett, Lavoie, and O'Neill also observed that in the general bibliographic universe as represented by the *WorldCat* database, the portion of *work*s that fall into this category is not large; 6 percent had multiple *expressions* and 16 percent had multiple *manifestations*. The subset of *work*s that do have multiple *expressions* and *manifestations* are often part of the canon of *work*s in their particular discipline or musical genre and therefore constitute large and important bibliographic families with extensive holdings in the *WorldCat* database. The music bibliographic universe abounds with large bibliographic families. Two examples of such families found in the *WorldCat* database are Beethoven's *Symphony* No. 9 and Handel's *Messiah,* which, in April 2005, were represented by approximately 1,114 and 1,806 bibliographic records, respectively.

Aggregates, Integral Units, Unified Works, and the Whole/Part Relationship

The *aggregate work* was later added as another class of *work* to the three classes identified by Bennett, Lavoie, and O'Neill and is defined as an entity comprised of multiple *work*s.[9] FRBR states that "from a logical perspective the entity *work,* for example, may represent an aggregate of individual *work*s brought together by an editor or compiler... By the same token, the entity *work* may represent an intellectually or artistically discrete component of a larger *work.*"[10] Aggregates are plentiful in the music bibliographic universe, for a large proportion of sound recordings are aggregates, and printed music anthologies by definition are aggregate *work*s. Sound recordings that contain two or three complete *work*s, such as the compact disc (CD) containing two of *Mozart's* symphonies, or the CDs of most popular genres of music such as rock, folk, and jazz, are comprised of multiple *work*s and fit the first part of the FRBR definition. Aggregate works can also be comprised of *parts* of *work*s. For example, the CD containing instrumental excerpts from Italian operas by Verdi, Giordano, Puccini, Mascagni, and Leoncavallo does not contain any one *work* in its entirety, but only parts (i.e., excerpts) of *work*s. In this case the aggregate CD conforms to the second part of the FRBR definition. A whole/part relationship exists between the aggregate work and the individual works that it contains. This is the most numerous type of relationship found in the music bibliographic universe.[11]

The specific place of the aggregate *work* in the FRBR model continues to elude us. Some suggest that an aggregation of works is not a *work* in and of itself, but rather a physical manifestation that contains multiple works.[12] This view does not account for the intellectual process involved in selecting the works to include in the aggregate. Others view an aggregate as a *work* in its own right, or a "*work of works*" that should be treated like any other work in the FRBR model.[13] Thus, defining the aggregate *work* still presents problems for the FRBR model, as well as the music community. An IFLA Working Group is reviewing various options for how aggregates should be defined and modeled within the FRBR structure.

Larger musical *works* such as operas, cantatas, and symphonies with artistically discrete components (i.e., acts, sections, movements) are not generally considered aggregate *works,* but rather "integral units" according to FRBR. The report does not define what is meant by an integral unit; however, it can be inferred that such *works* are comprised of component parts, which derive their meaning within the context of the complete *work.* Such a definition would be helpful for distinguishing an "integral unit" from a "unified work" (discussed later). Nevertheless, the relationship between a complete musical *work* that is considered an integral unit and its component parts is also considered a whole/ part relationship.

In the current MARC/AACR2R structured catalog, it is the uniform title that implies the relationship by using the conventional form "Complete work. Subordinate part," for example, *Schmücke dich, o liebe Seele. Jesu, wahres Brot des Lebens.* Many of the newer metadata schemas that use an XML encoding structure use the tags <isPartOf> and <hasPart> to identify this relationship. For example, the chorale *Jesu, wahres Brot des Lebens* <isPartOf> *Schmücke dich, o liebe Seele* by J. S. Bach; and the cantata *Schmücke dich, o liebe Seele* <hasPart> *Jesu, wahres Brot des Lebens.*

FRBR identifies two types of whole/part relationships: dependent and independent. The dependent whole/part relationship is what FRBR refers to as the "integral units" discussed previously.

> Dependent parts are component parts of a *work* that are intended to be used in the context of the larger *work* and as such depend on the context provided by the larger *work* for much of their meaning.... Independent parts are those that do not depend to any significant extent on the context provided by the larger *work* for their meaning.[14]

From these definitions it is obvious that the individual pieces in a musical anthology have an independent part/whole relationship to the anthology, for each individual piece in the collection continues to stand as an independent work. The definition of "dependent parts," however, does not provide enough clarification for large musical *works.* According to the FRBR Report, the primary criterion for determining if a part is dependent or independent is whether or not it has a distinctive name or title.[15] This criterion for independence presents problems for some large musical *works* that are integral units. A large vocal *work* such as an opera or cantata usually has parts such as arias and choruses with distinctive titles, although these are not always official titles, but rather opening lines of text. Many such sections can be and are performed independently. Are these considered independent parts because they have a textual title, or are they dependent because they occur within the context of a larger work? We have also seen that many instrumental musical *works* do not have distinctive titles and their movements or sections do not have distinctive titles. Yet many symphonic movements are performed separately from the entire work and played independently by radio stations. Should these be considered dependent parts because they do not have distinct titles and they derive their context as part of the larger *work?* The music community's concept of the "performable unit" deals with this problem in a more realistic way. A performable unit is any work or part of a work that can stand on its own in a performance. This alleviates the problem of determining independence or dependence based on context and the existence of a distinctive title.

When a part is separated from the complete *work* in which it appears, we refer to this as extraction. The FRBR Report identifies two extraction models for dependent whole/part relationships: segmental and systemic. According to FRBR, "segmental parts are discrete components of a work whose content exists as a distinct identifiable segment within a whole."[16] In fact, this is a vertical extraction and frequently represents the concept of a performable unit of a *work* such as an aria from an opera or a movement from a symphony. Thus in music, this type of extraction is not always confined to a dependent-part status. The horizontal or linear extraction (referred to as systemic by FRBR) is seen in the music world as the practice of extracting the music for one instrument or voice part across the entire *work,* providing that instrument or voice with a part, separate from the full score, from which to perform the music. This linear extraction, while published as a separate part, has no meaning out of context of the complete *work* and is, therefore, a dependent part.

As noted, there are four different ways to model a *work* (elemental, simple, complex, and aggregate). There is one additional class of *work* that presents special problems for music catalogers. The "unified *work*" contains characteristics of an aggregate *work,* but differs conceptually. An aggregate *work* brings *works* (and independent parts of *works*) together to form a collective work, but each component *work* in the aggregate retains its independent identity. A unified *work,* however, has two types of semantic content that are integrated to become one single unified *work.* This type of *work* can be found in the musical bibliographic universe in the form of vocal music and presents a conceptual difficulty for the practical application of the FRBR model to music catalogs.[17] FRBR touches on the concept of a unified *work* when it identifies the "work-to-work complement relationship." The term *complement,* however, can be confusing, for it can mean that two works are joined to make one complete whole, or it can mean that two works remain separate but enhance each other. A unified *work* refers to the former.

It is often the case with unified musical *works* that one work already exists and the new unified *work* is created by adding new content to the existing work. One example of this is *Wessex Graves: Five Settings of Poems by Thomas Hardy for Voice and Harp* by Michael Berkeley. Hardy's poems existed before the music was composed and were the inspiration for the new unified *work.* The opposite method of creating unified *works* is also common. For example, the song *Goin' Home* used the existing musical theme from the Largo movement of Dvorak's *New World Symphony* to which William Arms Fisher added lyrics to create a unified *work*. In other cases the text is written in collaboration with the composer. A few examples of this collaborative process include the opera *Don Giovanni* for which Mozart wrote the music while collaborating with the librettist Lorenzo da Ponte; the well-known team of Gilbert and Sullivan who collaborated on many operettas, for which Sullivan wrote the music and Gilbert wrote the lyrics; and the collaboration between the composer Richard Rogers and the lyricist Oscar Hammerstein, which created some of the best known Broadway musicals, including *South Pacific* and *Oklahoma*. Of course not all vocal *works* are collaborative efforts, and for many popular songs the words and music are by the same person.

When the music and text are not created by the same person, researchers and practitioners raise the question "what constitutes the *primary work?*" Is the music the primary *work;* is the text the primary *work;* or do the text and music combined constitute a new *work?* Primacy is necessary for the selection of a main entry, which is usually a question of who is primarily responsible for the intellectual or artistic content of the *work*. Throughout various sets of cataloging rules, the issue of primacy has shifted back and forth between the text being the primary work (with author as main entry) and the music being the primary work (with the composer being given the main entry).[18] The issue of primacy is also dependent on how the *work* is viewed by catalogers and users. In other words, is a vocal *work* a single unified *work* with two types of semantic content (text and music), or is it an aggregate *work* consisting of two different *work*s that have been combined? The definition of a unified musical *work* is one attempt to address this problem, for a unified *work* is a new *work* of mixed responsibility. The unified *work,* therefore, may have a derivative relationship with one or more other *works,* as is the case when one portion of the unified *work* has a previous existence, or it may be simply a new *work* that contains words and music, as is the case with many popular songs.

Discussion and confusion over the issues of definition and primacy will continue as long as the cataloging community retains the concept of main entry and continues to seek a single operational definition of a *work*. Although studies have identified different classes of *works,* there is no one definition that fits all types of *works* and will satisfy all cultural communities. Catalogers' judgment must be exercised in the case of these complex works. The use of role identifiers to indicate the part that each person or corporate body played in the creation of the *work* would alleviate the dependence on main entry.

Musical Expressions

The *expression* level entity causes the most consternation for catalogers in general, but music catalogers have an innate understanding of the concept, as they deal with it on a daily basis. The FRBR Report defines an *expression* as "the intellectual or artistic realization of a *work* in the form of alpha-numeric, musical or choreographic notation, sound, image, object, movement, etc., or any combination of such forms."[19]

Earlier in this chapter we discussed the different types of *expressions* that may exist for a musical work, that is, notation, sound, and moving image with sound. Figure 12.1 shows that the musical *work* "Symphony No. 9" (FRBR Group 1) was composed by the *person* "Beethoven" (FRBR Group 2). The *work* has two forms of *expression:* the music notation created by Beethoven is the primary *notation expression* (E1); the second type of *expression* is the musical *performance* (E2).

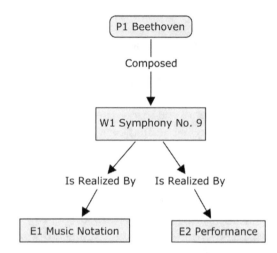

Figure 12.1. Musical work with two expressions.

Just as there can be multiple *expressions* of music, some forms of music *expressions* can be represented in a variety of ways. It can be problematic if the FRBR Group 1 entities are interpreted literally as representing a single tier for each entity type because the model does not restrict the structure in that respect. A better way to view the model is as having four *primary* entity levels, with some entity levels capable of having subentities. This allows for a much richer structure that better accommodates the musical bibliographic universe and still remains within the boundaries of the original model.

A musical *work* expressed as notation can have different presentation formats. The notation may appear as a full score, with a separate staff for each instrument or vocal part. It may be presented as a condensed version of the *work,* such as a vocal score or conductor's score. The notation might appear as individual instrumental parts for the *work.* The notated music could be a transcription of the *work* from one form of notation to another, from the original instrumentation to different instruments or voices, or transpositions of the *work* that change the tonal key of the original to another key. These diverse types of music presentations, or versions, are all *expressions* of the *expression* "music notation," in other words they are subentities of an *expression* entity. All of these different transformations are considered different *expressions* of the same *work.*

In this respect musical *works* differ from other types of *works,* for although the semantic or semiotic content has changed to a greater or lesser degree, the ideational content is regarded as identical to the original *work* and therefore is still considered the same *work.* These transformations are essentially "near equivalents" of the musical *work* that in some ways correspond to language translations of textual *works.*

Figure 12.2 provides an example of the possible complexity of musical *expressions.* The example shows four different ways that the music notation is expressed: as a full score (E1.1), as a set of instrumental parts (E1.2), as a miniature score (E1.3), and as a condensed (conductor's) score (E1.4). Each of these is a *subexpression* of the *expression* "music notation." In addition, the *sub-expression* "instrumental parts set" is itself an aggregate and includes a different *subexpression* for each separate instrumental part. In each of these *expressions* and *subexpressions* the notational content varies to a greater or lesser degree, yet all are considered *expressions* of the same *work.* These variations are what

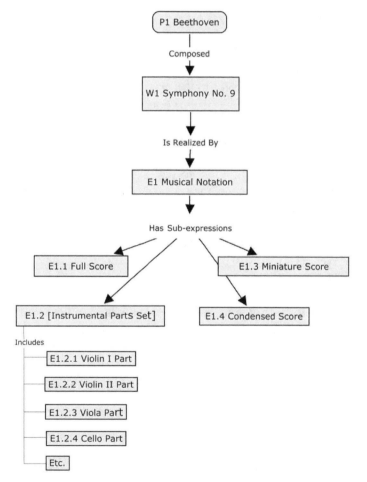

Figure 12.2. Musical expression with complex sub-expressions.

Le Boeuf refers to when he says that subcategories can be further transformed without loss of identity for the initial *work*.[20]

Expression Level Attributes, Titles, and Records

The FRBR Final Report provides an extensive list of *expression* level attributes. As with *work* attributes, some *expression* attributes are general in nature and are applicable to many different types of *expressions* including musical *expressions,* whereas other attributes are specific to *musical expressions.* The attributes that are most important for musical *expressions* include the following:

- *Form of expression:* The form of *expression* is the means by which the *work* is realized. The form of a musical *expression* can be music notation, sound, or moving image with sound. This should not be confused with the musical form of the *work.*
- *Date of expression:* The date the *expression* was created. A musical *expression* date might refer to the date the *work* was performed, or the date the work was arranged, transcribed, transposed, etc. For expressions that are performances of works, the performance date commonly appears in a note in the metadata record.
- *Language of expression:* This attribute applies to musical *works* with text and may refer to the original language in which the work is sung, or to translations into other languages. Texts may also use two or more languages as is the case with macaronic texts that use a mixture of languages, a common practice in medieval carols and motets.
- *Type of score:* This refers to the presentation format of the music notation that represents the musical composition. As discussed previously, scores can be in the form of full scores, miniature scores, condensed scores, vocal scores, parts, etc. The type of score may represent more than just a change in the physical layout of the music staves, as it may also present the musical content in a way that differs from the original.
- *Medium of performance:* This critical attribute provides information on the instrumental and/or vocal medium of performance represented in the *expression* of a musical *work* (e.g., two pianos, chamber orchestra, mixed voices). The instruments and/or voices represented in a particular *expression* of a *work* (e.g., a transcription, an arrangement, or a performance) may differ from the medium of performance for which the *work* was originally intended.

According to FRBR, the "Title of the *expression* is a word, phrase, or group of characters naming the *expression.* There may be one or more titles associated with an *expression.* The title of an *expression* that forms part of a larger *expression* may consist solely of a number or other generic designation that is dependent on the title of the larger *expression*."[21] A distinct *expression* title, or lack thereof, is currently a major obstacle to creating discrete *expression* level records that will serve the functions of the catalog and the needs of the users. This section examines the prevailing problems of creating *expression* level titles and metadata records within the context of the attributes associated with the *expression* entity.

A uniform title is constructed for most musical *works* and performs the tasks of identifying, distinguishing, and collocating *works* in the catalog. Because a *work* is realized by an *expression,* in many cases an *expression* title is created by adding data elements that identify the entity as an *expression* to the uniform title for the *work.* Unlike uniform titles for *works,* however, the additional information prescribed by the current cataloging rules does not provide enough detail to identify a specific *expression.* This is partially because the cataloging code was developed with the older *work-item* model in mind, before the development of the four-level FRBR model that included the *expression* level entity.

Authority files currently contain nascent name/uniform title *expression* level authority records in addition to w*ork* records. Traditionally, the term *heading* is used to refer to this name/title data combination. The new *Resource Description and Access* (RDA) code currently under development will use the term *access point* instead of *heading.*

> Access point for work: Britten, Benjamin, 1913–1976. Ceremony of carols
> Access point for expression: Britten, Benjamin, 1913–1976. Ceremony of carols; arr.

As seen in this example, the addition of the term *arr.* to the uniform title of the original *work* for women's voices indicates that this title represents an *expression,* but it does not provide enough information to identify a distinctive *expression.* It does not distinguish this arrangement from other arrangements of the *work* (for SSAATTBB or SSATB), nor does it identify the arranger (Julius Harrison). In fact, information that is necessary to identify a specific *expression* is scattered throughout the metadata record, making it difficult to create *expression* level records from MARC records by automatic conversion.

The Joint Steering Committee for Revision of AACR (JSC) created the Format Variation Working Group (FVWG) to explore ways to facilitate collocation at the *expression* level.[22] The group identified two possible methods to achieve this: (1) adding cataloging rules to include instructions for the construction of *expression* level headings, and (2) automatic collocation at the system level based on existing data in the MARC record.[23] The first method will be addressed in some way by the new RDA code. Researchers are addressing the second method of automatic collocation in a variety of ways. OCLC developed a FRBR conversion algorithm for MARC records to collocate *works,* the Library of Congress offers a FRBR display tool, and the vendor VTLS, Inc. developed an OPAC system capable of switching between the standard MARC record structure and a FRBR record structure. Another recommendation of the FVWG was to change the ambiguous term *uniform title* to a more specific term. As of this writing, it appears that the JSC will adopt the term *preferred title* for use in the RDA. The term *uniform title* will continue to be used in this chapter, for the new term has not yet been formally adopted.

The FVWG viewed *expression* headings as extensions of *work* headings with information added to identify and distinguish *expressions*. Additional elements suggested by the FVWG that are applicable to music entities include language, mode (form) of *expression,* and date of *expression.* For musical *expressions,* FRBR's medium of performance attribute would also be a useful element to include in the heading. For *expressions* in the form of music notation the subentity "type or format of score" could also be added as part of the heading. In addition to recommending attributes for the *expression* heading, the FVWG recommended adding Group 2 entities (persons or corporate bodies) involved in the creation of the *expression* to the *expression* heading. The use of relator codes would clarify any confusion over the contributing roles of each person involved. Based on the FVWG recommendations, with the addition of role indicators and score format, an *expression* heading might look something like this:

Britten, Benjamin, 1913–1976, cmp. Ceremony of carols; arr., mixed voices (SSATB). Vocal score. 1948. (Harrison, arr.).

A distinctive *expression* heading will help facilitate the conversion of music catalogs to a FRBR-based structure; however, a heading is only part of a metadata record and the goal of FRBR implementation is to have separate records for each Group 1 entity, or to be able to extract automatically on-the-fly data attributes for each entity from the existing MARC record. Although algorithms and FRBR display tools have been successful in converting MARC records to *work* sets, the lack of consistent use of data fields for *expression* information hinders progress at automatic *expression* record generation. Following are examples of separate *work* and *expression* level records for Britten's *Ceremony of Carols.* Each *expression* level record is linked back to the *work* record by means of a *work* identifier, and each *expression* record has its own identifier.

Work Record	
Work ID	BRCC025
Composer	Britten, Benjamin, 1913–1976, cmp.
Title	Ceremony of Carols
Medium of performance	Treble voices, SSA with harp.
Date	1943

Expression 1 Record	
Expression ID	BRCC025/01
Arranger	Harrison, Julius, 1885–1963, arr.
Medium of performance	Mixed voices, SSATB with keyboard.
Date	1948

Expression 2 Record	
Expression ID	BRCC025/02
Conductor	Hill, David, cnd
Performer/group	Westminster Cathedral Choir; Williams, Sioned, harp.
Medium of performance	Treble voices, SSA with harp.
Date	Performed in the Cathedral, June 26–27, 1986.

The problem of redundancy and data scatter is exacerbated by the ambiguous use of terminology. For example, the "type of score" attribute may refer to *expressions* and *subexpressions* that seem the same, but are conceptually different. The current phrase "musical presentation" leads one to believe that it refers solely to the presentation format of the music notation (e.g., full score, miniature score, score, and parts), when in fact it can also refer to the way in which the *work* has been arranged (e.g., from SSA to SSATB voices). The confusion over the meaning of the term *musical presentation* fostered discussions among the communities involved in the RDA development.[24] The American Library Association (ALA) representative to the JSC clearly laid out some of the problems when she stated that:

Current practice according to AACR2 and various *Library of Congress Rule Interpretations* requires catalogers to decide whether to place musical format information in:

- [ISBD] Area 1, as part of the Statement of responsibility (for those terms or phrases that imply a modification of the music)
- [ISBD] Area 2, as an Edition statement (for "book type" edition statements) or
- [ISBD] Area 3, as the Musical presentation statement (for statements that indicate the physical presentation of the music).

…Music publishers' practices also contribute to this problem. Scores do not always include a printed statement of musical format for catalogers to transcribe. For example, when using AACR2, "vocal score" will sometimes first appear in [ISBD] Area 5, and not at all in [ISBD] Areas 1–3.[25]

This problem also contributes to the difficulty of automatic conversion of MARC records to *expression* level records because of *expression* attribute data scattered throughout the MARC record. Data dispersion makes it difficult to identify and normalize the data elements with consistency, a necessary component of automatic conversion. The following table shows some data fields where *expression* information can be found. Also, the MARC record contains *expression* data coded fields such as 008–20 (Format of music), 008–33 (Transposition

ISBD Area	MARC Field
Area 1	245 … / ‡c vocal score arranged by the composer.
Area 1	245 … / ‡c arranged by Mozart with additional instruments.
Area 2	250 2-piano edition.
Area 3	254 Partitur.
Area 7	500 Arranged for SSATB; original work for women's voices.
Area 7	500 Vocal score based on Mozart's arrangement with additional instruments
Area 7	500 Sung in Korean
Area 7	500 Full score with German and English texts + instrumental parts

and arrangement), 041 (Language of expression), and 048 (Number of musical instruments or voices).

Solutions to these *expression* level problems will depend in large part on the development of the RDA cataloging code and the record and database structures of future catalogs. The conceptualization of the *expression* entity in the FRBR model, however, remains one of the most important contributions to music cataloging, for it provides a logical foundation for better understanding the music bibliographic universe and a meaningful basis for clustering music catalog record displays.

On a final note, when the different FRBR entities and the many possible types of relationships are taken into consideration it becomes evident that FRBR is capable of supporting a more complex design structure than that associated with a simple hierarchy. In the digital environment music researchers are experimenting with new ways to integrate the FRBR model with content-based music information retrieval systems. Diet and Kurth have added a *file* entity layer below the FRBR *item* level in order to accommodate complex multimedia objects, because a digital *item* can contain several *files*. The researchers also use new relationships to indicate the "start" and "end" of temporal files.[26] The ability to support a complex bibliographic universe, with all its entities and relationships, is especially important to the field of music. Figure 12.3 shows the relationships among several

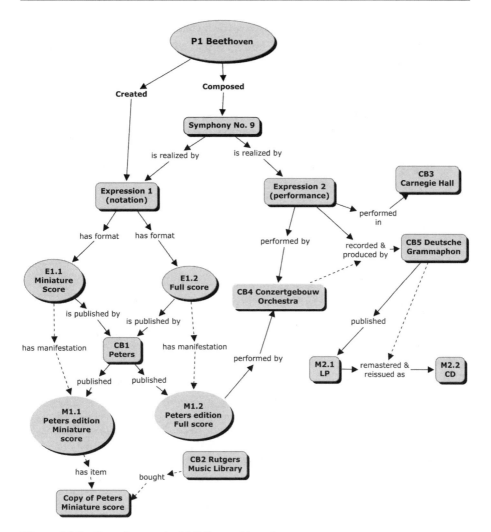

Figure 12.3. Complex musical bibliographic universe.

entities and subentities in FRBR Group 1, including the *work, expressions, mani-festations,* and *items,* and between the entities in Group 1 and Group 2.

Conclusions

This chapter discussed the complexity of the music bibliographic universe. It addressed the musical *work* and the special challenges it presents for catalog-ers, and the musical *expression* with the problems of distinctive *expression* titles and data attribute scatter in existing metadata records. Despite these challenges, FRBR is the first conceptual model to acknowledge the structural complexities that are such a large part of the music bibliographic universe. Perhaps most important, the FRBR model emphasizes the existence of bibliographic families and bibliographic relationships, concepts that are critical to music catalogs. FRBR does not solve all of the problems associated with cataloging complex music resources, but it does present a more logical approach to the problems. This is a period of evolution for the cataloging rules, metadata schemas, and catalog database structures. In the last analysis, flexibility in interpreting the FRBR model and dealing with the thorny issues of defining *works*, aggregates, primacy, and hierarchies can only benefit the user by providing more meaningful catalog displays and making navigation through large musical bibliographic families easier.

Notes

1. Patrick Le Boeuf, "Musical *Works* in the FRBR Model, or, "Quasi la Stessa Cosa": Variations on a Theme by Umberto Eco," *Cataloging & Classification Quarterly* 39, no. 3/4 (2005): 103–124.

2. A more detailed discussion of the complexity of music documents can be found in Sherry L. Vellucci, *Bibliographic Relationships in Music Catalogs* (Lanham: Scarecrow Press, 1997).

3. Seymour Lubetzky, "The Objectives of the Catalog." In *Foundations of Cataloging: A Sourcebook,* eds. M. Carpenter and E. Svenonious (Littleton, CO: Libraries Unlimited, 1985), p. 189.

4. *Functional Requirements for Bibliographic Records: Final Report*/IFLA Study Group on the Functional Requirements for Bibliographic Records/[International Federation of Library Associations and Institutions. IFLA Universal Bibliographic Control and International MARC Programme, Deutsche Bibliothek, Frankfurt am Main] (München: Saur, 1998), p. 34.

5. Rick Bennett, Brian F. Lavoie, and Edward T. O'Neill, "The Concept of a *Work* in WorldCat: An Application of FRBR," *Library Collections, Acquisitions, & Technical Services* 27 (2003): 45–59; Patrick Le Boeuf, "Musical *Works* in the FRBR Model," or "Quasi la Stessa Cosa: Variations on a Theme by Umberto Eco," *Cataloging & Classification Quarterly* 39, no. 3/4 (2005):103–124; Richard P. Smiraglia, *The Nature of "a Work": Implications for the Organization of Knowledge* (Lanham, MD: Scarecrow Press, 2001); Martha M. Yee, "What Is a Work? Part 1: The User and the Objects of the Catalog," *Cataloging and Classification Quarterly* 19, no. 1 (1994): 9–28; M. M. Yee, "What Is a Work? Part 2: The Anglo-American Cataloging Codes," *Cataloging and Classification Quarterly* 19, no. 2 (1994): 5–22; M. M. Yee, "What Is a Work? Part 3: The Anglo-American Cataloging Codes," *Cataloging and Classification Quarterly* 20, no. 1 (1995): 25–46; M. M. Yee "What Is a Work? Part 4: Cataloging Theorists and a Definition Abstract." *Cataloging and Classification Quarterly* 20, no. 2 (1995): 3–24.

6. *FRBR: Final Report*, p. 16.

7. Ibid.

8. Rick Bennett, Brian F. Lavoie, and Edward T. O'Neill, "The Concept of a *Work* in WorldCat: An Application of FRBR," *Library Collections, Acquisitions, & Technical Services* 27 (2003): 45–59.

9. Edward O'Neill, "Relational Models for Aggregates," Presented at the IFLA FRBR Workshop, Dublin, Ohio, May 2, 2005.

10. *FRBR: Final Report*, p. 26.

11. Sherry L. Vellucci, *Bibliographic Relationships in Music Catalogs* (Lanham, MD: Scarecrow Press,1997), p. 91.

12. Edward O'Neill, "Relational Models for Aggregates."

13. *FRBR: Final Report*, p. 28.

14. Ibid., p. 69.

15. Ibid.

16. Ibid.

17. Marie-Louise Ayers, "Case Studies in Implementing Functional Requirements for Bibliographic Records [FRBR]: AustLit and MusicAustralia," *Australian Library Journal* 54, no. 1 (2005). Available online: http://alia.org.au/publishing/alj/54.1/full. text/ayres.html.

18. For an explanation of the changing views in different versions of the cataloging rules, see the discussion of libretti by David Miller and Patrick Le Boeuf "Such Stuff as Dreams are Made on: How does FRBR Fit Performing Arts?" *Cataloging & Classification Quarterly* 39, no. 3/4 (2005):163–165.

19. *FRBR: Final Report*, p. 18.

20. Le Boeuf, p. 106.

21. *FRBR: Final Report*, p. 36.

22. Joint Steering Committee for Revision of AACR, Historical Documents, "Format Variation Working Group," Document collection: http://www.collectionscanada.ca/jsc/docs.html#ForVarWG.

23. Jennifer Bowen, "FRBR: Coming Soon to Your Library?" *Library Resources & Technical Services* 49, no. 3 (2004): 179–188.

24. See the JSC Document 5JSC/LC.4 and the associated responses. Available online: http://www.collectionscanada.ca/jsc/working1.html.

25. Memo from Jennifer Bowen, American Library Association representative to the Joint Steering Committee for Revision of AACR. Response to Rule proposals for musical format information (eliminating Musical presentation statement area (5.3)). September 15, 2005.

26. Jürgen Diet and Frank Kurth, "The Probado Music Repository at the Bavarian State Library." Proceedings of the 8th International Conference on Music Information Retrieval (ISMIR 2007), September 2007.

13

FRBR and Serials: One Serialist's Analysis

Steven C. Shadle

In this chapter my intention is to provide the reader with an overview of how serials can be modeled in Functional Requirements for Bibliographic Records (FRBR),[1] what has been done to date in the use of FRBR to provide access to serials, and how this analysis has the potential to improve access to the content that is embodied in serially issued resources. I've talked on the subject of serials and FRBR at two annual meetings (2005 and 2006) of the North American Serials Interest Group (NASIG) and in both cases roughly one-third of the audience was not at all familiar with FRBR (that presentation was their first exposure), half of the audience had some FRBR awareness and understanding, but weren't really sure how it would be useful for serials, and a relatively small number were comfortable with the concepts in applying FRBR to serial resources and wanted more information on applications and implementation. For a concept that has been in the information community for nearly 10 years, I was a little surprised to find this proportion of attendees with such a limited knowledge of FRBR until I realized that there has been very little work done to date that would directly affect the serials community. FRBR applications have primarily focused on helping the user identify and select works in multiple editions, translations, and versions (e.g., *Hamlet*) and works of performance available in multiple performances and recordings (e.g., *Brandenburg Concerto No. 1 in F Major*). To a lesser extent, serials are published in multiple versions and this is one of the areas where FRBR holds some promise to help improve access. But differing cataloging practices between monographs and serials means that much of the work to date on identifying monographic FRBR entities and relationships (through the use of existing monograph catalog records) cannot easily be adapted to the serial record. Even so, there is potential for FRBR to be a useful tool in the bibliographic control of and access to serials and other continuing resources.

Definitions and Characteristics

A few issues (pun intended) need to be clarified before we can talk about analyzing a serial using the FRBR model. One is related to the nature and definition of the serial. Although there are attributes more or less unique to serials that are defined as FRBR attributes (e.g., frequency, regularity, issue designation, publication pattern), the concept of a serial as defined by the *Anglo-American Cataloguing Rules, Second Edition*[2] (AACR2R; a resource with no predetermined conclusion issued in a succession of discrete parts that usually bear numbering) is not defined within the FRBR context. In the cataloger's world, the concept is critical, as it is used to identify which rule set is used to create and maintain a bibliographic description. Because FRBR is not a set of rules, but instead an entity-relationship model, however, there are no rules; there are only definitions of entities, relationships, and their attributes. In the same way, there is no definition of a continuing resource or serial, but instead there are entity attributes that describe the continuing nature of a resource. These include intended termination (of a work), extensibility (of an expression), and publication status (of a manifestation).

The AACR2R defining characteristics of a serial create a category that is very broad and not intuitively inclusive to anyone but a serialist. Put another way, how many individuals, if given an issue of *National Geographic* and a Seattle telephone book, are going to identify the fact that these two things share any common characteristics whatsoever? Instead, individuals are likely to note that they are very different things because:

- *National Geographic* consists of articles and the Seattle telephone book does not.
- An individual might consider keeping a complete run of *National Geographic,* but he or she would almost never consider keeping a run of the Seattle telephone book.

This example identifies two characteristics that are generally ignored by the serialist (or at least by the serials cataloger), but which are very important to a FRBR analysis of a serial:

- Is the serial work a collection of individual works (articles)?
- Is each issue of a serial a "revised" version of the previous issue?

Depending on the answers, FRBR analysis may produce different entity-relationship models.

The Journal and Article as Works

In 3.2.1, FRBR identifies the Work entity as a distinct intellectual or artistic creation and further characterizes it as an abstract entity that exists only in the commonality of content between and among various expressions of the work. Although there is not complete agreement in the serials community that a journal is an intellectual work in the same sense that a work of single-authorship is, there is general acknowledgment that a journal can be considered a work of collected works or shared authorship and thus can be modeled in FRBR.[3] A journal is more than just a collection of articles. Editorial control shapes the scope and content, and peer review often revises the draft content (or keeps content from appearing). Thus the journal as a whole can be considered an intellectual construct of shared responsibility consisting of a collection of individual works.

If we accept the premise that a journal can be considered a work, then what does it look like to apply FRBR to a journal and what benefits do we gain by doing so? A simple case would be something like:

$\mathbf{w}_1$ *Serials Librarian*

  $\mathbf{e}_1$ Textual expression (the only expression of this serial)

   $\mathbf{m}_1$ Print version

     $\mathbf{i}_1$ Copy in UW Libraries' periodicals collection

   $\mathbf{m}_2$ Online version

     $\mathbf{i}_1$ Files located on www.haworthpress.com

This could be considered the top-down, big picture view of a journal; however, individual articles are also works and a journal is an aggregation of articles. I wrote an article for *Serials Librarian* in 1998 that was simultaneously published in a monograph and revised in 2002 as part of a second edition of the monograph. I also deposited a preprint copy of the article in our digital repository. The Group 1 entity for that article could look something like this:

$\mathbf{w}_{1.1}$ Steve Shadle. *A Square Peg in a Round Hole: Applying AACR2 to Electronic Journals*

  $\mathbf{e}_{1.1}$ Original article

   $\mathbf{m}_{1.1}$ *Serials Librarian* 33, no. 1–2 (1998) p.147–166

     $\mathbf{i}_{1.1}$ Copy of article in UW Libraries' periodicals collection

   $\mathbf{m}_{2.1}$ *Serials Librarian (Online)* 33, no. 1–2 (1998) p. 147–166

     $\mathbf{i}_{2.1}$ DOI: 10.1300/J123v33n01_09

   $\mathbf{m}_{3.1}$ *E-Serials: Publishers, Libraries, Users, and Standards*, 1998. p. 147–166

     $\mathbf{i}_{3.1}$ Copy of article in UW Libraries' monographs collection

  $\mathbf{e}_{1.2}$ Revised article

   $\mathbf{m}_{1.2}$ *E-Serials: Publishers, Libraries, Users, and Standards. 2nd ed.*, (2002). p.119–139

$\mathbf{i}_{1.2}$ Copy in article UW Libraries' monographs collection

$\mathbf{m}_{2.2}$ Electronic preprint

$\mathbf{i}_{2.2}$ Copy in UW Libraries DSpace collection

In addition to the Group 1 entity relationships that are on display here (i.e., a work *is realized through* an expression, which *is embodied in* a manifestation, which *is exemplified by* an item), it is obvious there is some type of whole/part relationship going on between the journal and article entities. FRBR 5.3.1.1 clearly describes the whole/part *work* relationship and even uses journal article as a specific example of a whole/part relationship at the *work* level. In a similar fashion, FRBR 5.3.2.1 uses journal article as a specific example of a whole/part relationship at the *expression* level. The sections that describe the whole/part relationship at the *manifestation* and *item* levels (5.3.4.1 and 5.3.6.1, respectively), however, do not present journal article as an example of a whole/part relationship of those levels. The focus on *item*-level relationships (and to a lesser degree, *manifestation*-level relationships) is (correctly) on the physical "exemplification" of the work, and because journal articles are typically not published as physically separate pieces (apart from the issue), there is no (apparent) whole/part relationship between the copy of my article in the periodicals collection and all of the issues of the journal sitting on the shelves in the periodicals collection. FRBR, however, also states that in cases where the manifestation or item consists of more than one volume, there could be a whole/part relationship between the manifestation/item as a whole and an individual volume of that manifestation/item. In considering an electronic serial (where the article is typically a PDF or HTML file among a collection of files), it does appear that the article manifestation/item can be considered a "part" of the journal manifestation/item. FRBR 5.2.1 includes a statement:

> "It should be noted that although the relationships between *work, expression, manifestation,* and *item* are depicted in the entity-relationship diagram in a segmented way, they operate logically as a continuous chain....Thus when a relationship is made between an *expression* and a *manifestation* that embodies the *expression,* the *manifestation* is at the same time logically linked to the *work* that is realized through the *expression,* given that the *expression* has been linked to the *work* it realizes."[4]

It's difficult to know whether that "logical linking" includes whole/part relationships that might be related at the work or expression-level but also apply to manifestations and items of those works and expressions.

At this point, a picture might be useful. Figure 13.1 presents the three modeled resources (journal, article, and monograph) side by side with arrows showing the "Has Part/Is Part of" whole/part relationships. The whole lines indicate the relationships specified in 5.3.1.1 and 5.3.2.1, specifically the component (whole/part) relationship at the work or expression level. The arrows are double-ended to indicate the fact that the relationship (as all FRBR relationships)

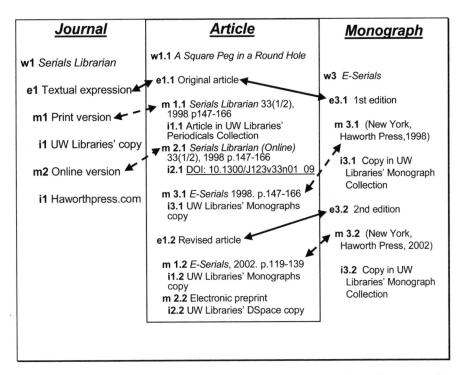

Figure 13.1. Whole/Part Relationships Between Journal, Article, and Monograph.

is reciprocal. Note that the article has been revised and republished. The revised expression of the work has never been published as an article in *Serials Librarian;* thus it is difficult to say (in this case) that the relationship between journal and article is characteristic of the *work,* as not all expressions of the article work have a relationship to the journal. This is indicated by the fact that the revised article (e1.2) does not have a component relationship with the journal, but only a component relationship with the revised expression of the monograph. The only expression of the article that has a component relationship with the journal is the one that was originally published in the journal (represented by the line between e1.1 and e1).

At the expression-level, one could consider the expression of the original article to have a whole/part relationship with the single *expression* of the journal. Remember, the *expression* consists basically of the content of the *work* (the specific words, phrases, figures, etc.) excluding aspects of physical form, such as page layout and typography. One image I like to use when discussing the nature of expressions is that if one were holding onto a physical information object—a book, a magazine, a DVD—and then suddenly the content floated out of the physical container and was suspended in the air, without specific form or substance, just the words and pictures floating there, *that's* what's being *expressed* by the physical manifestation.

In the case of Figure 13.1, the two manifestations of the original article that were published in *Serials Librarian* (print and online) have a pretty clear component relationship to the journal. But what about that third manifestation (the publication of the original article within the monograph)? In the case of Haworth republications, the monograph will typically have the same typeface, pagination, and so on as the original journal issue. But what if it doesn't? Is it the case that by its nature, the monograph-published article can be considered a component of the serial?

When thinking about the *expression* of the article and the journal, I believe the answer is yes; the expression (i.e., content) of the original article is a component of both the journal and the monograph, and the entity-relationship model should reflect that relationship. In Figure 13.1, this is represented by the fact that e1.1 has a component relationship with both e1 (the expression of the journal) and e3.1 (the 1998 expression of the monograph). Think about the users who are specifically looking for the original article. They likely don't care whether they get the monograph or journal issue, as long as they get the original article.

If one is uncomfortable with this line of thinking, one can always (or also) draw lines between the journal and article manifestation and items, as this represents the publication and physical item representations. These are represented in Figure 13.1 as the dotted lines between each article manifestation and the larger component manifestation in which the article appears. But why make these four manifestation-level relationships when the three expression-level relationships will serve the same purpose in presenting the relationships?

Why should we really care whether the relationship is represented by one link between expressions or three links between manifestations? Historically, libraries have forced users into searching silos (much like cattle through the stockyard). If one wants an article, one searches one set of databases or indexes; if one wants a book or a video, one searches the catalog; if one wants a digital image or manuscript, one searches a digital repository or a photograph or manuscript collection. But articles (or article-like writings) don't just appear in journals. They appear in books, in preprint, e-print or institutional repositories, and in conference proceedings. Figure 13.2 shows the result of an article title search in a library and information science citation database.

This is all fine and dandy if the library subscribes to the journal. But if it doesn't, then the user will have to pursue another service (like interlibrary loan), even though the library may have a copy of the monograph that contains the article.

Figures 13.3 and 13.4 show the result of a title search for my article in library catalog silos.

Because the WorldCat record contains indexed contents notes, the searcher can identify that a manifestation of the article appeared in this book. If the searcher's library doesn't own the book, however, the searcher will likely need to request the book through another service (again, such as interlibrary loan), even though the library may subscribe to *Serials Librarian*. Figure 13.4 illustrates that the library has never enhanced its catalog records with table of contents information resulting in an even worse experience for the user.

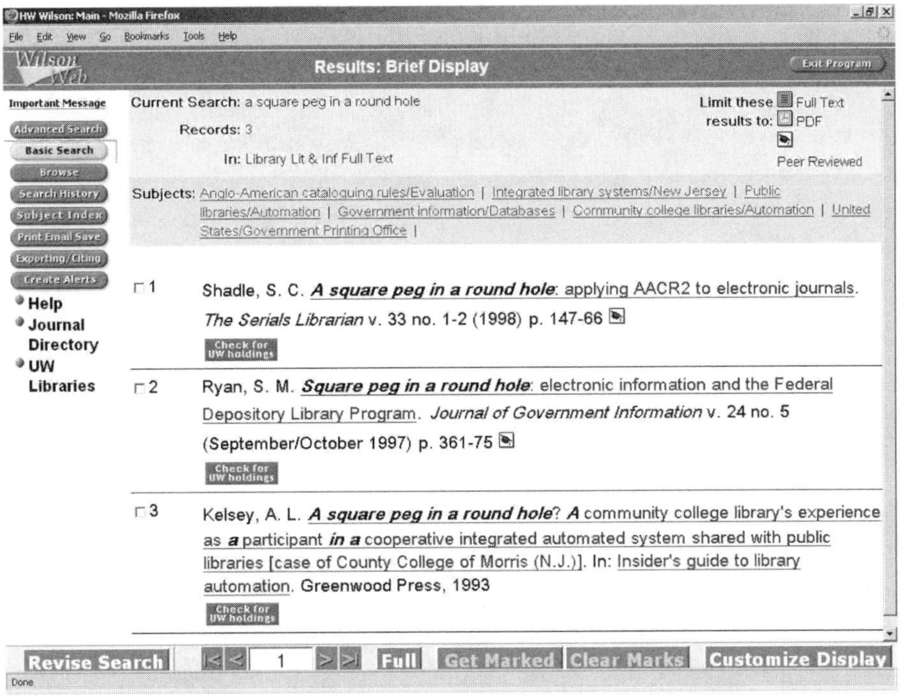

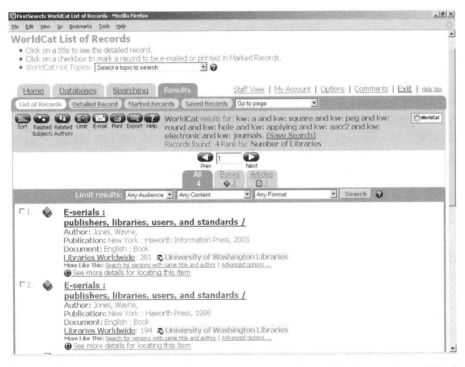

Figure 13.2. Search Results from *Library Literature & Information Science Full Text* (Source: http://vnweb.hwwilsonweb.com/hww/shared/shared_main.jhtml?_requestid= 35146).

Figure 13.3. Monograph Records Retrieved From Article Title Search from OCLC WorldCat (Source: http://firstsearch.oclc.org).

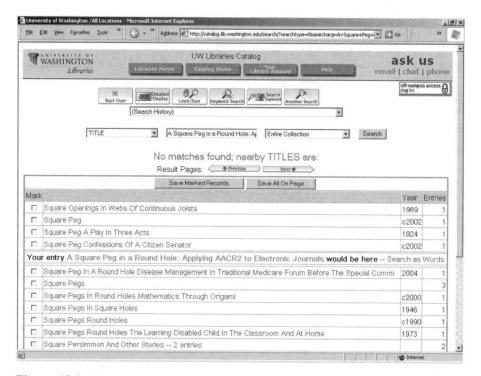

Figure 13.4. Failed Article Title Search from University of Washington Libraries Catalog (Source: http://catalog.lib.washington.edu/search~/?searchtype=t& searcharg=a+ square+peg+in+a+round+hole+applying+aacr2+to+electronic+journals).

Here, the only option given to the user is to repeat the search as a keyword search. The resulting "No Entries Found" display with no other options given is a dead end for users. Better at this point, to (shudder) point users to Google Scholar (Figure 13.5).

At least Google Scholar gives users a fighting chance, although most of the links won't result in (free) full-text for the user and the following related entries may be of interest to some users, but clutter for others. We are still in a delivery silo in the sense that the first entry refers only to the article as it appeared in *Serials Librarian.* There is a link at the bottom of the first page for the article as it appeared in *E-Serials,* so there is some hope that if the user's library doesn't have access to one manifestation, it might have access to another that can be provided to the user. But this display still presents the manifestations as separate entries, appearing in different places of the display. A better FRBR-based display would present the journal article as an entry and *then* present the fact that it is a component part of two publications (rather than to present the two publications separately and indicate the article is a component part of each).

Given the current Web searching environment (start with the single search box), it behooves the library community to eliminate as many searching silos as possible. With OCLC's purchase of Openly Informatics, there now exists an

Figure 13.5. Article Title Search Results from Google Scholar (Source: http://scholar. google.com/scholar?q=a+square+peg+in+a+round+hole+applying+aacr2+to+electronic+ journals).

organizational framework that can support the integration of article citation and library catalog data. The serials community should be more actively involved in research to identify whether FRBR can be used to support this integration with a goal of simplified data displays and more transparent access to article-level content, no matter the aggregation.

The Journal Issue as FRBR Entity

At my 2005 North American Serials Interest Group (NASIG) presentation, there was some discussion about the nature of the journal issue. Most attendees already understood that a journal article could be considered an independent work and most understood (or could be convinced) that a journal could also be considered a work. But what about the journal issue? Many attendees felt that the journal issue served the sole purpose of bundling together articles in a physical package that could be easily delivered to subscribers and added to library collections, that there was nothing about the bundling that affected user access. After all, many online serials lose their "issueness" when older articles are available only as a database. So how could a journal issue be considered a *work?*

As the discussion continued, however, examples of individual issues as *work* surfaced: the "proceedings" issue of a journal (which has a unity of purpose beyond the fact that it is a collection of articles), a monographic series volume which may consist of individual contributions (which is not a journal per se, but is an example of aggregation of articles, under editorial control, published within a serial/series), the theme issue (which typically has distinctive editorial control and frequently an analyzable title). We've already seen an example of a theme issue simultaneously published as a monograph (although in fact, the reality is a little more complex as the first edition of *E-Serials* consisted collectively of the two 1998 issues (numbered volume 33, no. 1/2 and volume 33, no. 3/4 and with analytic titles *E-Serials. Part 1* and *E-Serials. Part 2*). In the case of Haworth republications, most aspects of the manifestations (serial and monograph) are identical. Why would the monograph be considered a *work* and the journal issues not? If the content is identical, why do superficial differences (such as the fact that the monograph has a hard cover and cannot be purchased on standing order) make one a work and the other not a work? Of course, these differences don't matter. Volume 33, no. 1/2 of *Serials Librarian* is as much a FRBR work as the first edition of *E-Serials*. So then is it only analyzable issues of a journal that are considered works, or is any issue of a journal considered a component work of the serial? Each issue of a serial undergoes editorial or artistic control of some form (even monthly weather reports require decisions to be made about what data will be captured and how it will be presented). And in fact, the relationship of editor to serial may be more accurately modeled as a relationship to the issue (as the editor works to shape each issue) rather than as a relationship to the journal as a whole.

FRBR does include the concept of "journal issue as FRBR work" by indicating (in Table 5.2: *Whole/Part Work-To-Work Relationships*) that a volume/issue of a serial is a *dependent* work part (versus the previously discussed journal article or monographic series volume, which is considered an *independent* work part). 5.3.1.1 provides a description that explains the distinction between dependent and independent work parts:

> *Dependent* parts are component parts of a *work* that are intended to be used in the context of the larger *work* and as such depend on the context provided by the larger *work* for much of their meaning. Dependent components are often difficult to identify without reference to the larger *work* as they generally do not have distinctive names/titles. *Independent* parts are those that do not depend to any significant extent on the context provided by the larger *work* for their meaning. Typically, independent components have distinctive names/titles. It is assumed that in both cases, the *work* that represents the whole is an independent *work*.[5]

This description expresses two generalizable principles. First, a dependent work relies on the larger work for much of its meaning. I'm not sure this is really the case with a journal issue as: (1) we've already seen examples of journal issues that have a *meaning* independent of the journal itself, and (2) the *meaning* of a journal is typically not as important as the individual contribution within the article, so dependence between journal and article is not as critical when it comes to use. The second generalizable principle is that if a component part is analyzable, it's independent; if it's not analyzable, it's dependent. Even though *volume/issue of a serial* is presented in the table as a dependent part, it could likely be considered independent if it is analyzable. This generalization is also supported later in 5.3.2.1 where "issues of a journal" are presented as an example of an independent part (along with monographs in a monographic series and articles in a journal). The same distinction (dependent vs. independent) is made at both the work (FRBR 5.3.1.1) and the expression (FRBR 5.3.2.1) level, so the analyzable journal issue as independent component part of an *expression* is also identified.

The last sentence in the quote, however, raises a concern as it implies that FRBR doesn't allow a model of reality where a dependent work (e.g., journal issue) can have independent component work parts. This restriction makes some sense within the context of current national cataloging practices, as an unanalyzable issue of a journal is not cataloged separately but is represented only within the context of the serial record. This makes sense if the journal issue doesn't have a separate title. But what if the library has only one issue of a journal and that particular issue was edited or had a contribution by a faculty member and you've been asked to add it to the library catalog? In that case, the access points and/or bibliographic description of the issue may differ enough from that of the serial to justify a separate record for the issue. Over the course of my career, I've seen a number of records in OCLC for individual journal issues that have a title statement such as: *245 00 Industrial environment. $n Vol. 15, no. 12.* In the context of a flat file of database records, this type of standalone analytic record may introduce more confusion than it generates access, but within a linked environment that recognizes the component relationships, this type of record may be useful. Figure 13.6 is a slide taken from a demonstration of the implementation of FRBR in VTLS's Virtua catalog.

Figure 13.6 illustrates the fact that FRBR relationships are used to "drill-down" from serial to issue to article and allows the user to browse table of contents (a virtual shelf browsing of the issues of a journal). The MARC record shown in the figure describes an article as *manifestation,* which is linked to an *expression* of a journal issue, which is linked to the journal *work* record. It works just fine in creating this piece of functionality (table-of-contents (TOC) browsing), but it doesn't recognize the fact that there are two different types of hierarchy (abstract to specific vs. whole/part).

Type of issuance (and its consequent numbering pattern) is not necessarily tied to an *expression.* Online and print manifestations may have an identical set of articles, but they may not share a numbering scheme or issuance pattern. It's not uncommon for the online version of a journal to consist of an article database (sometimes lacking any reference to the print version's original numbering or pagination), and I've seen more than one case of a continuously published e-serial (meaning articles are published online as available) that has a regularly published print cumulation of articles (with a corresponding print issue numbering not appearing in the online version). What does this tell us about issue-level

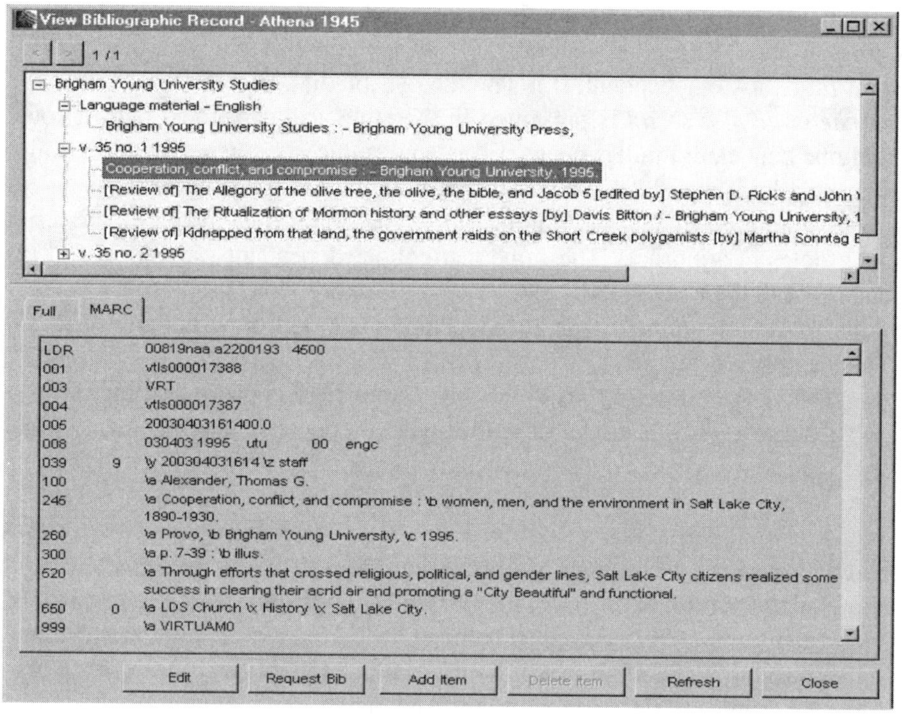

Figure 13.6. Implementation of Table of Contents Browsing from VTLS (Source: http://www.vtls.com/documents/FRBR9.PPT).

attributes such as numbering? They obviously are not attributes of the work, as different expressions (e.g., translations) do not necessarily share a common numbering. They are also not necessarily attributes of the expression, as different manifestations (print and online) may have different numbering schemes and different published "units." So these issue-level characteristics must be attributes of the *manifestation,* as all items (e.g., the same set of files or all copies of a particular issue) will carry the same numbering.

To implement TOC browsing (as VTLS has done), there has to be "something" at the untitled, issue level (or put another way, the line presented as *v. 35, no. 1 1995* in the VTLS display has to come from somewhere). If the journal issue is an actual living, breathing bibliographic entity, one might model the entity relationships as in Figure 13.7.

Figure 13.7 attempts to illustrate the FRBR entities that are presented in Figure 13.6. Note that the whole/part relationship is generally modeled at the work and expression level, similar to Figure 13.1, but including an "issue" entity that sits between the journal and the article. In this figure, w35.1 and w35.2 are issues that are both parts of the larger journal work w1. The two journal articles represented (w3 and w4) are components of the issue w35.1. Again, the difference between Figure 13.1 and Figure 13.7 is that in Figure 13.1, the articles are modeled as (direct) components of the journal, whereas in Figure 13.7 the articles are modeled as components of an issue that is a component of a journal.

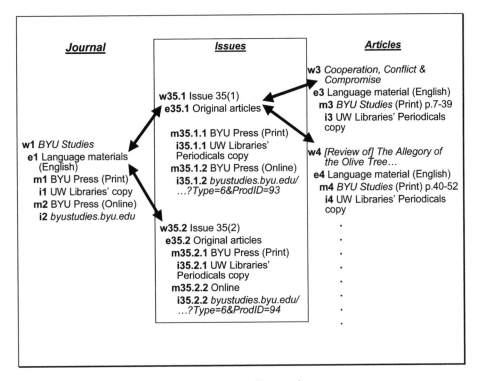

Figure 13.7. Dependent Part (Issue) as Work/Expression.

Also note that this model does not include an online manifestation for each of the articles because none (apparently) exists. *BYU Studies* presents article PDFs for some (but not all) articles. There is a Web presence for the issues (represented by m35.1.2 and m35.2.2), but individual articles from these issues are not (yet) digitized. This model supports the creation of a browsable, drill-down table of contents display similar to Figure 13.6, but it does not meet the previously discussed "analyzable" criteria, and in addition it uses issue numbering to identify a work. If the online manifestation of the journal consisted of an article database that lacked any reference to the numbering of the original print issues, then it would be difficult to justify numbering as a *work* attribute of the issue (or to have the online version be a *manifestation* of an issue when no online issue exists). Put another way, if the online version lacks issues, then where is the line drawn between any online manifestations of articles (which aren't modeled here, but would be appearing in the right column of Figure 13.7 as additional manifestations of the articles) and the online manifestation of the journal? Not through an issue *work* because no issue work exists for the online manifestation. So, if not all manifestations of an article are related to a specific journal issue, then is the journal issue really a work?

Figure 13.8 illustrates another possible model that doesn't consider the dependent part (e.g., journal issue lacking separate title) to be a separate work, but instead to be a manifestation (in part) of the larger journal. In this figure, the issue is considered a component *manifestation* of a particular journal *manifestation,* rather than a component *work* of a journal *work.* FRBR 5.3.4.1 describes a whole/partrelationship at the manifestation level and one of the examples used in the accompanying table (FRBR Table 5.8) is *Volume of a multivolume manifestation.* So even though there is no journal example specifically represented in the accompanying table, one could state that the journal issue is a *manifestation* that has a component relationship with the larger journal *manifestation.* Considering that "issueness" doesn't appear to be something inherent in the *expression* (as shown by the fact that the print manifestation may be organized into "issues," whereas the online manifestation may not be organized into those same issues even though the *expression* may be identical), then it may make sense to model the issue as a component *manifestation* of a journal manifestation, rather than as a component *work.*

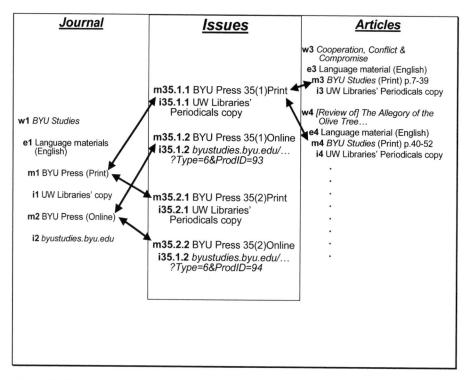

Figure 13.8. Dependent Part (Issue) as Manifestation.

If this is the case, then what about the relationship of the journal article to the journal issue? If there is no journal *issue work* or *expression,* does it make sense to propose a component relationship between the issue *manifestation* and the article *work,* or is the component relationship between the issue and article manifestations (as indicated in Figure 13.8)? Figure 13.1 shows a component relationship between works and between expressions, but this was before the concept of a journal issue entity was introduced. As previously stated, the need to provide information about all manifestations of a given article (published in a serial vs. published in a monograph) still needs to be met, but is it met sufficiently by modeling the component relationship between manifestations rather than between works or expressions?

Put another way, what is lost if one redraws the lines in Figure 13.8 so that the lines from the article (w3/e3, w4/e4) connect directly to the journal (w1/e1) rather than to the issue entity (m35.1.1)? After all, FRBR 5.3.1.1 and 5.3.2.1 indicate the article is a component (specifically an independent part) of a journal, not an issue. The piece of functionality that is potentially lost is the drill-down browsing presented in Figure 13.6. If the article does not have some type of relationship to the issue, then the information needed to create this display must be found elsewhere. And that elsewhere is the article manifestation.

Notice in Figure 13.1, m1.1 and m2.1 (the manifestations of the original article that appear in the print and online versions of *Serials Librarian*) specify the issue they are published in, whereas in Figures 13.7 and 13.8, I only specified the manifestation ("BYU Studies (Print)") in the entries labeled m3 & m4. The difference in the labeling of the entries in these figures illustrates a concept that is presented elsewhere in this monograph, that sometimes a characteristic of a resource can be modeled as an attribute of an entity, as a relationship between entities, or possibly both. A commonly referred to case in point is publication information. In the United States, we tend to look at publication information (place of publication, publisher) as an attribute of a manifestation (i.e., descriptive information transcribed from a book). In Europe (where publisher information tends to be under authority control in library systems), publication information is often considered a relationship between the publisher (Group 2 entity) and the manifestation published (Group 1 entity). There is no right and wrong model here, but there may be consequences to the modeling decision that should be considered, a primary one being "How does the modeling decision support user tasks identified in FRBR?" In the case of publisher information, if a user needs to be assured of a high-recall, high-precision search when identifying works by a particular publisher, then it is probably best to model publisher information as that of a relationship so that variant forms of publisher name are all controlled.

In a similar fashion, we can ask the same question about issue numbering. Is it sufficient to provide issue number/date as an attribute of an article manifestation, or does it serve the user better to model a journal issue *manifestation* that provides a controlled form of issue numbering, and this manifestation has a component relationship to the article? Does publication pattern data perhaps play a role somewhere in here? Looking at Figure 13.8 one more time, one has to wonder whether entities m1, i1, m2, and i2 (the manifestations and items of the serial) are even necessary, as they consist of nothing more than the collection of the individual issues. Why not simplify the model and relate the journal issue component parts directly to the journal expression (e1 in this case) rather than through a component manifestation? A simpler version of Figure 13.8 would posit that the manifestation of a journal is nothing but its component parts.

Figure 13.9 presents a model that assumes that the issue of a journal is simultaneously a manifestation of a particular journal expression and a component part of a particular expression. The article *manifestation* is directly related to the issue *manifestation* (which is an expression of the journal). In some respects this is similar to Figure 13.1, which models the component relation between article and journal (without an intermediate issue *work*), but the relationship is between *manifestations,* not between *works* or *expressions* of a work. This model lacks an entity for the journal manifestation. An assumption here is that all of the manifestation-specific information about a journal is identified with the *issue* manifestation (or put another way, in terms of *manifestation*-specific information, the journal is the sum of all the issues). This is likely not the best way to model the journal/issue relationship, however, as there is information about the journal manifestation (e.g., ISSN), which may not be manifest on the individual issue. Is it necessary to repeat publication information, title, and so on each issue manifestation entity if that information can be represented once in the journal manifestation entity?

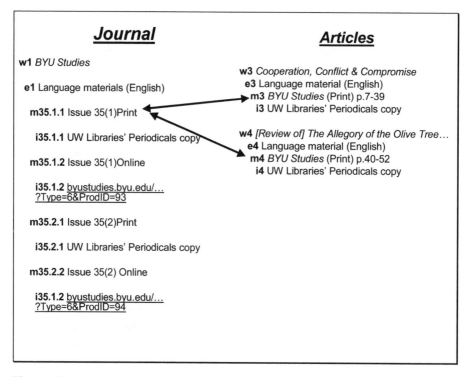

Figure 13.9. Dependent Part (Issue) as Component of Journal Expression.

If the reader is completely lost at this point, it is perfectly understandable. Two different types of hierarchical relationships are evidenced simultaneously in this discussion—one that describes abstract to concrete (*work, expression, manifestation, item*) and the other that describes resource components (journal, issue, article).

It is not yet clear how best to model the unanalyzable journal issue. FRBR is maintained by the FRBR Review Group, a committee of the IFLA Cataloguing Section Standing Committee. In 2005, the Working Group on Aggregates was established to investigate practical solutions to the specific problems encountered in modeling aggregations (including journals).[6] The Working Group is currently developing several models for aggregations that were discussed at their meeting in Durban, South Africa, in August 2007. Stay tuned for further developments!

The Journal Title Change

Successively issued works have the potential to change over time, and one element the serials cataloger focuses on is the title. A monographic set can clearly be identified as a single work (even if the title changes over time), as there is a unity to (and interdependence within) its content. But what about a journal that changes title over time? Being composed of separate, individual titles, it doesn't carry that same unity and interdependence. Single work? Separate works?

Serials cataloging practices cannot really help inform us on the question of work, as they have been developed more as a reaction to existing library catalog technologies (e.g., book catalog, card catalog, online catalog) than to any real theoretical examination of the serial work. Successive entry cataloging was developed "to prepare an entry that will stand the longest time and will permit the making of necessary changes with the minimum of modification."[7] Lubetzky recognized that this practical approach to cataloging violated the Paris Principles' second objective of relating and displaying together the editions a library has of a given work.[8] Tillett has suggested the use of authority records containing a complete history of a serial title as one way (within the existing bibliographic standards and system framework) to preserve the integrity of journal title history and citation, while at the same time bringing together that history to support information system displays.[9] Throughout these (and other) discussions, it is a common assumption that there are users whose needs will be best met by considering the serial to be a single work issued over time and that a title change does not necessarily reflect the creation of a new work.

So how can we model such a change? Frieda Rosenberg and Diane Hillman[10] (and others) suggest that one way to easily model this history is to consider the individual title (as currently considered by serials catalogers) to be an individual work, but for there to be a "superwork" that encompasses the instances of a serial title over time and could be used to collocate related expressions and manifestations of a serial. Figure 13.10, from another VTLS demonstration, shows a possible staff display (although the user displays would be similar) that results from a search for *Atlantic Monthly*.

In this example, *Atlantic Monthly* is considered a work. Each of the titles carried by the work over time are considered component works of the "super" work. An experienced serials cataloger will see that the component titles are the uniform titles that have been assigned to each serial record as the title has flip-flopped back and forth between *Atlantic* and *Atlantic Monthly*. This display presents the expressions and manifestations associated with each *work,* and it also presents the works chronologically and (importantly for many users) includes the range of

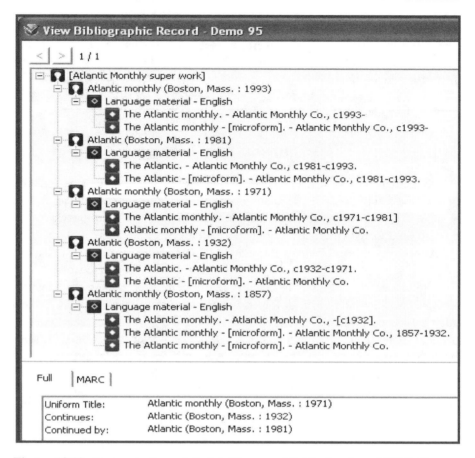

Figure 13.10. Demonstration of Serial "Superwork" Display from VTLS (Source: http://www.vtls.com/documents/FRBR12.PPT).

dates associated with each work. Compare Figure 13.10 and Figure 13.11, which presents the search results without an overarching structure or context.

Figure 13.11 represents much of what is wrong with our current library catalogs. One of the complaints about successive entry cataloging in the card catalog environment was that it required users to thread their way through several drawers of catalog cards, manually compiling the information necessary to identify the titles and dates involved in a serial's publication history. This has not improved in the online catalog represented in Figure 13.11 where the catalog user is required to (1) identify which of these entries is for the journal *Atlantic Monthly* (not an easy thing to do, as several of these results are generated from related work added entries on monograph records, requiring the user to examine many apparently unrelated monograph records before finding a record for the journal), and (2) click through links possibly labeled *Continues* and *Continued By* to find the specific title or dates sought (and this is only if the catalog has hot-linked these fields and if they are readily apparent in the record display). If not, the user must manually rekey each title and go through the same laborious process to find what is wanted.

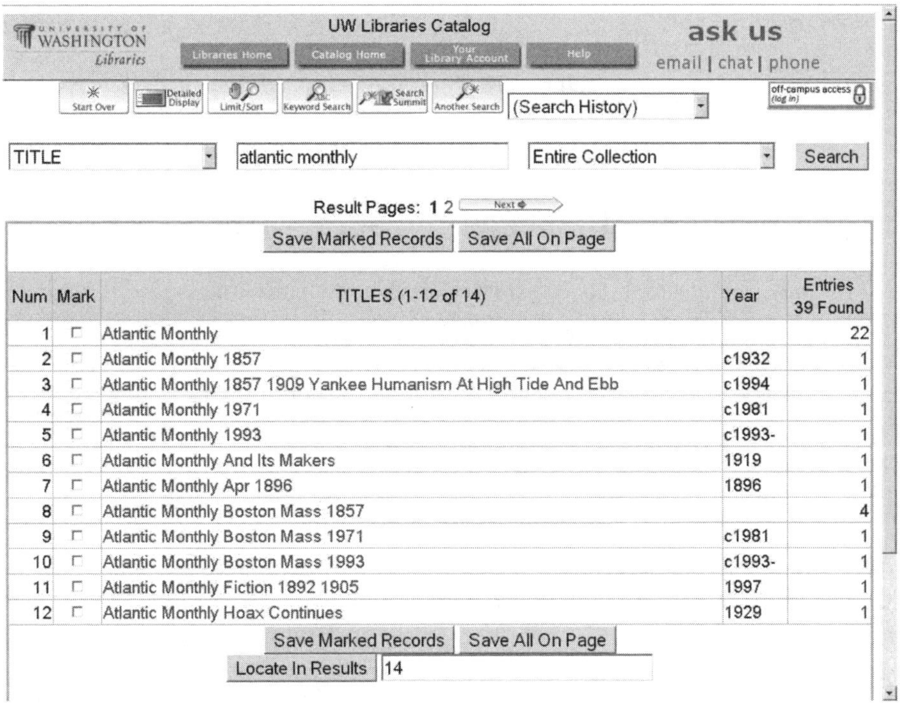

Num	Mark	TITLES (1-12 of 14)	Year	Entries 39 Found
1		Atlantic Monthly		22
2		Atlantic Monthly 1857	c1932	1
3		Atlantic Monthly 1857 1909 Yankee Humanism At High Tide And Ebb	c1994	1
4		Atlantic Monthly 1971	c1981	1
5		Atlantic Monthly 1993	c1993-	1
6		Atlantic Monthly And Its Makers	1919	1
7		Atlantic Monthly Apr 1896	1896	1
8		Atlantic Monthly Boston Mass 1857		4
9		Atlantic Monthly Boston Mass 1971	c1981	1
10		Atlantic Monthly Boston Mass 1993	c1993-	1
11		Atlantic Monthly Fiction 1892 1905	1997	1
12		Atlantic Monthly Hoax Continues	1929	1

Figure 13.11. Catalog Search Results From a Title Search for Atlantic Monthly from University of Washington Libraries Catalog (Source: http://catalog.lib.washington.edu/search~/?searchtype=t&searcharg=atlantic+monthly).

So how do we get to a serial record display (such as the one in Figure 13.10) without reinventing the wheel? The serials cataloging community needs to do the analysis (similar to that already done by others in the areas of literature and music) to identify the elements in existing MARC serial records that can be used to generate this data and these displays. For example, the use of the MARC 130/240 fields to collocate manifestations and expressions generally doesn't work, because the uniform title is typically used to distinguish works, expressions, and manifestations from each other. In fact, a typical serial uniform title may perform both collocation and identification functions, for example:

130 0 Reflections (Cambridge, Mass.: Online)

In this case, the portion of the uniform title preceding the colon serves to collocate this electronic serial's entry with the print version, whereas the portion after the colon serves to distinguish the online manifestation from its print counterpart. The OCLC work set algorithm (described elsewhere in this monograph—see Chapter 5) doesn't analyze this uniform title in a way that produces the expected FRBR relationships. In addition, there are MARC fields commonly used in serials cataloging (primarily the linking fields) that have been used in the place of uniform titles and related work entries to describe relationships that are now considered FRBR relationships. For example, the grouping of five *works* in Figure 13.10 was likely generated from MARC 780/785 fields. Ed Jones provides much more information on how MARC linking fields can be used to support the generation of FRBR relationships and displays.[11]

Final Thoughts on Succession

It may be that serials catalogers will be able to work within a FRBR environment with only a small number of changes to existing practice. It's hard to know at this point because there is still quite a bit of work that needs to be done in developing models and examples before we can truly get a sense of what will be required to support FRBR-like information systems. I would like to note that it is understandable that serialists did not immediately jump on the FRBR bandwagon. Over the years, serials catalogers have codified how to describe change in a serial resource over time that takes into account the successive issuance nature of the serial publication (and more recently, for single-part continuing resources, the iterative nature of publication). As mentioned in the beginning of this chapter, FRBR does broadly take seriality into account (by defining such attributes as intended termination, extensibility, and publication status) but otherwise doesn't provide a whole lot of guidance for the serials cataloger coming from the traditional AACR2/ISBD context. In the general discussion of entity attributes, FRBR 4.1 states:

> A given instance of an entity will generally exhibit only one value for each attribute...In some cases, however, a given instance of an entity may have multiple values for a single attribute (e.g., a book may contain more than one statement indicating the "title of the *manifestation*"). There are also cases where the value of an attribute of a given instance of an entity may change over time (e.g., the "extent of the carrier" for a serial will change as new volumes are issued).

It appears that an entity will not generally have multiple values for the same attribute, and the one example of a continuing resource entity with a changing attribute is one in which the single value (*extent*) is changed to reflect the current extent of a still-being-published serial (serials catalogers gave up on that a long time ago by resorting to a physical description of "*v.*" until the publication ceased). When one has dozens (if not hundreds) of successive issues over time, however, characteristics will change in a way that will require multiple values for any particular attribute. Another example of this lack of serials world view is in the explanation of the four Group 1 entities that is presented in FRBR 3.2. There are various references to resource change, but they are generally in the context of "this change signals that you may have a new entity." For example, a discussion of the manifestation entity in FRBR 3.2.3 includes the following:

> Where the production process involves a publisher, producer, distributor, etc., and there are changes signaled in the product that are related to publication, marketing,

etc. (e.g., a change in publisher, repackaging, etc.), the resulting product may be considered a new *manifestation.*

Serials catalogers may very well interpret that statement to mean that they are required to create a successive *manifestation*-level record whenever there is a change of publisher in a serial. This practice would never work within the context of the ISSN (which claims to be a manifestation-level identifier) as a change of publisher is not a trigger for the assignment of a new ISSN. No wonder some in the serials cataloging community are a little confused.

I do hope that, in addition to expected benefits to the user, FRBR will provide the serials cataloging community with an opportunity to reexamine why we do what we do in a more principled way. For example, if we require an "authorized" form of heading for citation and identification, maybe it makes more sense to work with an authority system (rather than bibliographic systems) to provide that reference structure. For what elements is exact transcription of data still important? Serials catalogers typically track title from chief source (or most likely the cover as first choice of chief source substitute) religiously and have professional disagreements about what constitutes "the title." Maybe the "title" as it appears on the piece is a characteristic of the manifestation and can be transmitted in publisher-supplied, issue-level data, but the "title" (as in citation form) is a characteristic of the work and it's a cataloger's job to provide the authoritative form of that data element. More modeling is needed to determine whether our concepts of successive and integrating issuance are really necessary and important within a FRBR approach. Work can also be done on the differences between successively issued article collections versus revised editions (we use the same set of cataloging rules, but users look at these two classes of material as very different things). In kicking the tires of FRBR, the serials cataloging community might be able to better inform future cataloging codes (such as *RDA: Resource Description and Access*). I encourage everyone to get out there and kick the tires in whatever way possible!

Notes

1. *Functional Requirements for Bibliographic Records: Final Report,* IFLA Study Group on the Functional Requirements for Bibliographic Records (Munchen: Saur, 1998). Also available: http://www.ifla.org/VII/s13/frbr/frbr.pdf.

2. *Anglo-American Cataloguing Rules, Second Edition, 2002 Revision,* prepared under the direction of the Joint Steering Committee for Revision of AACR (Chicago: American Library Association, 2002).

3. Kristin Antelman. "Identifying the Serial Work as a Bibliographic Entity." *Library Resources & Technical Services* 48, 4 (Oct. 2004): 239–244.

4. *FRBR Report,* p. 60.

5. Ibid., p. 69.

6. IFLA Cataloguing Section, FRBR Review Group, Working Group on Aggregates, [home page] available: http://www.ifla.org/VII/s13/wgfrbr/aggregates_wg.htm.

7. *Anglo-American Cataloging Rules. North American Text* (Chicago: American Library Association, 1967), 231.

8. Seymour Lubetzky. *Code of Cataloging Rules: Author and Title Entry. An Unfinished Draft for a New Edition of Cataloging Rules Prepared for the Catalog Code Revision Committee* (Chicago: ALA, 1960), p. 83.

9. Barbara B. Tillett. *FRBR: Serials and Beyond.* http://www.ala.org/ala/alctscontent/serialssection/serialscomm/contresourcecata/CRCC_serialsFRBR.pdf (accessed January 27, 2007).

10. CONSER Task Force on Universal Holdings. *An Approach to Serials with FRBR in Mind.* http://www.lib.unc.edu/cat/mfh/serials_approach_frbr.pdf (Accessed February 3, 2007).

11. Ed Jones, "The FRBR Model as Applied to Continuing Resources." *Library Resources & Technical Services* 49, 4 (Oct. 2005): 227–242.

Index

About the Editor and Contributors

MURTHA BACA holds a PhD in Art History and Italian language and literature from the University of California, Los Angeles. She is Head of the Getty Vocabulary Program and Digital Resource Management department at the Getty Research Institute in Los Angeles. Murtha has published extensively on data standards and controlled vocabularies for indexing and accessing cultural heritage information, especially with a view to providing end-user access to images and related data on line. In 2002 she edited *Introduction to Art Image Access: Issues, Tools, Standards Strategies*; a revised edition of *Introduction to Metadata* is planned for early 2008. Murtha has taught many workshops and seminars on metadata, visual resources cataloging, and thesaurus construction at museums, universities, and other organizations in North and South America and in Europe.

SHERMAN CLARKE is currently Head of Original Cataloging at New York University Libraries, with previous positions at the Amon Carter Museum, Rhode Island School of Design, Cornell University, and the University of Pittsburgh. He founded Art NACO in 1993 and continues to coordinate it. Sherman received the 2005 Distinguished Service Award from the Art Libraries Society of North America. He is also active in the American Library Association, Visual Resources Association, College Art Association, and Society of Architectural Historians. His undergraduate and graduate study of art history continues to richly inform a lifetime of art and architecture sight- and site-seeing.

WILLIAM DENTON is Web Librarian at York University in Toronto, Canada. He also runs the FRBR Blog at www.frbr.org. He thinks about FRBR more days than not, but he thinks about other things too.

MARY LYNETTE LARSGAARD is Director of the Map Library and Assistant Head of the Map and Imagery Laboratory, Davidson Library, University of California at Santa Barbara. The Map and Imagery Lab has a collection of remote-sensing imagery and maps of approximately 6.5 million items, and is the largest of its kind in any university library in North America. Mary has published extensively in the field of geospatial data in libraries, most notably with a widely used text, *Map Librarianship: An Introduction* (third edition published in 1998 by Libraries Unlimited). Her specialties within that broad area are cataloging/metadata creation, and twentieth-century and more recent topographic and geologic maps. In 2000, she was promoted to Librarian, Distinguished Step, a promotion given only to librarians who have demonstrated superior competence and are internationally recognized as an authority in an area of library science.

EDWARD T. O'NEILL is a Consulting Research Scientist at the Office of Research, OCLC Online Computer Library Center. He received his B.S.I.E., a M.S.I.E., and a Ph.D., in Industrial Engineering from Purdue University. His research interests include authority control, subject analysis, database quality, collection management, and bibliographic relationships. He is active in IFLA and is on the Standing Committee of the Classification and Indexing Section and is member of IFLA's FRBR Review Group. He may be contacted at oneill@oclc.org.

GLENN E. PATTON is Director of WorldCat Quality Management at OCLC where he has spent more than 25 years doing support, training, product development, and quality and standards activities for OCLC services and products. He serves as OCLC's liaison to the American Library Association's Committee on Cataloging: Description and Access. He currently serves as a member of the IFLA Bibliography Section and of the IFLA FRBR Review Group. He chairs the IFLA Working Group on Functional Requirements and Numbering of Authority Records.

STEVEN C. SHADLE is Serials Access Librarian at the University of Washington Libraries. Previous to his current position, he was an ISSN Cataloger in the National Serials Data Program at the Library of Congress and Technical Services Librarian at the U.S. Agency for International Development Library. Steve is an active trainer in the Serials Cataloging Cooperative Training Program (SCCTP) and co-authored their Electronic Serials Cataloging workshop. His articles on serials cataloging, electronic serials cataloging and FRBR have appeared in Serials Review, Serials Librarian and the Journal of Internet Cataloging and he frequently talks on these subjects at NASIG (North American Serials Interest Group) and American Library Association meetings.

RICHARD P. SMIRAGLIA, Ph.D., is Professor at the Palmer School of Library and Information Science at Long Island University in Brookville, New York. He teaches courses in knowledge organization and in research methods at the masters and doctoral levels. He has been with the Palmer School since 1992. He is the author of many books and monographs in the fields of knowledge organization, cataloging, and bibliography. He is currently editor of the quarterly journal *Knowledge Organization*. His 2001 monograph, *The Nature of "A Work"* was the first monograph-length treatment of the topic of works and their role in knowledge organization. In 2002 he edited *Works as Entities for Information Retrieval*, in which an international panel of authors focus on domain-specific research about works and the problems inherent in their representation for information storage and retrieval. His most recent monograph is *Metadata: A Cataloger's Primer* (2005).

ARLENE G. TAYLOR is Professor Emerita, School of Information Sciences, University of Pittsburgh. She has held professional positions in three libraries and has taught part-time or full-time in schools of library and information science for more than 35 years. Her numerous publications include the text-books *Introduction to Cataloging and Classification* and *The Organization of Information*; and recent articles have included research on importance of controlled vocabulary in keyword searching, as well as several articles on teaching different aspects of organizing information. Dr. Taylor has been the recipient of two Fulbright Senior Specialist Program Grants, and was the recipient of the 2000 ALA/Highsmith Library Literature Award and the 1996 Margaret Mann Citation, among other honors.

BARBARA B. TILLETT, Ph.D., is Chief of the Cataloging Policy and Support Office (CPSO) at the Library of Congress and Acting Chief of the Cataloging Distribution Service. She currently serves as the Library of Congress representative on the Joint Steering Committee for Development of RDA (*Resource Description and Access),* chairs the IFLA (International Federation of Library Associations and Institutions) Division IV on Bibliographic Control, and is the LC coordinator for the project to develop a Virtual International Authority File. Dr. Tillett currently serves as a member of the IFLA FRBR Review Group and the IFLA Working Group on FRANAR, as well as leading the worldwide initiative within IFLA to update and replace the 1961 "Paris Principles". Her awards include the Library of Congress's distinguished service award, the prestigious U.S. federal Fleming Award, and in 2004 she was the recipient of the distinguished Margaret Mann Citation in recognition for her many contributions in the areas of cataloging and classification.

ALEXANDER C. THURMAN is a catalog librarian at Columbia University, and previously worked at the Burke Library (Union Theological Seminary), Bobst Library (NYU), and the New York Public Library. He has a B.A. from the University of Virginia and an M.A. and a Ph.D from NYU (all in English literature), as well as an M.L.S. from Long Island University. He is the author of "Metadata Standards for Archival Control: An Introduction to EAD and EAC" in *Metadata: A Cataloger's Primer.*

SHERRY L. VELLUCCI, Ph.D., is a member of the faculty at Rutgers University, School of Communication, Information and Library Science, Department of Library & Information Science, where she teaches courses in Information Organization, Cataloging and Classification, and Metadata. She holds a doctorate in Library Science from Columbia University and a Master's Degree in Library Science from Drexel University. Dr. Vellucci has received several awards for her metadata research and publications, including the American Library Association's *Best of LRTS Award* for her article on "Metadata and Authority Control." She is an internationally renowned conference speaker and has most recently taught courses and workshops in New Zealand and Vietnam. Dr. Vellucci has published books and articles in the area of bibliographic relationships, authority control, cataloging and metadata. She is co-chair of the Advisory Board of the Metadata Education and Research Information Center (MERIC), serves on the editorial board of the journal *Cataloging & Classification Quarterly,* and is a member of the ALA/ALCTS Cataloging Committee: Description and Access.

MARTHA M. YEE has worked since 1983 as Cataloging Supervisor at the UCLA Film & Television Archive. She has a Ph.D. in Library and Information Science with a specialization in cataloging of moving image materials from the Graduate School of Library and Information Science at UCLA. Every two years, she teaches a quarter-long course on the cataloging of moving image materials as part of the UCLA Moving Image Archival Studies program. She has also been active in the Cataloging and Classification Section of the Association for Library Collections and Technical Services at the American Library Association; she has served as member of both the Cataloging Committee: Description and Access and the Subject Analysis Committee at various times in the past, and has also served as chair of the Machine Readable Bibliographic Information Committee.